The Soviet Union

The Soviet Union

Internal and External Perspectives on Soviet Society

Vladimir Shlapentokh, Eric Shiraev,
and Eero Carroll

THE SOVIET UNION
Copyright © Vladimir Shlapentokh, Eric Shiraev, and Eero Carroll, 2008.
All rights reserved.

First published in 2008 by
PALGRAVE MACMILLAN™ in the United States - a division of
St. Martin's Press LLC, 175 Fifth Avenue, New York, N.Y. 10010

Where this book is distributed in the UK, Europe and the rest of the world, this is by Palgrave Macmillan, a division of Macmillan Publishers Limited, registered in England, company number 785998, of Houndmills, Basingstoke, Hampshire RG21 6XS.

Palgrave Macmillan is the global academic imprint of the above companies and has companies and representatives throughout the world.

Palgrave® and Macmillan® are registered trademarks in the United States, the United Kingdom, Europe and other countries.

ISBN-13: 978-0-230-60777-4
ISBN-10: 0-230-60777-2

A catalogue record of the book is available from the British Library.

Library of Congress Cataloging-in-Publication Data

Shlapentokh, Vladimir.
   The Soviet Union : internal and external perspectives on Soviet society / Vladimir Shlapentokh, Eric Shiraev and Eero Carroll.
     p. cm.
   Includes bibliographical references and index.
   ISBN 0-230-60777-2
  1. Soviet Union—Foreign public opinion, American. 2. Public opinion—United States. 3. Public opinion—Soviet Union. I. Shiraev, Eric, 1960– II. Carroll, Eero. III. Title.
   E183.8.R9S45 2008
   947—dc22   2008019399

Design by Westchester Book Group.

First edition: December 2008

Contents

List of Tables	vii
Preface	ix
1 Introduction	1
2 Thinkers from Overseas: How Western Experts Described the Soviet Union over Its 74-Year History	13
3 Homegrown Russian Elites and Soviet Realities	49
4 The Soviet Union in the Mirror of American Public Opinion from the 1930s to 1990	77
5 Ordinary Citizens' Perceptions of the Soviet System from Within	113
6 Conclusion	141
Notes	145
Bibliography	157
Subject Index	171
Name Index	179

List of Tables

4.1	Americans' knowledge about the Soviet Union in the mid-1940s, the mid-1980s, and 1991	83
4.2	Sympathy, antipathy, and other attitudes regarding the Soviet Union in a comparative perspective (from the mid-1930s to the mid-1940s)	86
4.3	The dynamics of trust in Russia during and after World War II	88
4.4	Wartime and immediate postwar approval or disapproval of particular policies of Russia or U.S. policies affecting Russia (in percent)	89
4.5	Wartime and immediate postwar approval or disapproval of particular policies of Russia or U.S. policies affecting Russia (in percent)	89
4.6	American attitudes about academic and cultural exchanges with the Soviet Union (from the late 1950s to the late 1980s)	91
4.7	Five polls that examined people's attitudes (in percent) about the Soviet Union with respect to Reagan's "evil empire" declaration (1984–1987)	92
4.8	Reasons for why the Soviet Union could be considered an enemy nation in 1984	93
4.9	U.S. survey estimations in 1985 on the number of envisioned emigrants from the Soviet Union upon exit liberalization	96
4.10	Percentages of Americans supporting particular opinions of the Soviet Union (Russia)	98
4.11	Agreement with the opinion that Russia is a dominant and expansionist country	99
4.12	Opinions about Russia as a potential threat, enemy, or warmonger	101
4.13	Personal ratings and other assessments of the Soviet leaders	103

4.14 American attitudes about Soviet leaders' intentions and/or anticipated changes in Russian politics due to changes in leadership (in percent)   104

4.15 U.S. respondents' trust in Russians in relation to social background characteristics   108

Preface

The Soviet Union: Internal and External Perspectives on Soviet Society

Our book is a humble attempt to make a small contribution to social sciences and history. This is a brief study of how people perceived, explained, and interpreted information available to them about the social and political developments in a country that no longer exists. We chose the Soviet Union as an example to demonstrate to our readers how different observers at different times looked at the same society, the same political institutions, and the same facts, and yet perceived everything they saw so differently. Which of these perceptions were accurate, correct? Was the "red terror" of 1918 a necessary political action to bring stability to Russia, or was it a clear act of genocide against its own people? Were political repressions of Stalin's era unavoidable symptoms of a totalitarian regime, or were they brave policies of national consolidation? Opinions varied dramatically depending on who saw the facts and from which angle.

Many people conveniently assume today that diversity in human knowledge is a sign of society's intellectual strength. In the West, we praise societies that promote diversity. In fact, cultural diversity that encourages tolerance to other people's opinions plays a very useful and important social function. If a society respects other people's customs and encourages understanding of traditions and beliefs of other groups—this makes the threads of this society's fabric stronger. However, despite our shared principal support for diversity and tolerance, people commonly reserve the right to criticize and reject the customs that are rooted in physical abuse, blatant discrimination, and violation of basic human rights. In other words, cultural tolerance has its limits. Arranged marriages practiced in traditional cultures, from the Western standpoint, are commonly viewed and even accepted as a cultural tradition. Yet most of us overwhelmingly reject domestic violence, blatant gender discrimination, infanticide, ritualistic murder, serfdom, or slavery—even though these abuses might appear to some as cultural customs practiced for centuries.

Many people also serf comfortably today on an intellectual wave of acceptance of diversity of opinions. In fact, diversity of opinions is one of the foundations of a democratic society. It is part of the democratic tradition to invite various opinions and recognize different points of view to interpret simple single facts and complicated chains of events. People, for example, have the right to like or dislike, support or criticize a government's policy. Some people believe that every rich and democratic nation should have a universal health care system paid for by taxpayers. Others hold an opinion that only private sector, not the government, is capable of providing a competitive and efficient medical system. Some people believe that free-market societies should learn something positive from the experience of former socialist countries, such as the Soviet Union or Poland. Others insist that the socialist experience was a global failure and that the only lesson we should learn is that we should not repeat the socialist countries' experience at all. Most of us commonly believe that the diversity of evaluations and opinions expressed individually or through a collective effort helps to understand the complexity of social and political realities.

Today most of us acknowledge that people may have different values. Many, if not most Muslims in traditional communities in their countries perceive their own life in somewhat dissimilar ways than Americans or Britons do. Many people living in the West tend to believe that it is an individual's fundamental and universal right and responsibility to exercise control of our government, support political equality, and be socially and politically active. However, many (again, if not most) people in traditional societies are largely faith-centric and think that everything happens for a "higher" reason and there is little that one can do to influence politics or change society. As an example, some of us, the Westerners, who are demanding a better life and more political and social freedoms for women living in traditional societies often encounter that many Muslim women reject our advocacy on their behalf. They perceive their life not as a self-realization of individual potentials but rather as a fulfillment of a duty and an obligation before God and the family. Different values show dissimilar paths that people choose in their lives.

However, there is an area of human perceptions that deals with facts. There are events of yesterday and today that have actually happened regardless of our personal values and irrespective of what we think of these facts. The Declaration of Independence was signed by the delegates of the Second Continental Congress in 1776. Several Bolshevik armed detachments took over the Winter Palace in St.Petersburg in 1917. Joseph Stalin often drank wine and spoke Russian with a heavy Georgian accent. The Soviet space program was under the control of the Defense ministry.

These are facts. If, however, someone published a report suggesting that the Bolshevik Party had nothing to do with the Russian revolution of 1917, that Stalin was allergic to alcohol, and that the Soviet Space industry was funded by Israel, will we easily accept these statements as proven facts? Unlike in most cases related to cultural diversity or diversity of opinions, a routine acceptance of all kinds of facts or assigning to them an equal value—just because of a false premise that we have to be tolerant to different opinions—is not an encouraging development.

But where is the problem here? Who would challenge, for example, the obvious facts such as the sponsorship of the Soviet space program? True, the structure of the Soviet government and Stalin's personal habits do not stir up disagreements and heated discussions. Other topics, however, do.

For example, how many people have been arrested and killed for political reasons under the Stalin's regime? Was it 10 million or 10,000? It is certainly fair to say that some researches blatantly deny the magnitude of Stalin's repressions (counting the victims in hundreds or even tens of thousands) while others wholeheartedly believe that the Soviet Union gave the world the worst example of mass terror in the twentieth century: The regime was responsible for tens of millions of politically motivated deaths. It is also fair to say that some researchers switch their estimations sometimes when new evidence convinces them to do so. Others, however, find the same evidence unconvincing. Does this mean that we have to go ahead and, in the case of Stalin's political repressions, call it a "draw" and give the estimation of the casualties somewhere at midpoint? Will it be three million then?

This "middle of the road" approach is seldom practiced, however. Let us turn, for example, to the judiciary system. When two sides disagree about a legal dispute, or when the persecution and defense present two different versions of a criminal case, the judge normally does not allow the diversity of opinions to thrive in the final verdict. The judge announces the verdict and, as a result, one side wins and the other loses. The suspect is either guilty or not guilty. Imagine what would happen, if the judge decides to embrace all the arguments of the prosecution and defense as "correct facts" and refuses to announce a verdict in the name of "accepting all points of view." Of course, in some cases the judge may ask the disputing sides to settle their disagreement and find a middle ground. But such cases are relatively rare and far between.

The diversity in perceptions of facts is usually beneficial when people share similar social and political interests and agree to be mutually respectful and tolerant to each other (Putnam, 2007). The diversity in perceptions may lead to a conflict and can deepen antagonisms when the opposite sides share different philosophies of life or are torn apart by intolerance, mistrust, and profound mutual disagreements. In other words, accepting all views in the name of mutual respect does not necessarily bring accord and peace.

How did those people who question the historical facts of the Holocaust (or simply deny its existence) help to bring worldwide understanding and tolerance and to promote international cooperation and global peace?

Did the "diversity" of the absolutely opposite opinions about the Armenian genocide of the early twentieth century help both Armenia and Turkey to establish normal, productive, and mutually beneficial relations?

Did the dissimilar and mutually exclusive opinions about who came first to Judea and Samaria—the Jews or the Arabs—help to bring peace and stability to Israel and Palestine?

Did all those dissimilar opinions about the real causes of the Iraq war promote harmony and common understanding between U.S. political forces on the "left" and on the "right"?

History shows that instead of embracing the diversity of perceived facts, very often, the competing sides had to put aside their ideologies and agree to accept certain perceptions of reality so that they could see the world events from a similar standpoint. For example, most of the time during the cold war, political leaders in Washington and Moscow saw international relations through the thick lenses of their ideological glasses. Moreover, they persuaded their own people to see the world and the U.S.-Soviet relations in a similar, ideological fashion. Both sides, however, were able to agree to see the nuclear arms race as a potentially lethal development for both countries and for the entire world. They both agreed to accept the "reality" of a forthcoming nuclear disaster. As a result, both Washington and Moscow put their ideological "glasses" aside and took several strategically preventive measures to avoid an approaching nuclear confrontation. The fragile peace was achieved.

Imagine what would have happened if one side did not see the danger of the nuclear armament and believed it could win a nuclear war. In fact, something similar happened with the way the United States and the Soviet Union approached President Reagan's Strategic Defensive Initiative ("star wars"). Reagan did not see the potential threat of this program to the Soviets. They, on the other hand, saw it as a grave threat to their own security. Who knows, if the sides agreed to see star wars from a similar perspective, and if Reagan promised to abandon the SDI during the 1986 summit in Reykjavik, both countries by the end of the century would have liquidated most of their nuclear arsenals.

Of course, it is naïve to think that in the future, most governments and people, unified by a common goal, would overcome their deep ideological and political differences in perceptions and embrace one vision of the global social and political reality. Most probably, this will never happen. Political cognition of an individual, the way we see the world of politics around us—no matter whether this person is a president of a country, an accountant, or a college professor—is affected by ideology, specific political beliefs, and pure pragmatic considerations of the day. People often defend their views not only because they believe in the evidence that supports their position but also because they don't want to appear wrong or acknowledge their own mistakes. A Communist Party veteran in today's Russia does not want to accept the fact that his life-long struggle was useless because he fought for the "wrong" ideas. This veteran believes today that there was nothing fundamentally wrong with the Soviet Union, and the only problem was the corrupt political leaders who abandoned Marxism, embraced the West, and let their power slip into the hands of new and greedy political elites. On the other hand, this veteran's neighbor today might see the Soviet Union as a sick, pathological society run on a fuel of mass fears and hallucinations held together by an oppressive government. These two individuals do not ever speak to each other. Who of these two holds a more accurate view?

Every person has a right to have an independent view on anything she or he pleases. Nevertheless it is possible to reduce the gap in people opinions and perceptions, especially in the situations in which such perceptions could fuel antagonisms and confrontations. If we gradually agree to accept some common perceptions of the facts, we can share some common ground in the interpretation of these facts. The authors of this book want to be part of this process.

THE TASKS OF THE BOOK

First, we focus on the diversity of evaluations of current events in history. We hope that the reader could realize how complex people's perceptions were about seemingly simple historic facts and events taking place in one country. Those of us who grew up in the Western culture should not be too confident about the validity of our own perceptions of other countries. It was common, for instance, for an average American to interpret the lives of the people in the Soviet Union as miserable and full of frightening uncertainties. Most of the Soviet people, conversely, believed that they had lived in the freest society in the world, free of racism, unemployment, and market uncertainties. They believed they were protected by reasonable social policies provided by the strong and benevolent government. When food shortages and other economic difficulties occurred, most ordinary people generally considered them as caused by mistakes or misfortunes and not by the deeply seated deficiencies of the socialist system.

People may like or dislike their lives and the circumstances surrounding them. A poor person may be happier and more optimistic than a millionaire. However, let us not deny the fact that that the poor person has no money and the millionaire has some. Similarly, if we follow this analogy, despite their subjective feelings, Soviet people had very little political freedom and very limited access to material possessions. Like Americans were wrong to believe that most Soviet people had miserable lives, the Soviets were equally wrong to believe they lived in a free society.

Second, in this book, we try to stay away from relativism and its postmodernist assumptions, which we will discuss in chapter 1. We believe that different perceptions of reality are welcome but they are not "equal" to each other. Some of them are more accurate depictions than others! Even the most objective eyewitnesses of historic events, from their own view, may reflect reality less accurately than other witnesses did. Some perceptions are incomplete while others are more comprehensive. There have been falsified reports and deliberate lies about specific facts or major historic developments. For instance, some people in Russia still believe that the 1940 massacre of thousands of Polish officers was orchestrated by the Nazis and not by the Soviet authorities. Others until today deny the existence of the secret protocols to the Molotov-Ribbentrop pact on 1939, which guaranteed the massive territorial expansions for Germany and the Soviet Union.

Third, it is often apparent that various observers in the past tended to see the Soviet Union through the prism of their own professional and ideological affiliations. Some of their views evolved with time and some did not. Most Russian liberal intellectuals, those who were able to leave the Soviet Union, were very critical of their former country, its institutions, policies, and even social customs. Many American conservatives eagerly supported these critical views. Some Soviet critical thinkers in the 1960s saw the pitiful state of the Soviet system and its moral bankruptcy. On the other hand, scores of Western liberal intellectuals continued to adore the socialist principles of the Soviet economy and praised the social policies of the Communist state. The debates about the causes of the Soviet Union's collapse are very often based on pure ideological and political positions: When conservatives praise Reagan as the winner of the cold war, liberals commonly say that Reagan had nothing to do with the victory over Communism. In fact, they say, it was not a victory.

Neither country won. It was a draw. We do not want to describe the results of the cold war in football terms, however. We believe that facts of the past should not be twisted to satisfy one's emotional attachments or nostalgic feelings.

Fourth, we believe that even despite "unevenness" of perceptions and their obvious political undertone, our collective political cognition should get richer if we expand our intellectual curiosity and invite the views and theories that contradict our own outlook. Like a judge during a court hearing, we accept the evidence from both sides and question witnesses' testimonies from many walks of life. In this book, for instance, we will separate the perceptions of the Soviet society held by experts and other professionals, on the one hand, and by ordinary people, on the other.

WHY THE SOVIET UNION?

It is difficult to find a country other than the former Soviet Union that drew so many diverse perceptions of its institutions, economy, education, or foreign policy. The reader will be amazed to see how the same historic events were perceived so differently inside and outside the Soviet Union.

First, it was the revolutionary origin of the country that caused heated debates about the nature of the radical changes in Russia after 1917. Russia was the first country in the world in which one political party established the strictest control over the entire population. In fact, Soviet authorities abolished private property, moved the country's peasants into collective farms, suppressed religion, shrunk social inequality, established political censorship, ordered mandatory employment, and placed education under state control. However, people inside and outside Russia, both educated and not, interpreted these developments from their personal positions. Most Russians and most Americans saw the same events—the forceful collectivization in the 1930s, the massive casualties of the 1941–1945 war, the beginning of the cold war in the late 1940s, Khrushchev's reforms in the 1950s, Brezhnev's economic and political stagnation of the 1970s, or Gorbachev's perestroika of the 1970s—very differently.

The choice of the Soviet Union was also predictable because of the authors' personal and professional interests. Two of the authors have spent a significant chunk of their adult life in the Soviet Union and thus can rely on their own rich personal experience. Vladimir Shlapentokh, for example, was a leading Soviet sociologist. He was among the first in the nation who received permission from the government to conduct national polls in the 1960s–1970s and to publish some of the polling data he had obtained. These results—whether available in other published sources before or not—are used in this book. Another author, Eric Shiraev, was doing research on the changing political cognition of the Soviet youth and published his first book in the Soviet Union in 1988. The two met in the United States and cooperated on several books related to political cognition, perceptions of the United States, and other countries. The third author, Eero Carroll, as an independent observer and researcher, brought his scholarly view to the general debate of this book.

We hope that—while reflecting on these various images of the Soviet society—our readers would eventually turn their attention to the global world of today. We all may have similar or different values and opinions. An important goal remains to find more agreement about the facts. Who was more and who was less accurate in their perceptions of facts is the matter of constant reevaluation, of course.

East Lansing, Michigan
Washington, DC
Stockholm

For additional information about this book or to voice your opinion, please visit www.eshiraev.com.

CHAPTER 1

INTRODUCTION

A FEW WORDS ABOUT EMPIRICISM AND RATIONALISM

Red Square. This eclectic architectural assembly seen through the eyes of many people was associated with an evil political regime ruled by authoritarian dictators who were spreading fear across borders. To others, the image of Red Square was always associated with peace, inspiration, and hope. Whose perceptions were more accurate and whose were more misleading? Were they all accurate? Are people's hopes and fears, as related to the world around them, products of pure imagination?

The "true" nature of reality has interested philosophers of all times and places. In Western thought, the struggle between empirists and rationalists has gone on incessantly since the ancient Greeks began their intellectual inquiry into the nature of human perception. For empirists, the human mind reflects or perceives the external world "as is." Rationalists, however, insist that various features of the perceived world are, to some degree, products of the human rational mind. Democritus's empirical line of thought was rooted in recognition of the "material" reality that atoms exist outside of and are reflected in our mind, which also consists of atoms. Plato's line derived from an assumption about the existence of eternal "ideas" that reveal to humans only the "shadow" of the world. Aristotle played the role of a mediator between the materialist and idealist lines explaining that we reflect reality like wax carries the form and shape of an engraved seal. These and other philosophers, however, said little about human perception of society.

In the modern era, the thinking, comprehending individual became the focus of an innovative approach to science. This approach, developed by René Descartes, influenced the development of several scientific branches and specific research methods, including introspection, which would become one of the most popular methods of psychology at the end of the nineteenth century. Descartes was certain that people could make an accurate impression of the external world. Although he believed in the power of science to deliver accurate knowledge, he still used an ontological justification for his optimism: God is perfect and cannot deceive humans in their quest to obtain truthful knowledge.

English philosopher Thomas Hobbes represented the school of empiricism. Hobbes believed that the essence of human behavior and perception is in physical motion and that the principles of Galileo's mechanics should be applied to every social process that people examine. He shared a common view among scientists that the human body was primarily a working machine and that this same principle could be used to describe a community or society in general. For Hobbes, there was one reality and we humans were capable of understanding it accurately.

Other philosophers objected to this position. For the Dutchman Benedict Spinoza, human beings were part of nature. They were carriers of nature's two attributes: objective and subjective. The human mind corresponded to the world of material objects. Ideas and objects were two sides of the same substance: nature. Both Spinoza and Gottfried Leibnitz in Germany defended the view of rationalism. They believed that reason was the prime source of knowledge and that the thinking mind, not human sensations alone, should provide justification of truth. In other words, they insisted that an individual's rational interpretation of facts was superior to his or her subjective perceptions of facts.

In Prussia, Immanuel Kant tried to appease both camps, empirist and rationalist, proposing a compromise that supposed the existence of the objective world, which can be perceived, but not entirely, and only by special logical categories of "pure reason." He believed that we, as humans, can never understand the order of the world by making observations and relying on our senses alone. We make numerous mistakes by attempting to explain the world and asking questions about causation, God, nature, the soul, happiness, history, and so forth. To reduce confusion, people have to switch their attention from general inquiries about the world to specific studies of facts. Even if we the people cannot prove or disprove some facts or beliefs, we should agree to accept particular points of view for practical reasons, in the name of our community.

This theoretical struggle regarding the nature and character of human cognition, however, did not bother social scientists until the end of the nineteenth century. They did not pay serious attention to the empiricism-rationalism debate and almost unanimously shared the position of the naïve realists, that is, the belief that they were capable of producing a true picture of reality just because they studied it. In fact, the position of most social scientists could be explained by a simple formula or principle, that is, "one reality generates one subjective reality." This means that the objective external social reality generates in the mind of an educated and careful observer a "true" image of this world. If a cruel monarch is engaged in brutal actions, the scholar should describe these actions as they are. The cruelty of the monarch lies in his actions.

Serious early inquires into the subjectivity of social perception took place in the nineteenth century. Germans Ludwig Feuerbach and, later, Karl Marx were among the first to suggest that people pursue their interests and, therefore, create reflections of social reality, such as religion, social science, or art, to justify these interests. People who pursue different interests perceive the world differently. Feuerbach created an anthropological view of religion and saw God as a necessary compensation for human weaknesses. Marx emphasized class interest—an objective goal of a large social group—as a major motivational force stimulating people's use of knowledge. A ruling royal family may see a war and a foreign conquest as glorious events; yet for the army recruits fighting it, the war could be a major devastation, causing and deepening poverty. In fact, Marx was among the first scholars to propose the new formula "one objective reality—many subjective realities." The French philosophers of the eighteenth century who believed in the power of opinions to change the world clearly influenced Marx when he discussed how the same reality produced in the minds of economists and politicians quite dissimilar perceptions. This formula "one objective reality—many subjective realities" was elaborated by Marx in several of his publications.[1]

Marx's approach to the interaction between reality and its reflections in the human mind was practically neglected by most social scientists. They continued to equate objective reality to its perceptions by the "educated" human mind. Almost none of the great sociologists of the nineteenth century—not Auguste Compte, Adolphe Quetelet, or Émile Durkheim—dealt with the quality of knowledge and other epistemological problems in their social analysis. Max Weber was rather an exception with his interest in the impact of values on social cognition and his call for "value-free social science." Only occasionally, they turned to discuss the possibility that even a great social scientist could display a very unique and even biased perception of the world.

SOCIAL SCIENCE AVOIDS THE QUESTION OF SUBJECTIVITY

The inclination of social scientists to ignore the complexity of social and political cognition (the way that people perceive social and political realities) became evident when scholars began to develop and utilize survey methods as early as the 1930s. Most pollsters, and others who made interpretation of survey results a profession, generally assumed that their respondents, either ordinary people or elites, displayed accurate reflections of social reality.

Naïve empiricism was a dominant paradigm in American social sciences in the twentieth century, almost until the time of the "cognitive revolution" in psychology in the 1960s. In fact, in most academic debates that took place among social scientists—for instance, between functionalists and advocates of the conflict approach, between neo-Marxists and their opponents—epistemology and the questions of how and why we perceive the world in a particular way were almost absent. Absorbed with the enticing complexities and popularity of empirical studies, most American scholars were accomplished positivists who had little interest in the subtleties of cognitive process in their own minds or in the minds of their respondents. The works of representatives of the Chicago school in the 1920s and 1930s show this tendency.

The phenomenological revolution attempted in the works of Edmund Husserl and his followers in Germany in the beginning of the twentieth century was almost unnoticed in the mainstream of American sociology and psychology. American psychologists did not give any substantial support to the views of William James, a prominent scientist and one of the founders of American experimental psychology. James operated with the term *multiple realities* (or *sub universe*), which also included the realities of religion and mythology. He endowed each sphere with the status of reality if it was the object of the interest and attention of the individual.[2] Even the arrival on American shores of Alfred Schutz, a leading German phenomenologist with a clear interest in social process, exerted only some influence on the minds of the majority of social scientists. (It is remarkable that Schutz mentioned the impact of James on his views.) However, most thinkers of the twentieth century continued to pay little attention to how social factors influenced perceptions of society and how individuals shaped their fundamental perceptions of history, social institutions, and politics. Even later, despite some remarkable studies conducted in social psychology, most social and political scientists in the 1960s–1970s continued to discount the importance of social and political cognition. Alvin Gouldner's book *The Coming Crisis of Western Sociology* (1970), in which the author debunked the objectivity of American sociologists and showed the impact of an assortment of factors on their scientific perceptions, had very little impact on his own contemporaries or on the next generation of social scientists.

In the 1960s, American psychologists in their experimental studies of attitudes showed the importance of the subjective component of people's reflections of the social world. Yet scores of political scientists, historians, sociologists, and pollsters continued to remain in the mainstream of naïve materialism. Very few researchers before the 1980s, including pollsters, had serious doubts about the veracity of their respondents, eyewitnesses, and "area experts." It is significant too that many social scientists also neglected the probable impact of their own values on their observations and their interpretation of seemingly objective "hard facts." In effect, if we look at textbooks on sociology or public opinion published before the 1980s, we will find that only a few scholars paid some, mostly perfunctory, attention to the empirical validity of the survey data and to the effects of the desirable values on people's responses. Leading figures such as George Gallup and Hadley Cantril paid only lip service to the issue. The work of Donald Campbell published in 1968, who preached the need for critical attitudes toward sociological information and insisted on the importance of the multisource approach in social studies, was mostly ignored by social scientists.[3] In the 1960s–1970s, only a few researchers working in the fields of the social and political sciences used terms such as *validity* and *reliability* in regard to collected data. The most prominent publications in sociological literature related to surveys and published before the 1980s basically ignored the correspondence between the beliefs of respondents and their survey answers. Take, for instance, Melvin Kohn's famous book *Class and Conformity* (1968). Discussing people's attitudes about their work, the author did not even mention that the respondents' answers could have been strongly influenced by outside factors such as "political correctness," deeply seated religious values, or some immediate individual concern.

One major cause of the dominance of naïve realism in American social and political sciences was researchers' lack of attention to the role of ideology in shaping the human mind. This tendency persisted to some degree in the twenty-first century as well. Such inattention to ideology clearly contrasted with the position of Soviet social and political scientists, especially in the 1960–1970s. Despite the Soviet social and political scientists' limited theoretical and research experience (empirical sociology, for example, was not "permitted" in the Soviet Union until the late 1950s), they accepted the belief that survey respondents were strongly influenced in their answers by the dominant ideology of their society. In particular, the Soviet scholars believed that respondents in capitalist countries, in fear of giving politically incorrect answers, were frequently and deliberately insincere with the researchers.

Soviet sociologists, in effect, were aware that they had to deal with several "realities" accepted by most people in the Soviet Union. One was the reality of their everyday life with all its difficulties, absurdities, and happy and distressing developments. Another reality appeared in people's opinions given to pollsters. It was a more optimistic and positive vision of their lives and the world around them. Harsh criticisms and pessimistic views were carefully avoided. Finally, the third reality was the censored reality of party officials and ideologues. It was a reality containing perceptions of a strong and prosperous country supported by its people. In that picture, the Soviet Union was a country looking forward to its days of prosperity, international respect, and ideological unity. People lived in and knew only one social reality but reflected and spoke differently about it based on their individual ideological beliefs and specific position in the society.[4]

Another evidence of the sensitivity of Soviet intellectuals regarding the nature of the human mind was their positive reaction to the works of George Orwell. To many readers in the Soviet Union, Orwell's analogies related to a totalitarian society were almost perfect. They described the life and the mind of Soviet residents fairly accurately. For many Western authors, however, Orwell's book *1984* had almost nothing to do with the Soviet reality. Christopher Hitchens, one of Orwell's leading biographers, defined *1984* as "an admonitory parable or fantasy."[5] The same tendency to diminish or deny the ability of the government in *1984* to brainwash Oceania's residents is reflected in various works by Jeffrey Meyers and other critics who saw Orwell's ideas as a reflection of his own problems or as a poor caricature of the Soviet regime.[6] However, for scores of Soviet social scientists and sociologists as well as for many other of Orwell's readers in the Soviet Union, one of his greatest contributions was his profound insight into the functioning of the totalitarian ideology. He showed that the ruling elites were capable of creating an alternative reality and of persuading so many people in its validity.[7]

One of the authors of this book, Vladimir Shlapentokh, began his career as a Soviet sociologist who studied how the Soviet people developed their perception of the surrounding social world and which factors influenced their views. Of course, surveys could provide valuable information, but could the Soviet people tell a pollster what they truly thought? When Shlapentokh began to design the questions for the first national surveys in 1966–1969 (the respondents were the subscribers of the daily *Izvestia*, one of the most circulated papers in the Soviet Union), he tried to use several methodological devices to find out the actual, uninhibited views and feelings of the respondents. He compared the answers that the respondents gave at work, at home, in written mailed questionnaires, and in face-to-face interviews, answering both multiple-choice and open-ended questions.[8] Shlapentokh and other Soviet sociologists (among them Boris

Grushin and Vladimir Yadov) were able to describe, on the basis of their empirical data collected in the 1960s, how the Soviet people perceived the official image of Soviet society and how they tried to "adjust" their answers to the questions in the surveys: Many respondents did not accept the official picture of their society but tried not to reveal their true, mostly critical, views. Using various survey techniques, the Soviet sociologists were able to describe a variety of critical views of the regime: Some of them were ultraconservative and demanded "more Leninism" and "more communism"; others were nationalistic and chauvinistic; and others were clearly pro-Western. Contrary to what the Soviet propaganda claimed and many people in the West believed, there was no monolithic opinion about their country held by all the Soviet people.[9]

EMERGENCE OF THE CONCEPT OF SOCIAL CONSTRUCTION

Several schools of thought—all challenging naïve realism—began to emerge in more recent times, including ethnomethodology; symbolic interactionism; management of impressions; and cognitive sociology, with its concept of construction of social reality. In *The Social Construction of Reality: A Treatise in the Sociology of Knowledge,* Peter Berger and Thomas Luckmann made a decisive leap forward from the formula "one reality generates one subjective reality" to another formula, "one reality—many subjective realities," which, in fact, was close to Marx's view of the role of ideology in the human perceptions of the world.[10] The authors did not deny the existence of objective reality. However, they wrote about the construction of reality by individuals who have their own preexisting assumptions about the world.

Since the 1980s, the interest among American social scientists in the influence of various factors affecting an individual's perception of reality has somewhat increased. The impact of "desirable values" on scholars' and ordinary people's perceptions of facts was widely recognized. Psychological research set the tone of further discussions. However, naïve realism died hard and continued to dominate American social and political science. Many sociologists, historians, and political scientists were aware of but generally unwilling to take into serious consideration the tendency of people to misperceive the facts and social events around them. Take, as an example, the World Values Survey carried out by the University of Michigan in 1997–2002. The authors of the project assumed that respondents in all countries—from the United States to China and from Denmark to Ghana—would tell the interviewers their genuine reflections on social and political events at home and in the world. Doubts about the empirical validity of the responses have been raised neither by the authors of the World Values Survey nor by many of those who have used the data in their discussions.

Other intellectual developments, and there were several, were supportive of the idea of social construction of people's perception. One such development was the school of thought founded by Swiss psychologist Jean Piaget. He drew attention to a seemingly trivial fact, that children in the process of their intellectual growth change their fundamental reflections of the world. According to Piaget, children go through several stages of development and develop different kinds of mental operations that allow them to see and interpret the world differently at each stage. Piaget showed that each psychological construction emerging inside the developing child's brain is tested against reality in the same way that a scientist tests the validity of a hypothesis!

The works of Piaget did not have an impact beyond the field of cognitive and developmental psychology. In order to compel American social and political scientists to be involved in the epistemological debates and cast doubt on their naïve realism, American social science needed a boost. Such a boost was given by the school of so-called French structuralism. It was rooted also in the outburst of postmodernist ideology—deconstructivism—and, in particular, the multicultural movement, with its focus on the total "equality" of values and perceptions regardless of their social contexts.

ONE SUBJECTIVE REALITY—ONE OBJECTIVE REALITY

While empiricists, materialists, and orthodox Marxists assumed that an objective reality shapes perceptions in the individual's subjective world, French structuralists reversed the direction of causation: To them, it is the dominant structure of the human mind that creates the reality that some, if they choose, later call "objective"! Focusing on the processes within the human mind, Claude Lévi-Strauss and Michel Foucault each looked at the mental functions that create social structures. In their view, mental functions cause the reproduction of most cultural patterns, including beliefs and customs. These mental structures are responsible for the cross-cultural similarity of some phenomena such as fairy tales or myths. In a way, structuralists declared their allegiance to the formula "one subjective reality—one objective reality." Thomas Kuhn, the most famous American follower of French structuralism (along with Paul Feyerabend), was in the same "idealistic" league and reversed the traditional materialist belief that the gradual accumulation of objective scientific facts changes a scholarly methodology. He showed that people's understanding of reality changes under the impact of new, emerging scientific paradigms. In some way, the concept "one subjective reality—one objective reality" was also shared by the many American social scientists who propagated in the 1970s the belief that labeling social phenomena or groups of people (for example, the mentally ill or criminals) was in fact an act of questionable reality-creation and subsequent discrimination against these groups. They believed that people should therefore stop using such labels.

MANY SUBJECTIVE REALITIES—MANY OBJECTIVE REALITIES

Meanwhile, supporters of the new intellectual trend called deconstruction refused to recognize the existence of general meanings as well as the criteria for social consensus about meanings. The deconstructionists proclaimed a new formula, "many subjective realities—many objective realities." The new school celebrated a form of "absolute" relativism submerged within the infinite chain of contexts. The troubadours of the new trend in social sciences declared that all people operate in a special world of individually and socially constructed objects, that is, the objects whose meaning is created by the human mind. For example, in their interpretations, gender and race have become such constructs.

These ideas would have remained in relative obscurity had they never been reinforced by the powerful political winds of the second half of the twentieth century. Deconstructivism received an unexpected encouragement from supporters of social theories proclaiming the essential equality of the abilities of all human beings of all cultures in their reflection, understanding, and interpretation of reality. In other words, there is no right or wrong, simple or sophisticated, advanced or less advanced perceptions, skills, or theories of reality. Every view should be equal to the next and thus should be celebrated. Again, as in the case of deconstruction, the roots of this super-egalitarian social relativism are found in the remote past, in early socialist utopian theories, and in Marxism for which social equality was the ultimate goal and tool of social progress. Since the 1980s–1990s, an idealistic concept of the construction of social reality and multiple realities has also become popular in American social sciences. The terms *objective reality* and even *reality* have disappeared from sociology textbooks; they are conveniently avoided. This transformation passed two stages: In the first stage, the objective reality lost its supremacy over subjective reality; in the second, the objective reality lost its very existence.

The multi-realities approach influenced a number of interesting works in American social and political sciences. Relativism focused on different views of the same social events; it brought to attention a multi-view perspective. Several interesting works have appeared. These multi-perspective studies have dealt with the ideological and political tendencies of the International Monetary Fund (Horowitz, 1985), contradictory accounts of lethal school shootings in Paducah, Kentucky, and Jonesboro, Arkansas (Roth and Mehta, 2002), and the reasons for the failure of the Israeli-Palestinian peace process since the late 1970s (Kacowicz, 2005). There is a stimulating book-length treatise about how to understand the environmental accident at Love Canal in New York State (Mazur, 1998). A series of works by Christian Davenport and his colleagues also uses a multi-perspective approach and multisourced accounts of repression against the Black Panther Party in Oakland, California, between 1967 and 1973 (Davenport and Litras, 2000) as well as the Rwandan genocide of 1993 (Davenport and Stam, 2003). The authors argue that social scientists who use eyewitness accounts as evidence tend to ignore the fact that different eyewitnesses use different explanations about what has taken place and why. The analysis of five different newspaper accounts (local and national), as Davenport and Litras (2000) concluded, results in different conclusions about why repression against the Black Panther Party took place. Similarly, numerous eyewitness accounts about the Rwandan genocide differ when the researchers interview representatives of different ethnic groups in that African country.

Two authors of this book along with Joshua Woods published a monograph based on a multinational research project about the attitudes about America in the aftermath of September 11, 2001.[11] The data collected in that project showed that perceptions of the same dramatic event varied immensely from country to country and across social groups in these nations. People around the world were clearly at odds with one another regarding the causes of the terrorist act, the September 11 perpetrators, and the motivations of the perpetrators. Opinions varied about who was the actual victim of the attacks and, quite predictably, how the world should have responded to prevent similar attacks in the future.

OUR POSITION

Looking at multiple perceptions of the Soviet Union, we try to avoid relativism and deconstructivist claims about the existence of many equally accurate depictions of social reality. We assume that a scholar, like any other individual, deals with "hard reality" comprised of many objective indicators ranging from actual events to empirical statistical data reflecting tangible events and developments. Of course, this "hard reality" can be interpreted and explained in great many ways.

At the same time, we do not want to share the position of "naïve realists." We generally accept the formula "one objective reality—many subjective realities." We recognize that different people tend to perceive the same "hard reality" in different ways. We agree with Searle, who suggests the importance of dealing with two groups or two categories of facts. These categories are (1) the facts (he calls them "brute facts"), which exist independently of what people think about them and (2) the facts that depend for their existence on human thought (he calls them "social facts.").[12] Social facts are socially constructed. As the saying goes, freedom fighters in one person's eyes are terrorists in the other person's view. Yet there are "brute facts" out there too, and the denial of their existence does not, as Kant would have said, advance the interests of the human community.

From this point of view, we state that Soviet society in each period of its existence and development was a "real fact." The various structural and dynamic elements of that society are also real facts, such as the one-party political system; political censorship; or the state monopoly on economic assets, media, science, and education. The Soviet political police (named in different periods Cheka, NKVD, and KGB) existed. Similarly, the gulag and the prison system were real facts. It is also a fact that millions of people perished in the Soviet Union; they were killed by deliberate state terror, collectivization, and several wars. We can also mention several other "objective facts" as the leading role of the party, the planning character of Soviet economy, the militarization of society, and so forth.

We also try to show how dissimilar the images (held by different groups inside and outside this country) of the Soviet society were. These images influenced the social and political behavior of millions of people, including top government officials, managers, journalists, and powerful elites. The official images of Soviet society created by the ruling elites were installed, like software, in the minds of the people; this certainly helped the Soviet rulers to run the country. On the other hand, the perceptions of the Soviet society shared by the dissidents or liberal intellectuals within the country fueled their desire to tell the world their version of what they believed was "real" truth. Some of them even dared to oppose the communist system openly.

Outside the Soviet Union, the images of the Soviet society appearing in the press, in government statements, or in eyewitness accounts made some people either supporters or enemies of the Soviet Union as a political regime or a country. Many intellectuals in the West admired the Soviet anticapitalist system that eliminated private property, destroyed free market, condemned individualism, and limited individual freedoms. Others in the West saw these policies as a reflection of the toxic totalitarian nature of the Soviet political system.

We believe that a discussion of the multiple images of Soviet society held by contemporaries should help scholars, journalists, and educators to understand better the nature and developments in Russia today. People carrying different ideologies—a main factor influencing the perceptions of the world—may focus their attention on different aspects of Soviet life in the past. Comparing the views of people with the different ideological orientations, "the soft views," we can extract essential information that should help us to form a more comprehensive, balanced approach "to hard reality" of Soviet society.

In using multiple "soft realities" to understand the unique "hard reality," we also attempt to use a multisourced approach. With the extensive use of the multisourced views in our study of the Soviet society, we also need to question the validity of each view offered by both experts and ordinary people. Because we are not the advocates of relativism and believe in the existence of "hard reality," we need to check constantly how far these "soft realities" went to distort and disfigure "the hard reality."

Thus far our attempt to examine multiple views is not an ultimate solution to the problem of an accurate portrayal of social and political life in the former Soviet Union. We tend to believe that critical views of Soviet society are more "realistic" than the visions of society based on its apology. From this perspective, we assume that the Soviet government's official image of society (shared and supported by many people in the Soviet Union) as well as the perceptions of a few Western admirers of the Soviet Union were the images farthest from "real facts" compared with many other, critical views of that country. Although we attempt to maintain a critical view of Soviet society, we do not assert that the apologetic visions of the Soviet Union were all wrong while the critical perceptions and model were all accurate and right. Those Sovietologists in the United States and other countries who saw the Soviet Union as an "evil" totalitarian society also made many mistakes in their assessments. The apologists of the Soviet system, on the other hand, made many significant contributions to scholarship and a better understanding of the country.

In any case, we hope that this book, which displays the panoply of visions of Soviet society, will contribute to a better understanding of that great country and to the evaluations, choices, and policies that we make today related to Russia.

CHAPTER 2

THINKERS FROM OVERSEAS: HOW WESTERN EXPERTS DESCRIBED THE SOVIET UNION OVER ITS 74-YEAR HISTORY

INTRODUCTION

At least two major schools of thought regarding the Soviet Union have existed. The first was the totalitarian school, which emphasized the abnormal, pathological, and exceptional nature of the Soviet system. The other was the revisionist school, which has largely presented the Soviet Union as a "normal" society, one among many with similar features. The totalitarian theorists, as a rule, overestimated the Soviet regime's strength, threats, and stability. They also miscalculated the Soviet people's disaffection with the Communist regime. Revisionists, on the other hand, while giving many important insights about gradual changes within the Soviet regime, were sometimes too eager (for ideological or political reasons) to portray the Soviet Union as an ordinary society, not much different from any other country. When theorists of the totalitarian school (we will call them totalitarianists) tended to condemn the Soviet regime, the revisionists (we will call them normalizers) were inclined to treat it in a rather kindly and accepting way (Shlapentokh, 2001).

Overall, American and European totalitarianists (despite their ideological limitations), working in the atmosphere of the cold war, have generally benefited from their use of critical attitudes about the Soviet

Union. Government funding and other financial support, after all, is easier to obtain if a researcher identifies foreign threats and warns about his own country's vulnerabilities. Yet many experts from the normalizers' camp shared their own measure of intellectual and financial support, primarily from the liberal circle of intellectuals, think tanks, and the media.

We will analyze developments of Western (mostly American) expert-observers' views over two major periods, with some subdivisions, lasting from 1917 to 1991. You will see that the differences in the elite's perceptions of the Soviet Union and its political and ideological system are simply remarkable.

EARLY ADVOCATES AND CRITICS (1917–1945)

American experts have been very much interested in the Soviet Russia after the October Revolution of 1917. Right from the early days of a new state, the perceptions of it differed dramatically. Early Sovietologists (to be precise, the Soviet Union was formed in 1922) had already displayed noticeably contrasting views, which became the early theoretical sources used by both the totalitarianists and normalizers of the later periods.[1]

From the end of 1917, but mostly after the end of the Civil War in the early 1920s, a main tenet of official Communist ideology in Russia was that the new Communist society was superior to any form of Western capitalism and any other social system ever created in history. The view of the Soviet society's uniqueness and superiority was at the core of the state propaganda and a newly formed centralized educational system. Before the concept of totalitarianism had been constructed and explained, American and (more broadly) Western observers were already divided in their perceptions. Some of them saw the new Soviet regime as egalitarian and truly progressive while others described it as dictatorial and utterly oppressive. The debates between these two "camps" would continue over the seventy-three-year period of Soviet history. At the beginning, the ideological litmus test separating the two camps was either support or opposition to the Russian Revolution and to the Soviet political and social "experiment" (Burbank, 1991).

AMERICAN SUPPORTERS OF THE SOVIET OFFICIAL IMAGE

Until the 1940s, many American intellectuals (who were, generally, strong critics of American society and supporters of Socialist views) propagated the idea of the Soviet economic, moral, and ideological pre-eminence (Shlapentokh, 1998). They mostly dismissed critical reports about troubling events in Russia, such as mass murders, as inaccuracies, deliberate lies, or right-wing propaganda. Among several American admirers of the Soviet society were prominent writers and intellectuals such as Upton Sinclair, Theodore Dreiser, Lincoln Steffens, and Lillian Hellman. Upton Sinclair, for instance, dismissed anti-Bolshevik stories as sheer misinformation distributed by mainstream American and European newspapers and magazines (Lash, 1962). Others were critical of the violence but believed in the progressive nature of the Soviet social experiment. Steffens, after visiting Moscow in 1923, solemnly asserted, "Russia proved that you can change human nature sufficiently in one generation" (Steffens, 1938: 627–628).

Of course, some American Socialists and Communists, like journalist John Reed, were among the most ardent and consistent supporters of the Soviet Union. Many from the American Left accepted, at face value, almost everything that the Kremlin leaders were saying. For example, the American sympathizers demonstrated their full support for the Kremlin's repressive actions against rivalling Socialist parties and groupings, such as the Mensheviks and the Socialist Revolutionary Party (SR). They also accepted the Soviet government's version of the show trials staged to prosecute the Mensheviks in the 1920s and 1930s. For example, the Workers' Library Publishers (1931) reissued the translations of the trial of "the All-Union Bureau of the Central Committee of the Counter-Revolutionary Mensheviks." In the text's preface, the publishers expressed support for the charges brought by the Soviet government against the accused members of the political opposition. Edward Ross, a leading American sociologist in the beginning of the twentieth century and a strong self-identified opponent of private property and individualism, openly praised Russia's attempts to create a Socialist society (Ross, 1918). Many journalists like those of the *The Nation* voiced their support of the Russian and Soviet policies frequently viewed by the American side as a form of social progressivism. (Remember President Woodrow Wilson was elected in 1912 and 1916 partially because of his progressive domestic agenda, yet he was extremely critical of the Russian Revolution and despised Communism).

Russia's sympathizers were not at all concerned with the Bolsheviks' dissolution of the Constitutional Assembly—the highest legislative body at that time—in January of 1918. Some of them certainly recognized that these measures were clearly undemocratic. However, they also interpreted such actions as needed and necessary, especially after reflecting on the costs of building a new society in a backward country like Russia. For many American liberals like Lincoln Steffens, as well as for some young radicals, the absence of democracy in Russia was not an alarming sign at all. The masses in Russia, in their view, were not ready for democracy yet. Moreover, many American admirers of the Soviet regime did not appreciate capitalism and liberal democracy in general. They believed that the Soviets were developing a new social and political system, something truly superior to the corrupt and antiquated parliamentary democracy of the French, British, or American type. Former Trotskyites, like James Burnham, saw the Union of Soviet Socialist Republics as a vanguard in a vast managerial revolution—a direct result of the breakdown and gradual collapse of free-market capitalism (Burnham, 1941). The Soviet Union to them was a living example of a forthcoming global socioeconomic and political transition.

Besides the true admirers of the Soviet Union, many politically moderate observers and authors did not necessarily support the Communist experiments of the young Soviet state. They were, however, against Washington's harsh rhetoric and policies toward Russia. They also believed that the Soviet society needed understanding and, possibly, acceptance. In the 1920s, they began to portray the Soviet Union Soviet as a country undergoing increasing "normalization" in all areas of life after an initial "shock" of the revolution. William Chamberlin praised the Russian *Thermidor* that had liquidated "crude" Bolshevism and began to transform the revolution into "a settled order" (Chamberlin, 1930: 334–338; 1944). Eugene Lyons, a future critic of Communist Russia, had found during his visit to Moscow many signs of normalization and even some features of a new conservatism. It seemed to him that the revolutionary zeal began to settle down. He even ventured the prediction that the dissolution of the entire Communist Party in the next few years was in the works (Lyons, 1935).

Several authors of the 1920s and 1930s looked at the Soviet Union as an increasingly pluralistic society (American Sovietologists returned to this idea one more time in the 1970s). Samuel Harper, professor of Russian languages and institutions at the University of Chicago, denied the totalitarian and antidemocratic character of the Soviet Union. He described numerous political and social organizations in the Soviet Russia, such as the Komsomol (The Youth Communist League), the Young Pioneers' organizations (engaging children politically from 10 to 14 years old), the trade unions, and manufacturing cooperatives as effective institutional means for civic training and mass participation in politics. Harper also believed in the benefits of Socialist collectivism, which was perceived as an individual's sincere dedication to collective goals for the sake of Socialism. Harper described collectivism as a new form of collective freedom, which was different from the Western individual's liberties and the resulting selfishness (Harper, 1929; 1938). These views predate, but also prefigure, the ideas of American Sovietologists such as Jerry Hough or H. Gordon Skilling in the late 1960s and 1970s.

Another admirer of the Soviet Union, Heinrich Alexander Freund, supported many of Harper's conclusions. He contended in 1945 that despite all the changes that had occurred (the repressions against peasants in the early 1930s, political purges of 1936–1938, and, of course, the intrusive social and economic experimentation of Five Year Plans), the general progressive character of the Soviet state remained unchanged (Freund, 1945). Overall, the observers' tendency to accept uncritically the Soviet political repressions, state and party institutions, and laws, such as the Constitution of 1936 (Webb and Webb, 1937), was already in place by the 1930s.

Another group of American sympathizers of the Soviet regime emerged in the 1930s among the supporters of the FDR's New Deal. When the Great Depression hit the United States, calls for a new re-evaluation of capitalism became widespread. Some American intellectuals, expectedly, became very critical of free market capitalism and its uncertainties. They turned their attention back to social progressive ideas of the early twentieth century including the calls for a strong state control over the economy and state-run economic distribution policies—something that the Soviet Union, from their point of view, had been already doing for some time and doing effectively.

It was a favourable time to promote such ideas. In the 1930s, the prestige of the populist idea of the "strong state" reached its peak in Europe and in the United States of America. The short-lived yet widespread popularity of Italian dictator Benito Mussolini in the United States during its own difficult economic times was quite indicative of this mood. The Soviet super-centralized planning system found a number of American and international admirers, reflected in Harper's (1931) enthusiastic account of the Socialist "offensive" in Russia. Walter Duranty, head of the *New York Times'* Moscow bureau between 1922 and 1936, wrote that a real Socialism had been already achieved in Russia. Socialism, in his account, had woken up the new and dynamic forces of invention, initiative, and discipline—all used for the sake of everyone's community (Duranty, 1935). It took almost 70 years for the *New York Times* to recognize that its correspondent in Moscow had grossly distorted the Soviet reality in the reports in which he was describing the progress in the Soviet countryside and ignoring the famine in 1932–1933. His articles about Soviet life had brought him the Pulitzer Prize in 1932. While acknowledging these inaccuracies only in 2003, the *New York Times* still did not admit that Duranty had also tried to legitimize the show trials in 1936–1938 and many other civil rights violations in Russia before World War II.

The New Deal's gradual success in the United States was strengthening many American intellectuals' positive attitudes about the Soviet Union. Many perceived Franklin Delano Roosevelt's plans for ending the Depression as a proof about an increasing role of the state in economic affairs and in social security. Furthermore, supporters of Socialism often interpreted the New Deal and Stalin's industrialization as two national versions of the same policy.

Another factor that strengthened support for the Soviet Union among many intellectuals was the growing danger of Nazi Germany after Hitler's ascendance to power in 1933. Some American intellectuals did not want to criticize Stalin's Russia because of his role (at least until the highly demoralizing Molotov-Ribbentrop Pact of 1939) as the major restraining force against Hitler. In this prewar period, the most prominent New York intellectuals, many of the Jewish origin, staunchly defended the first Socialist country as a bulwark against Nazism and anti-Semitism. These intellectuals bluntly rejected almost any negative or critical information about the Soviet Union and its policies (Howe, 1982; Podhoretz, 1979).

EARLY AMERICAN CRITICS OF THE SOVIET SYSTEM

Despite the waves of sympathy toward Soviet Russia, many observers maintained a cautious and even negative view of the new regime. Several distinguished foreign-policy experts, such as Robert Lansing, the U.S. Secretary of State from 1915 to 1920, as well as prominent intellectuals like William Walling and Charles Crane were deeply concerned with the horrors of the Russian civil war, which ended by the early 1920s. Critics frequently predicted that the Bolshevik regime would fall apart in the matter of months, or maybe a few years. Editorials published in the *New York Times,* for example, predicted the impending fall of the Soviet regime during its early years of consolidation between 1917 and 1920[2]. Many American critics were also concerned about the circumstances of the Soviet regime's creation: They believed in the crucial role of the German Kaiser Wilhelm II in the making of the Bolshevik establishment through Germany's top paid agents such as Vladimir Lenin (1870–1924), future head of the state (Lash, 1962). The animosity of many Americans toward Bolsheviks and Russia, fuelled in the beginning by fears of a separate peace between Russia and Germany, was so strong that many intellectuals and politicians supported the American invasion of Soviet Russia from 1918 to 1919 (some of them, of course, also viewed this invasion as a preemptive move directed against Germany but not against Russia). They also argued that the United States should postpone diplomatic recognition of the Soviet Union as a sign of Washington's rejection of Russia's policies (Batsel, 1929). The diplomatic ties between the two countries were restored only in 1934.

Several conservative authors who visited the Soviet Union in the 1920s and 1930s depicted the horrors of the collectivization in villages and the industrialization in cities and towns. Among such commentators was Maurice Hindus (1929, 1931, 1933), an American journalist of Russian ancestry. He was probably one of the first Western observers to grasp the full scope of the unfolding tragedy of collectivization. On the other hand, he expressed some support of agricultural policies and believed in the leading role of the working class in society. Sober reports about the life of working people in the Soviet Union came from McCormick (1929). Other commentators expressed doubts about the official Soviet depiction of the 1930s political trials in Moscow (Lyons, 1940). A significant number of American authors believed that the Soviet Union was promoting an imminent world Communist Revolution (Taracouzio, 1940).

Such fears were to some extent unfounded, however. The most radical and hawkish leaders of the early Soviet regime had already left the country by the 1930s. Soviet Russia's first war commissar (or defence minister) Leon Trotsky (1879–1940), after leaving Russia, had drastically changed his view on the nature of Soviet society. He declared that Soviet society was deviating from Socialism because of Stalin's counterrevolution launched after his ascension to power. Initially, Trotsky hesitated to label this new form of society, but eventually named it, "Bonaparte-like" and "bureaucratic." As an orthodox Marxist, he believed that an anomalous society built in the Soviet Union was neither Socialist nor capitalist because state bureaucracy became the new ruling class in Russia. Thus, in Trotsky's view, the Soviet regime under Stalin had only two viable long-term options: to develop itself into a true Socialist nation, or return to a kind of bourgeois society (Trotsky, 1937). Trotsky's followers in the United States and around the world continued to portray the Soviet society as a degenerated workers' state, and predicted a quick ending of that system.

Supporters and Critics in Wartime and the First Postwar Years

The initial embattlement, and the final triumph, of the Soviet Union in the Second World War has silenced many critics of Moscow in the United States. The most prominent publications dedicated to the Soviet Union were generally friendly and described the allied country as somewhat akin to America. Wendell Willkie, the Republican opponent to Franklin Roosevelt in the presidential election of 1940 (Willkie had travelled to Russia during the war) defended the Soviet Union against its critics (Willkie, 1943). The writings of Alexander Werth, also favourable toward Moscow, became very popular among liberal intellectuals in the United States and Britain (Werth, 1942). Many actions of the Soviet government found their apologists. Louis Fischer (1941), an American correspondent in Russia, assessed the Molotov-Ribbentrop pact very positively as a way to preserve peace in Europe. Joseph Davies, the U.S. ambassador to Moscow from 1936 to 1938, presented a view exemplary of the prewar period, depicting a very optimistic picture of a young country building a new progressive society (Davies, 1942). In trying to present the Soviet Union as a typical society, Davis suggested that it was actually not a Communist state, but rather a moderate Socialist society. He and others tried to show that Moscow used quite innovative methods of management, combining some capitalist principles together with a massive and highly centralized industrialisation of its economy (Duranty, 1944).

However, the final collapse of Nazism in 1945, Stalin's expansionist policy in Eastern Europe, and the early cold war rivalries have strengthened the position of those Western observers who saw the Soviet political and social system as anomalous and dangerous. In the postwar years, supporters of the totalitarian model of the Soviet Union gained significant strength in American Sovietology. As we will see, this trend changed by the mid-1970s, when a second "wave" of normalizers attained a strong and even dominant position.

The "Clash of Schools" (Late 1940s–1991)

While most American people held, in general, critical views of Socialist Russia (we will describe this in chapter 4), the postwar American elites were somewhat divided in terms of their perceptions of the Soviet Union. These disagreements increasingly appeared as reflections of dissimilar schools of thought, with their inner logic, facts, arguments, and theories. At different periods, some arguments dominated to be later replaced by other arguments and theories. In retrospective, from the mid-1940s to the early 1960s, as the cold war developed, a critical school of thought became dominant among Sovietologists. The next subperiod (from the late 1960s into the 1980s) coincides with détente (relaxation or easing) of U.S.-Soviet relations, as well as with the student political turbulence in the 1960s and the antiwar movement. During this period, American political debates had polarized considerably. A large group of university intellectuals embraced far-reaching critical theories and ideas. These ideas frequently contained pro-Socialist views and carried sympathies toward Moscow's political and social system. During this period, most totalitarianists were on the defensive.

THE MID-1940S TO THE EARLY 1960S: RELATIVE DOMINANCE BY TOTALITARIANISTS

Understanding the Soviet Union as a totalitarian society was introduced by several scholars including, among others, Hannah Arendt (1951), J. L. Talmon (1952), Carl Friedrich, and Zbigniew Brzezinski (1956). One of the assumptions of some representatives of this school was an equation of Nazism and the Soviet regime. This postulate would later become the major target of criticism and even denunciation by many "revisionist" Sovietologists in the 1970s and later. Meanwhile, the critics of the Soviet system formulated several elements or features of a typical totalitarian society. These features included the absolute dominance of the supreme leader in the decision-making process; the political monopoly of one party; the political police as the most powerful instrument of the regime; the militarization of society; aggressive imperial policy; the totalitarian ideological indoctrination of the population; the ban on religion; the complete state monopoly on media, education, science, and culture; the dominance of the central administration over the provinces; the absence of democracy; the official class morale; the centralized control of the economy; and the rejection of private economic activity. All these elements were present in the Soviet Union, totalitarianists argued.

The totalitarianists' academic prestige grew especially in the early postwar period. Political scientists and historians found support for their ideas among experts from other disciplines. A few prominent economists such as Ludwig von Mises and Friedrich von Hayek, who worked in the United States in the 1950s and early 1960s, used economic data and statistical formulas to launch their own criticism against totalitarianism. They argued with numbers and formulas that the Socialist economy was doomed to fail (von Mises, 1951; von Hayek, 1944). Von Mises also argued that Socialist regimes could not establish workable methods of calculating the value of different economic activities, and were unable to stimulate people to work (von Mises, 1951; Hubbard, 1938). Von Hayek was confident that the Socialist economy could not function successfully for an extended period because ordinary people would have no influence on economic activities (von Hayek, 1944; Shlapentokh, 1988).

The totalitarian school was not homogeneous and its members frequently shared the opposite views on many subjects such as the role of ideology, the imperial historical past and Russian nationalism in the Soviet Union. One group of totalitarianists strongly rejected the important role of Marxist ideology in the creation and functioning of the Soviet system. They were advocating the "power" approach and argued, for example, that the Russian Social Democratic Workers' Party (Bolshevik) and their leader Vladimir Lenin strived for power for its own sake. Walter Rostow defended a belief that both Lenin and his successor Stalin wanted to increase their own power by simply using Marxism and prerevolutionary Russian traditions to achieve their goal (Rostow, 1953). Robert Conquest (1967) insisted that behind the Soviet leaders' ideological arguments, there were power-driven, pragmatic policy motivations to strengthen the Soviet state and tighten the control over the population. Richard Pipes (1984) also did not believe in the important role of Socialist ideas in Soviet history, seeing them only as a thin cover for Russo-centric authoritarianism; he also disregarded the Socialist dimensions of the 1917 October "coup" and a number of political developments that followed. Pipes also reduced the significance of the Marxist ideology in the belief systems of the original Russian revolutionaries. Socialist ideology, in his view, was only a convenient rationalization for power-thirsty Bolsheviks to grab control of the country. In his monumental work published in 1990, Pipes devoted only a few perfunctory sentences to Marxism. He did not even substantially analyze Lenin's views on history, economy, or politics. He treated Lenin's exercises in Marxism as almost irrelevant to his activities for seizing power (Pipes, 1990). Zbigniew Brzezinski (1956), a scholar who later served in President Carter's administration, was another supporter of this approach. Other scholars emphasized several major features of a power-driven political system such as institutional violence against dissenters, a highly organized bureaucracy, and the charismatic role of the leader.

A significant group of totalitarianists defended an opposite view. They saw the Marxist ideology as the major driving force of the Bolsheviks. These observers reminded their critics that a global revolution had always been among the top goals of the Soviet Communists especially in the early years of the Soviet Union. These experts overemphasized the ideological importance of Marxist internationalism and Moscow's calls for the world revolution.

These fearful expectations of the Soviet international behavior first occurred in the 1920s and were further reinforced by the Soviet acquisition of nuclear weapons right after World War II. In the 1950s and in the following decade, many Western experts strongly believed that the Soviet leaders were exceptionally ideological in their actions and dedicated to a global Communist takeover. One of them was George Kennan. He considered that the triumph of Socialism was the central element in the Soviet strategic worldview, although he was sceptical that Moscow would try to achieve this goal by staging a global war against the West (Kennan, 1961). Others were confident that the Soviet Union, as an empire, was on a mission to build a global Communist system by all means (Ulam, 1963). They were convinced that the Soviet regime, during its first 40 years of existence, constantly applied this militant ideology to its foreign policy and would do the same in the future.

Critics also pointed out the dangerous irrationality and strength of the Soviet Union's ideology. There was an assessment of the Soviet experiment as the greatest fantasy of the century (Kolakowski, 1978) or the tragic victory of ideology over common sense. After the collapse of the Soviet Union, in the special issue of *The National Interest*, Martin Malia argued that Socialism meant, above all, moral ideas, and that the essence of Socialism, such as its collectivist institutional forms, derive from this idea (Malia, 1993). There were arguments that one of the reasons of the Soviet regime's implosion was the erosion of the official ideology (Bialer, 1987).

Totalitarianists also disagreed about the nature of the historical link between the Soviet Union and the Russian empire. Some totalitarianists overlooked or rejected an assumption that the Soviet Union was in many senses a continuation and extension of the Russian empire. Some insisted that the Bolshevik regime was a historical accident, a sudden interruption of Russia's steady progress toward a constitutional democracy (Daniels, 1987). It was a radical interruption in the steady process of political power evolution. In other words, despite various flaws of the imperial regime that existed before February 1917, the Bolshevik Revolution was an anomaly, an illogical historical development.[3]

Other totalitarianists, however, saw the Soviet Union and the October Revolution as a logical result of many complicated social, economic, and political processes. The new system was rooted in the contradictions within the old Russian regime. Supporting this view, historians and political scientists did not discount the importance of the Communist ideology and were generally reluctant to describe the Bolsheviks as a power-grubbing bunch of thugs (Fainsod, 1963).

Among the most prominent supporters of the continuity hypothesis was Robert Tucker (1961), who saw the regime that emerged under Lenin and Stalin as a type of neo-Tsarist order that labelled itself socialist. He considered developments that took place in the 1930s as a setback to the Russian imperial order of developments and saw the later Soviet policies as attempts to overcome the country's historical backwardness (Tucker, 1990). Overall, prominent totalitarianists writing after the mid-1960s portrayed the Soviet Union as a system rooted in prerevolutionary Russian authoritative traditions, although the Bolshevik regime was born out of a radical coup d'etat (Inkeles, 1968).[4]

Although totalitarianists were able to present a complex and comprehensive description of the Soviet system, they also exposed their own serious weaknesses. Many of them often disregarded many accomplishments of the Soviet Union, such as social stability. Nevertheless, the Bolshevik's ability to restore order had been highly appreciated by many contemporaries of the Russian Revolution even in the Russian monarchists' ranks.[5] In the 1930s, American authors like L. E. Hubbard had been well aware of the Bolsheviks as a powerful force capable of restoring order and able to take the country out of chaos (Hubbard, 1938). Still, many totalitarianists did not want to acknowledge the fact that the restoration of social order was an achievement of the Soviet regime. Totalitarianists paid, for the most part, little attention to the attempts of the Soviet regime to modernize the society in both economic and social spheres. Despite grave military setbacks in 1941–1942, the Soviet Union has defeated the Nazi military machine in 1945. The Communists undeniably modernized the country turning it into a powerful industrial and welfare state with a strong military and an expansionist foreign policy.

Most supporters of the totalitarian models also paid relatively little attention to Russian nationalism as one of the regime's powerful motivating forces. In most of Richard Pipes's publications before 1991, he never viewed the Bolsheviks after 1918 as proponents of Russian nationalism. The totalitarianists tended to ignore that Soviet people accepted the patriotic goals of building a strong state. When, for example, W. W. Rostow (1967) described the evolution of ideology in the Soviet Union and its role in the postwar period, he practically disregarded its nationalist and imperial components (Shlapentokh, 2001). Patriotism often played a more prominent role than Socialist ideas did. Many totalitarianists overlooked the facts that Stalin actually eliminated much of Socialist phraseology from Soviet propaganda during the war against Germany (1941–1945). Instead, the Soviet World War II propaganda embraced strong nationalist ideas. A new blend of Marxism and Russian nationalism became an essential feature of the official Soviet ideology.

In the early postwar years, these weaknesses of totalitarianists' views were largely unnoticed. A majority of scholars holding these views at that time did not face a serious opposition within universities. Although Leonard Schapiro (1960), John N. Hazard (1953), and Isaac Deutscher (1950) criticized the mainstream totalitarian approach, there was no serious scholarly "battle" about the Soviet Union's nature at that time. Some intellectuals such as Merle Fainsod (1953, 1958), based on archival work, even attempted to combine the elements of the totalitarian perspective with other theories.

An important reason for the ascendance of the totalitarianists in the United States was political. The 1940s was a new age of hardening of superpower rivalry. A wave of anticommunist campaigns and investigations shook Washington, D.C. To be uncritical of the Soviet Union at that time was, at best, questionable or unpatriotic. However, after the death of Stalin in 1953, and Nikita Khrushchev's coming to power in the late 1950s, and the change of the administration in Washington in 1961, serious changes took place in Sovietology as well.

THE "NORMALIZATION" OR "REVISIONIST" SCHOOL FROM THE MID-1960S TO 1991

By the early 1960s, American Sovietology showed real signs of fragmentation. In the second half of the 1960s and the 1970s, the views of the Soviet Union as an abnormal and totalitarian regime were no longer dominant. Instead, the Soviet Union emerged as a "normal" society with a specific set of political and economic features, a country led by a government prone to mistakes but capable of remarkable accomplishments—something that was part of any state's history.

CRITIQUES OF THE TOTALITARIAN MODEL

One of the most significant points of disagreement was the scope of mass repressions and political persecutions that took place in the Soviet Union during Stalin's time. Observers focused on the atrocities of collectivization (1929–1932), the prosecution of intelligentsia in the late 1920s and early 1930s, and, of course, the mass terror campaigns carried out since the mid-1930s. First, in the absence of reliable data, scientists continuously disputed the overall number of victims. Both sides, expectedly, used different calculation methods and produced different numbers. The leading figure among the totalitarianists, Robert Conquest (1968) put the number of prisoners in prison camps (Gulag) by the end of 1938 at 9 million—an estimation that probably lacks basic demographic credibility.[6] Many totalitarianists accepted Conquest's figures at face value and thus became easy targets of criticism.

Many critics, particularly from the political liberal wing, argued that their conservative opponents, historians, and political scientists, who wanted to emphasize the gloomiest features of the Soviet regime, most likely exaggerated these large numbers. The reason for the exaggeration was their anti-Soviet and anticommunist ideological motivation.

Opponents of totalitarianists argued that the real number of victims, in their accounts, was measured in tens of thousands, at most in hundreds of thousands but not in millions and ten millions as Stalin's critics insisted (Lewin, 1974; Getty, 1985).[7] This tendency of many critics of totalitarian models (normalizers) to minimize or obscure the suffering of the Soviet people under political repressions, and particularly mass political killings, was later emphasized by Stephen Cohen (1985).

Disagreements between the supporters of totalitarian models and normalizers also focused on Stalin and his political and social roles. Several authors refused to recognize that Stalin was the sole ruler of the country and that there were no serious oppositional forces in the Soviet Union after the 1920s. The researchers denied the extraordinary nature and importance of state intervention in Stalin's era. They also attempted to remove the label of "tyrant" from Stalin's historic accounts. Instead, increasingly often, he was portrayed as a state leader making tough decisions in the most extraordinary circumstances (Kenez, 1986; Fitzpatrick, 1986). Much like postwar German "functionalists" who denied Hitler's key decision-making role in Nazi Germany, many normalizers tried energetically to de-demonize Stalin and re-create his image as an outstanding political leader.

Such descriptions, however, were often inaccurate. Sheila Fitzpatrick (1984) for example, suggested, without presenting any serious evidence, that the dreadful anti-intelligentsia campaigns of the late 1920s and early 1930s, were very similar to the campaigns pursued during the Chinese Cultural Revolution in the 1960s. Rank-and-file Communists, not the upper echelon, initiated both these campaigns, in her view. Stalin, in her analysis, was practically unaware of these purges. However, why did they occur? Because the noncommunist intelligentsia posed a serious political threat to the new regime, the system was motivated to take action. In her analysis, these campaigns were also a mass response from society as a whole. Her approach to Stalinism did not change after 1991. Sheila Fitzpatrick, continued to discount Stalin's role in massive ethnic and social cleansings that took place in the Soviet Union during its first 40 years of existence (Fitzpatrick, 1992).

Descriptions of the collectivization campaign offered by most normalizers in the 1970s and 1980s also tended to de-dramatize this policy, as Sheila Fitzpatrick did in the first (1982) edition of *The Russian Revolution*. She recognized several serious flaws in the collectivization campaign. However, she saw the "positive side" of collectivization as well. She accepted Stalin's theory that the most serious difficulties during the process of confiscation of peasants' lands were caused by private agrarian landholders, or *kulaks,* who fought against the Soviet state (Fitzpatrick,

1982, 1994). In contemporary terms, as we interpret her views, those private agrarian landholders were rural terrorists destabilizing the country and who forced the regime to react against them. Surely, the reaction of the state against kulaks was harsh.

Normalizers also believed that the Soviet system had a set of unique features that did not fit in most definitions of totalitarianism. Some argued about the existence of a liberal opposition to Stalin (Cohen, 1985). In similar terms, Getty and Manning (1993) rebuked totalitarian theories for portraying people in the Soviet Union as passive participants in state-society relations. Others refused to see resemblances between the totalitarian nature of the Nazi regime in Germany and Stalin's political system, the resemblance that most totalitarianists and other critics of the Soviet system considered obvious (Getty, 1985; Dallin, 1973).

The most common assumption was that after Stalin's death, totalitarianism in the Soviet Union significantly diminished and the Khrushchev era of the 1960s was a radical departure from the earlier periods. Stephen Cohen (1979), for instance, refused to see the Soviet society after 1953, even with a conservative turn during Brezhnev's regime, as totalitarian. In the eyes of the revisionists-normalizers, their opponents such as Merle Fainsod, Richard Pipes, Paul Hollander, and Robert Conquest were wrong in believing the fundamentally totalitarian nature of the Soviet state.

High respect for Lenin's and Stalin's opponents, especially for Nikolai Bukharin (1888–1938), was common among many Sovietologists-critics of the totalitarian model. They often expressed compassion about Socialism, and reflected on various counterfactual alternatives and "what-if" scenarios to show that Russia could have taken a different path of development after Lenin's death in 1924. As did many observers within the Soviet Union, these experts tried to separate a "true" Socialism, which was better and "cleaner" than a somewhat "distorted" version of Stalin's creation (Cohen, 1973; Lewin, 1974). They also believed in a diminishing power of Soviet top leaders who emerged on top of the political ladder after Stalin's death.[8] Unfortunately, these experts did not recognize the crucial role of social coercion within the Soviet system, refused to see the aggressiveness of the Soviet foreign policy (Dallin, 1973; Welch, 1970), and shared the view that Soviet political life had developed many distinct elements of political pluralism (Fainsod and Hough, 1979; Tucker, 1981).

Overall, when many critics believed that the Soviet Union remained, in essence, a solid totalitarian state, the revisionists from the normalizers' camp saw that country and its political system as dynamic, evolving, and improving.

Modernization Theories

Theories describing the process of socioeconomic transformation of the Soviet system and its gradual conversion to capitalism took a prominent place in Sovietology of the 1960s and 1970s. For example, Walt Rostow (1967) and Raymond Aron (1962) believed that the Soviet Union was just one of many other modern industrial societies. Daniel Bell (1973: 74) wrote that Communism had presented to the world a special model of industrialization with prevailing political rather than market mechanisms. In his view, the Soviet Union and the United States were, despite the remaining differences between them, somewhat congruent industrial societies different not in kind but in degree (Bell, 1973). The facts these exerts chose to use were apparently supportive of these claims. Many social changes were taking place in the Soviet Union: rapid urbanization, modernization, mass education, and rising living standards—all these were obvious changes apparent in the 1960s in comparison with the 1930s. Focusing on the Soviet economy and some socioeconomic changes, the normalizers, of course, played down the significance of the Soviet oppressive political system. They did not see the Soviet Union as a closed society with rampant political censorship, lack of political and individual freedoms, gender and ethnic discrimination, and intrusive administrative control over every element of social life.

Normalizers preferred to believe that Soviet society was changing radically after the 1950s. Based on this position, they also rejected their opponents' argument that the Soviet system was strengthening. They perceived this argument as too ideological and rooted in hawkish beliefs of the flawed cold war mentality.

Convergence or Cultural Pluralism

In the 1960s, the success of the Soviet Union in economic, space, and military fields appeared so obvious that many scholars began to claim that the Soviet Union and the United States must learn from each other and build on mutual experience. For them, Socialism was a social system that had a number of advantages over free-market capitalism. Similarly, normalizers suggested that the Soviet experience should also become a model for developing countries, especially those that had freed themselves from colonialism in Africa and Asia. By the 1970s, China had become an even more attractive developmental and inspirational model for some American "left," yet most of them preferred to use the Soviet Union as a more convenient case in point to which to refer.

Other supporters saw the differences between Moscow and Washington but suggested that the socioeconomic gap would eventually diminish. Pitirim Sorokin and C. Wright Mills, both distinguished sociologists, predicted that the social systems of the United States of America and the Union of Soviet Socialist Republics would gradually become similar. They also suggested that both societies were becoming more alike because of common requirements of economic production, the increased role of education, and the global character of universal technical knowledge (Mills, 1958; Sorokin, 1964; Bell, 1973). Alfred Meyer believed that capitalism and Socialism were moving closer together as economic and business systems. He used the model of the American corporation as a major building block for his analysis and showed similarities between American and Soviet enterprises. He argued that the increasing need for coordination and hierarchy would eventually create similarities in many economic areas (Meyer, 1970). In fact, these expressed views were an attempt at a reincarnation of the classic post-Marxian belief that technological, scientific, educational, and informational progress would help to dissolve the gap between dissimilar social systems (Schuman, 1957).

These ideas of Soviet-American equivalence lost their influence among Sovietologists in the 1970s due to primarily aggressive political actions undertaken by the Soviet Union in Czechoslovakia in 1968 and a general economic slowdown at home. Nevertheless, theories emphasizing U.S.-Soviet similarity continued to occupy the minds and hearts of many scholars who were foremost critical of the United States. Their logic was that both Western and Soviet-type societies actually had many similar social problems. For example, they claimed both countries had to fight poverty, censorship, thought control, bureaucracy, and environmental problems. Both Moscow and Washington offered different solutions to these problems. In fact, and this was most important, both American and Soviet societies were essentially oppressive. In other words, the differences were in an outward appearance, in policies, and not in substance (Lubrano and Solomon, 1980).[9]

A popular argument in the 1960s was that while Western capitalist economies produced higher per capita income and provided the consumer with choices, the Soviet-style economies freed people from fear of mass unemployment and saved them from the anxiety of inflation and many unpleasant vicissitudes of economic cycles. Open and secretive American supporters of Socialism (and their views were frequently discussed in the American media) saw Soviet-style economies as granting a secure future for all Soviet workers. This was something, which Western capitalism was unable to do. Similarly, while Western health care was of better quality than the medical system available in the Soviet

Union, the argument was that Soviet medicine was free and accessible to everybody. Another common argument of the Soviet Union proponents in the United States was that people in both countries were discriminated against and persecuted from time to time for their political views and political pluralism in the United States was compatible to the pluralism available to the Soviet people (Solomon, 1983). Translated into Russian, these and similar statements were enthusiastically discussed and praised in the official Soviet media as evidence of American and Western weakness.

Positivism

Critics of the totalitarian model often justified their views from the positivist viewpoint. Positivism as a dominant paradigm in Western social sciences encouraged quantitative research and statistical analysis in obtaining facts. Positivism also encouraged social scientists to avoid using labels or create broad, abstract categories. As you remember from chapter 1, positivism found support among some followers of deconstructivism who declared that the meaning of objects was attributed to them by the human mind. Therefore, many new Sovietologists-positivists, while focusing on facts, were sceptical about the use of broad definitions including *totalitarianism, an oppressive regime,* or *backwardness* and even considered these terms unscientific.

Today's scholars and media commentators debate the meaning of terms such as *imperialism, terrorism,* or *war on terror.* In an almost similar fashion, 30 or 40 years ago, the debate was focused on totalitarianism. One side eventually prevailed. As a result, *totalitarian* as a term almost disappeared from most Western sources for some time. Even scholars who believed that the Union of Soviet Socialist Republics was a totalitarian state almost stopped using the term. Some researchers even demanded an open revision of old totalitarian "dogmas" (Skilling and Griffiths, 1971). The term, however, made a big comeback in the mid-1980s, under the influence of newly emerged critics of Communism within the Soviet Union and Communist states in Eastern Europe. It is worth mentioning that Soviet editors censored any mention of the word *totalitarian* in conjunction to Communism or Socialism. The official *Soviet Encyclopaedia* in 1989 referred to this term as reflecting a "foreign" political phenomenon. Liberal intellectuals started to use this term in open press in the middle of the 1980s when censorship in the Soviet Union was defacto eliminated.[10]

Sovietologists-positivists were confident that they could create a more objective description of this society because they dealt primarily with statistical information, with undisputable facts. They were not much interested in attaching labels or playing blame games, in which they accused their scholarly and political opponents from the "right." They were trying to be rather careful investigators of the real fabric of society and to not conflict instigators or warmongers. Yet they could not avoid their own biases, from time to time, by focusing on primarily positive elements of life in the Soviet Union: schools built, apartments distributed, refrigerators owned, or milk consumed. They largely ignored many disturbing facts ranging from street crime, daily corruption, domestic spying by the KGB, industrial accidents, and ecological disasters.

Of course, totalitarianists were not bias-free. They also tried to focus on facts. Yet they frequently collected "solid" empirical data and ignored other facts in order to substantiate their critical vision of Soviet society. Sociologists, political scientists, historians, or journalists, despite their good intentions and dedication to truth searching, are very vulnerable to the bias of self-fulfilling prophecy, a tendency of the human mind to see and remember those facts that fit the mind's convenient expectations and beliefs. A scholar who believes that the imprisonment of Japanese-Americans during World War II was no different from Stalin's mass imprisonments in the Gulag (a comparison that is inappropriate in many respects) will certainly look for facts that would support this point of view. A diehard critic of the American health care system is likely to seek and find great examples of efficient medical care (which, of course, existed) in a Communist country. Likewise, a conservative pundit in the United States is likely to be critical of John Kennedy's and Lyndon Johnson's foreign policy toward the Soviet Union and will probably overlook Richard Nixon's and Reagan's mistakes in "handling" the Russians.

USING OFFICIAL SOURCES AND FOCUSING ON THE ECONOMY

One of the most serious weaknesses of commentators from the normalizers' camp was their trust in official publications released by the Soviet government or publications of Soviet scholars. While supporters of the totalitarian view considered official Soviet reports as almost useless (Dallin, 1973), their opponents disagreed. They studied official documents and analytical reports as somewhat credible and reliable sources. Some Sovietologists wanted to show that official Soviet authors were no less believable than, for example, American or French ones.

For example, Gail Lapidus cited Yuri Andropov (1914–1984), the top Soviet leader from 1982 to 1984, as the chief authority to understand Soviet ethnic policies. Lapidus respectfully mentioned Andropov's use of certain political terms, which should have, in her view, provided some important hints about the future policy of the Soviet Union (Lapidus, 1984). She also cited statements from editorials in the *Kommunist,* the main Communist Party's theoretical journal, as arguments supporting her views of Soviet policies. In addition, she cited works of Richard Kosolapov and other official ideologues of the Communist Party, whose writings were largely ignored by other Western scholars and ridiculed by most critically thinking scholars within the Soviet Union.

As a rule, the Sovietologists-normalizers dismissed most critical descriptions of Soviet realities offered by Soviet immigrants. Moreover, they saw Soviet dissidents (still living in the Soviet Union) and recent émigrés as people motivated to settle personal scores with the Soviet government and having little academic credibility. Of course, the credibility problem of certain experts is a persistent difficulty that foreign-policy officials and area studies experts have to face. A lot of information and, apparently, disinformation offered to the U.S. officials about Iraq in the early 2000s, for example, came from Iraqi dissidents, who were the victims and opponents of Saddam Hussein's regime. Back in the 1970s, some Soviet émigrés also appeared to many Americans as revenge-seeking individuals who wanted to discredit the government of their former homeland. Therefore, they appeared as not necessarily credible sources of information. Alexander Dallin wrote that many scholars of East European background as well as Russian refugees expressed their biased opinions and relied on preexisting conceptual schemes (Dallin, 1973). In other words, they could not tell the truth about the Soviet Union.

In a similar way, critical information about the deficiencies and atrocities of the Soviet government has been downplayed because this information could have come from an unreliable source and there was no way to confirm it. A systematic effort was made to discredit the reliability of the individuals who gave quantitative information about Stalin's repressions. For example, revisionists commonly rejected the publications of former prisoners of the gulag as unreliable sources. Alexander Solzhenitsyn's *The Gulag Archipelago* (1978) was under serious criticism because the author himself was a political prisoner and, as some of his critics argued, could not judge the whole situation objectively (Getty, 1985; Skocpol, 1979). At the same time, back in the Soviet Union, the KGB could send almost anyone to prison just for the possession of this Solzhenitsyn's book.

Another perceptual feature of those who attempted to "un-demonize" the Union of Soviet Socialist Republics was rather substantive. It involved choices and strategists about how to deal or compete with the Soviet economy. By the late 1970s, the signs were that the Soviet economy was clearly inefficient. However, back in the 1960s, when the Soviet economy grew rapidly (due to a number of factors including, probably, some economic liberalization policies), several sympathizers like John Kenneth Galbraith (1967) and Wassily Leontief (1960) praised the planning system as more advantageous compared to free market capitalism. Paul Gregory and Robert Stuart (1974: 2) wrote that, in their view, the Soviet system could function well without private ownership and without profit motivation. Moreover, the Soviet economic system was incredibly competitive. The authors even speculated that the Soviet Union could eventually become even stronger than the United States, and could offer solutions to a host of economic problems that the Western world was witnessing.

This point of view was not new. Earlier, even authors who were very critical of the Soviet economic system, such as David Granick, discussed the Soviet Union's chances of winning economic competition with the United States (Granick, 1960). In the 1970s, when the problems of the Soviet economy became obvious, there were many in the United States who argued that the Soviet Union's economic potential was still strong enough to guarantee the basic needs of their society, and provide for the country's national security (Lewin, 1974). By the late 1970s, however, even the most persistent admirers of the Soviet system had to acknowledge that Moscow had serious economic problems resulting in underproduction, hidden unemployment, inflation, and most importantly, food shortages in major cities. However, most optimistic forecasters maintained that these and other economic problems in the Union of Soviet Socialist Republics were temporary. The solutions had to be in reforms aimed at repairing and perfecting the Socialist model of production and distribution.

Some scholars praised the Soviet agricultural experiments. Arthur and Jan Adams (1971), for example, summarizing their impressions of the *kolkhoz* (collective) farm system, found that the main problem was that Soviet officials could not find appropriate ways to unleash human energy and to help to revive the Socialist structure of Soviet agriculture. Mentioning about serious problems facing the Soviet economy in the early 1980s, Seweryn Bialer concluded that the overall Socialist system had an enormous potential and that several reforms would have strengthened the system and provided additional stability (Bialer, 1980). Most American economists, with a few exceptions, ignored slowdowns in the Soviet economic growth indexes. Others relied on Soviet official statistics showing only economic improvements. As a result, miscalculations were rampant especially in the assessments of the Soviet GNP, which was estimated two or three times higher than it actually was (Ellman and Kontorovich, 1998).[11]

Scholars also paid insufficient attention to the Soviet military industries. In fourteen Western textbooks on the Soviet economy published between the 1960s and the 1980s (reviewed by M. Kontorovich in 1996), only three had a chapter or section on the Soviet military industry. It was common to overlook a large share that the military sector had within the overall economy.[12] Prominent American authors such as Abraham Bergson (1964) and Ed Hewett (1988), in their books on Soviet economy, barely analyzed the Soviet military-industrial complex. Even in publications specifically on research and development, as well as on technological change, Western authors tended not to see the necessity to mention the military economy of the Soviet Union.

Pluralism, Participation, Multiculturalism, and Detente

The revisionists often accused totalitarianists of instigating the inflammatory cold war rhetoric. As a result, they, as critics of the totalitarian Soviet Union, did not see many strengths of the Soviet economic and political system. First, they did not see the Soviet Union as a pluralistic society. Second, they rejected, as normalizers suggested, the idea of a democratic political system in the Soviet Union. Third, the also mistakenly saw Soviet ethnic policies as a new form of colonialism. In addition, the totalitarianists emphasized the aggressive nature of the Soviet Union's foreign policy.

Many scholars in the United States supported the view of the existence of the elements of pluralism in the Soviet Union. They also rejected the view that the Kremlin was the only source of important political decisions in the country. Geoff Eley (1986) wrote that scholars, in his view, had concluded that any political activity, by definition, is about reconciling plural interests. Therefore, political pluralism is an inseparable element of any complex political system. Some scholars defend the view that political liberalism is possible even in nondemocratic political systems. Furthermore, the Soviet Union under Stalin was an example of a pluralist democracy (Hough, 1971; Dallin, 1973).[13] Even some die-hard totalitarianists and outspoken critics of Communism argued that political participation of various groups in the Soviet Union was "for real" and that political pluralism was a good indicator of the existence of a weak but viable political opposition in the country (Brzezinski, 1966).

Meantime, most Soviet dissidents-insiders who could read about these experts' conclusions from smuggled printed sources (such as *Time* and *Newsweek* magazines) shook their heads in disbelief because neither did they see any signs of pluralism in the Soviet Union at that time nor did they find any viable political opposition within their country. Yet the American supporters of the pluralist idea argued that so long as the Soviet society had interest groups, with their interactions and conflicts, it was somewhat similar to any Western society. These Sovietologists saw in the conflict model of society and in institutional pluralism the most powerful challenge to supporters of totalitarian models (Skilling, 1966).

Many authors began to pick various groups and assign them their own political roles in Soviet society (Skilling and Griffiths, 1971). Jerry Hough insisted that there was a serious devolution of power in Soviet institutions due to the process of social growing (Hough, 1972). Challenging his conservative opponents, he concluded that the Soviet Union had several centers of decision-making. The top Soviet political structure was also, in his view, to a degree, pluralistic. Some scholars described the Kremlin as an arena of an elitist democracy and a place of conflicting ideas. Since the 1960s, dozens of leading scholars, journalists, and scores of graduate students studied various factions in the Soviet Politburo and the way they lined up during official ceremonies and receptions.[14] The fact that Khrushchev was removed from all his posts in 1964 was clear evidence to many that factions indeed existed within top leadership. The assumptions about a collective nature of the Soviet decision-making were extended to the fields of foreign policy (Bialer, 1983). Studying top Soviet leaders and their printed speeches, some scholars began to create subcategories within the Soviet leadership: There were "reformers" or "conservatives," "ideologues" or "pragmatics." These dichotomies were common in publications about the Soviet Union up until the end of the 1980s. These terms are not abandoned, however: They are used to describe top political leadership in countries such as China, Iran, North Korea, or Cuba.

These assumptions of a relative political pluralism, of course, indicated for normalizers that the Soviet Union was not supposed to be as dangerous as some warmongers in Washington tried to portray it was. A suggested policy implication was that because of the pluralism in decision-making, Moscow was supposed to be more predictable in the last quarter of the twentieth century compared to the situation in the 1950s when the country was under the total control of a totalitarian leader.

A special subfield of research involved empirical analyses of the changes taking place within the Soviet elite. Scholars from the normalizers' camp studied the rise of some Soviet leaders' educational and academic levels and spoke fervently of generational changes among party *apparatchiks*. The concept of "professionalization" of Soviet politicians became popular among a number of Sovietologists (Bialer, 1980). Several scholars began to identify the most powerful technical experts who could have quietly influenced the Kremlin's policies (Griffiths, 1972; Gustafson, 1981). Predicting the climate of diverse opinions within the ranks of top leadership meant better understanding the Soviet Union's future (Bialer, 1983; Hough, 1980).

Of course, in reality, political leaders who are more educated than other officials do not necessarily become more "democratic" or pluralist. In addition, most top party officials in the Soviet Union did not necessarily earn their doctorate degrees by going to school, taking night classes, earning credits, and writing papers. Their education was largely a farce, and the educational institutions that awarded these academic degrees to party bosses did not have much of a choice.

Other Sovietologists-normalizers also began to look for signs of civil participation in the Soviet Union. Their intention was to show that Soviet citizens actually participated in running their country and to find similarities between Western and Soviet democracies. The concept of civil participation was, in fact, a very popular element of Soviet propaganda for many years. There was one particularly difficult issue, about which most Western scholars agreed. There were no free elections in the Soviet Union since the late 1920s. Very few observers dared to deny that Soviet elections were a massive sham staged by the government.

While acknowledging that elections in the Soviet Union were not free, normalizers tried to find other examples of mass civil participation. They focused on labor union committees, employees' mandatory meetings, and even on election campaigns during which people vented their grievances to authorities. Letters to the media and government offices were also taken into consideration as evidence of citizenship. One of significant methodological difficulties was the inability to find reliable statistics about employees' meetings or letters of complaint sent to local radio stations. On the other hand, the Soviet official data, most probably distorted, were easily available. Using these data, some Western normalizers suggested that most Soviet citizens exercised freedom of speech and commonly enjoyed the right to criticize the authorities and complain about problems (Thurston, 1986). Another area where Soviet citizens were seen as actively participating was administrative management. Overall, the idea of mass participation in politics was used to draw parallels between the Soviet Union and Western countries and to describe the Soviet system as essentially democratic from the start of its existence (Rosenberg, 1988).[15]

Several Sovietologists from the normalizers' camp maintained that ordinary citizens in the Soviet Union contributed to politics substantially and, in some respects, more so than people do under any "classic" democracy. Gail Lapidus contended in 1975 that the level of popular political participation in the Soviet Union was increasing. Others saw the importance of public policy debates at workplace. These scholars enthusiastically discussed the official Soviet materials about people's active participation in labor unions and in Communist Youth League (Hough, 1977).

Like totalitarianists, normalizers overlooked serious ethnic problems hidden within the Soviet system. First, most scholars did not see the Soviet Union, since its beginnings, as a new empire. They also believed that the Soviet government was able to efficiently solve most ethnic problems within the country. In reality, because of Moscow's total control of the media, any information about ethnic tensions was suppressed. Disseminating information about ethnic conflicts was labelled anti-Soviet propaganda, which was a criminal offense. Building a peaceful multiethnic society (or creating an image of such a society) was a top priority of the Kremlin and any information challenging its expectations was "killed" immediately. People in the Soviet Union were aware of ethnic tensions in the regions yet they did not discuss them publicly. Western observers practically overlooked a growing number of ethnic problems in the Soviet Union, particularly in the early and mid-1980s (Colton, 1986). The strength of nationalist opposition in Soviet republics was also generally underestimated.

Finally, most normalizers did not see the Soviet foreign policy as interventionist and preferred to describe most Soviet actions as a response to the aggressive behavior of the United States or as a consequence of the cold war struggles. Arguing with the conservatives within the United States, the liberal scholars and public officials alike suggested that the threat from the Soviet Union was systematically exaggerated for political purposes. According to this view, the confrontation between the United States and the Soviet Union was unnecessary. Because of the mistakes committed by both Democratic and Republican (to a larger degree) administrations, and because of ideological warmongering in the United States, the Soviet Union had to respond accordingly. Furthermore, the actions of the United States, as critics argued, gave significant strength to the "cold warriors" within the Kremlin who, in turn, were eager to accuse the United States of aggressive intentions. In other words, irresponsible actions of Washington and Moscow created a very dangerous situation on a global scale.

While supporters of pacifism demanded the United States' unilateral disarmament, and most totalitarianists supported "peace through strength," most normalizers preferred to defend a flexible position suggesting that both countries should immediately engage in a sustained round of negotiations to reduce nuclear arms and to accept mutually agreeable principles of international behavior. Some even claimed that the Soviet Union was a great power in a phase of ascendance, which simply claimed a place under the sun, a place that should have been acknowledged (Bialer, 1980).

TOTALITARIANISTS OR NORMALIZERS?

At the end, both competing camps of totalitarianists and normalizers found each other somewhat unified about one issue. With only few exceptions, up until 1990, experts in both camps believed that the Soviet system was strong enough to sustain any destructive pressure from within or from outside. Even the most worrisome economic and political symptoms that occurred in the late 1980s did not indicate in the minds of a vast majority of experts a forthcoming implosion. It was a common understanding that a few "good" reforms should, like strong medical injections, improve the economy and open up the society politically. Moshe Lewin (1974), for example, ended his book on early economic reforms in the Union of Soviet Socialist Republics on a very optimistic note. Though the Soviet Union entered the post-Khrushchev period of counterreforms, he argued that the society and its economy were developing steadily and that the Soviet Union would eventually arrive at the age of political reason (Lewin, 1974). Critics of the Soviet Union also underlined Moscow's military and economic might, the country's accomplishments in space programs, a great scientific potential, and the country's technological advancements (Brzezinski, 1969; Pipes, 1984). Samuel Huntington and Zbigniew Brzezinski frequently referred to the Soviet system as efficient, reliable, and stable (Huntington and Brzezinski, 1964).

One of the key issues with policy implications was the assessments of the Soviet military potential. If the Soviet Union was a weak state and its global threat was diminishing, then there was no necessity to spend a significant portion of the U.S. federal budget on defense. On the other hand, if the Soviet Union, despite its growing difficulties in the late 1970s, had continued to pose a significant military threat, then the United States had to designate significant resources to respond to the challenge. If the Soviet system was inherently flawed, then the military might of the Soviet Union had been exaggerated. On the other hand, if the Soviet economy was competitive and efficient, then it could sustain a significant military build-up, that would have made the Soviet Union a permanent threat to the United States. At the end, economists argued that even a weak economy of the Soviet Union could have supported a strong military due to high levels of militarization at the expense of individual consumption (Birman, 1981). In other words, Soviet citizens did not eat well, but paid for a strong military. Richard Pipes, for example, asserted that the lack of economic growth did not mean the weakening of the system and its military strength (Pipes, 1984).

Again, like in the 1940s, the supporters of the totalitarian models, and a lot of them were political conservatives, generally prevailed in the 1980s. This shift to some degree helped the government set policy priorities and increase the United States' military build-up vis-à-vis Moscow. After the collapse of the Soviet Union in 1991, it was relatively easy for the conservative experts to claim that their research, lectures, articles, and books had influenced strong American foreign policy and contributed to the end of the cold war. Their logic was that the Soviet Union could no longer compete with the United States economically and militarily and was eventually forced to undergo significant economic and political reforms.

Only after 1989, when the Soviet threat had substantially diminished, could some conservatives like Martin Malia or Robert Conquest call the Soviet threat one of the greatest illusions of the century. They saw Soviet Communism finally collapsing like a house of cards because of the inherent weakness in the system. Its economic and social systems could not work properly (Malia, 1993; Conquest, 1993). Most conservatives, however, maintained that the cold war was over because of the increasingly tough American foreign and military policies. The Soviet Union, strong or weak, could not sustain the outside pressure. The opponents of this view typically referred to the complex social and political factors within the Soviet Union that contributed to its quick demise.

Conclusion

Significant political and ideological factors shaped American Sovietology developing from 1917 to 1991. Most American scholars had almost equal access to information in the United States, used similar research methods, and witnessed the same events taking place in the Soviet Union. What influenced the differences in their perceptions of that country?

Sovietology as an academic field has never been unified under an umbrella of one theory or a single approach. There were ebbs and flows of prevalent views and there were trends and fashions within the developing field. At different periods, some views were more "politically correct" than others.

Experts also knew about clear financial or professional applications of their theoretical views. For example, supporting a tough approach against the Soviet Union had never been popular on university campuses. On the other hand, any improvement in the relations between the United States and the Soviet Union could have resulted in reduced funding and diminished opportunities to receive additional money for teaching, travel, and research. Different presidential administrations required different research data to substantiate their policies. Richard Nixon's advisers needed research data that would have supported his policies of detente in the early 1970s. Supporters of the "tough" approach in dealing with the Soviet Union were certainly embraced by those experts who advised President Reagan in the 1980s. Similarly, President Clinton's advisers welcomed research data suggesting that Russia has lost its competitive edge to justify a period of general inaction in U.S. foreign policy toward Moscow.

A number of important political developments in the United States and abroad have also shaped the overall image of the Soviet Union among American scholars through the twentieth century. Among these development were the First World War and the Bolsheviks' separate peace with Germany, the growth of the Socialist movement in the United States in the 1920s and 1930s, the Great Depression and the New Deal, the rise of Nazism, and, of course, the Second World War. In the postwar period, other political events influenced Sovietology. Among these events were Moscow's acquisition of nuclear weapons; the Cuban Missile Crisis; the War in Vietnam; and the Soviet invasion of Hungary in 1956, Czechoslovakia in 1968, and Afghanistan in 1979. From the 1960s, the waves of liberalism and conservatism in the United States of America's political life have greatly influenced Sovietology, directly and indirectly.

As Abbot Gleason wrote, in remembering his own personal transition from a follower of the totalitarian vision of Soviet society to becoming a normalizer, three major factors that influenced his views were the JFK assassination, the civil rights movement, and the war in Vietnam. Later, he argued, a very close introspection of everyday life in the Soviet Union, which looked to him more like a Third World country than a totalitarian society, influenced his views and those of a new generation of Sovietologists, as he thinks (Gleason, 1995). While the cold war in the 1950s and early 1960s was a powerful factor influencing American images of the Soviet Union, the increasing dominance of progressive and liberal views in American universities and the media shaped the discussion about the Soviet Union and the threats, real and illusory, coming from that country.[16]

Most liberal Sovietologists, as a rule, were critical of U.S. foreign policy and, in particular, of policies toward the Soviet Union. During periods of confrontation between Moscow and Washington, they tried to disenchant the enthusiasm of the "hawks" and argued that there must be other, better, and peaceful ways to deal with the Soviet Union. The most convenient targets of criticism were, of course, Republican administrations and particularly Ronald Reagan (although Democratic presidents also received their share of serious criticism).

Having already taken an ideological position, many Sovietologists frequently interpreted Soviet society through the prism of ideology, thus overlooking many facts available to them (as they tend to do today). For almost seven decades, American Sovietologists displayed a variety of views of the Soviet Union ranging from praising it as a superior world power to denouncing it as a heinous historical aberration. Both camps made great observations but also committed serious mistakes in their observations and interpretations.

Most totalitarianists either ignored or underestimated the strength of the powerful international Socialist movement, with large and influential parties in Western Europe developing since the end of World War I. They did not see the impact of the international Socialist movement on the Russian Revolution and the development of Socialism in Russia in the first quarter of this century (Malia, 1994). Most totalitarianists also disregarded the crucial role of Russian nationalism in Soviet ideology and policy, and particularly in foreign policy. Totalitarianists did not understand well the role of the Communist Party and its leaders as the self-appointed "custodians" of order and tradition in Russia.

Looking at the Soviet foreign policy over the years, they saw it through the prism of Moscow's expansionism and discounted the importance of internal, domestic factors in other countries affecting their policies, especially during the cold war. For example, many observers could not acknowledge the popularity of Socialist ideas and the Soviet Union's policies around the world. For example, at different times, Moscow's policies found support in many countries including China, Cuba, Vietnam, North Korea, Laos, Yugoslavia, Albania, Angola, Cuba, and Ethiopia, to name a few. Totalitarianists had difficulty accepting the fact that a substantial proportion of Soviet people actually supported the Socialist regime. Most people in the Soviet Union, especially in the 1960s and 1970s, advocated only modest social and political changes, and did not want their country to disintegrate. On many occasions, totalitarianists criticized any positive view of the Soviet Union as politically biased or serving the enemies of the United States.

On the other hand, the normalizers had their share of miscalculations and blunders. While the advocates of the totalitarian model liked to equate the Soviet Union with Nazi Germany, fascist Italy, Maoist China, or Ho Chi Minh's Vietnam, the normalizers avoided such comparisons. Alexander Dallin, for example, rejected the very legitimacy of comparing the Soviet Union, at any time in its history, to Hitler's Germany (Dallin, 1973). Yet at the same time, the normalizers eagerly compared the Soviet Union with many democratic Western counties finding remarkable (yet mostly illusory) similarities already described in this chapter. Many Sovietologists of this group saw some social and political developments in the Soviet Union, where, in fact, such political pluralism did not exist. They exaggerated the importance of flashy Soviet propaganda labels such as guaranteed employment, fixed consumer prices, and free education and health care system and did not pay attention to what the majority of the Soviet people were actually getting out of these misleading social "perks."

Nevertheless, despite mistakes and misperceptions, the totalitarianists, in general, were much closer to painting a realistic picture of Soviet society than were their opponents.[17] The collapse of the Soviet Union and Communism was a less astonishing event for totalitarianists than it was for most normalizers. The forecasts made by some totalitarianists in the late 1950s and 1960s about the eventual end of the Soviet Union turned out remarkably perspicacious (Wolfe, 1981), although these forecasts were imprecise about the likely timings of the Soviet radical political changes. Eugene Lyons, for example, considered back in 1966 that a revolution against Soviet despotism was a serious and real possibility. He believed that the history of Russia was one of a constant civil war and that another one was coming soon (Lyons, 1966). David Sarnoff in 1968 was almost prophetic when he contended that within the next 20 years the Soviet Union would collapse, being unable to take care of its own economic and political problems and under the pressure of its discontented population. He also predicted the collapse of the multinational Soviet empire (Sarnoff, 1968). Robert Conquest (1967) also envisioned that a new and powerful leader could potentially transform the Soviet regime (he, of course, could not presume anything specific about Mikhail Gorbachev who at that time was a regional party secretary). It is remarkable that the views of an upcoming demise of the Soviet Union were harshly criticized (Dallin, 1973: 560–561). A prophet hath no honor in his own country.

Totalitarianists believed that they had a few reasons to celebrate their moral victory for their contribution to the end of the cold war, although they preferred to ignore their own profound analytic blunders.[18] Many Soviet intellectuals, as soon as political censorship ended in the late 1980s, embraced the views of American totalitarianists supporting their harsh and unsympathetic evaluations of Soviet society. The Soviet critics of their own regime made people like Robert Conquest and Richard Pipes their intellectual heroes. It was Pipes, after all, who was invited to the Russian Constitutional Court in 1992 to serve as a witness in the trial of the Communist Party of the Soviet Union. Perhaps the perceived victory of totalitarianists over normalizers was influenced by their overall critical attitude of the Soviet regime. While normalizers tended to be apologists for the Soviet Union, their opponents were inclined to find problems and conflicts there. For some reason, critical evaluations frequently appear superior to apologetic accounts in history. Soviet society was different from its Western counterparts, and the attempts to equate it with the United States or Western Europe have very little supporting evidence. However, those who insisted that Soviet society was essentially a deviation from the course of history were probably mistaken too. The Soviet system, particularly in its post-Stalin period, was a capable and functioning totalitarian society, supported by the majority of its citizens. It was a powerful state capable of conducting grandiose economic experiments, creating a vast bureaucracy, advancing arts and sciences, and building an omnipotent military machine.

Studies of foreign countries, as the case of American Sovietology has demonstrated, are often complicated and confusing tasks. If ideology and politics affect research and the expert's perceptions, how valuable is the knowledge obtained in such studies? It is necessary to rethink what can be done in order to make area studies more objective and less dependent on ideology and capricious political cycles that create "desirable" and less "desirable" outcomes of analysis.

A Case in Point: The Image of the Russian Revolution in Émigré Thought

Dmitry Shlapentokh

Émigré thought as an intellectual phenomenon had emerged at the beginning of the 1920s, after the end of the Russian civil war and the emergence of large Russian immigration communities in various parts of the globe. In the very beginning of the Soviet era, the Bolsheviks had been seen as foreign to Russia, and it was thought their rule would come to an end in the near future. The most popular view was the comparison of the French Revolution with the Thermidor, which undid the Jacobius Bolsheviks of the eighteenth century. While the "Thermidorian" model continued to be popular in émigré thought throughout the life of the Soviet regime, a new model had emerged. It maintained that the Bolsheviks were not a force artificial to Russia; rather, they were seen as a constructive force that had actually made Russia stronger. This trend of thought is usually known under the term *National-Bolshevism*.

National-Bolshevism

The National-Bolsheviks emerged from those members of the non-Bolshevik elite who had already engaged in the civil war and who saw in the Bolsheviks an actual force that reunified the state and brought a modicum of order. They also believed that the actions of the Bolsheviks—quite nationalistic, imperial by their implication—were more important than their official ideological proclamations; both Socialism and nationalism were not sworn enemies as before but actually complimentary doctrines. The assumption that Socialism and nationalism could be easily blended with each other was definitely not just a "product" of thinking coming from the Soviet Union. It was an international phenomenon.[19]

The National-Bolsheviks of the 1920s were either direct or indirect heirs of these earlier variations of the National-Bolshevism of the post–Civil War period. All National-Bolsheviks had a common ideological core praising the Bolsheviks for the resurrection of the Russian state and for asserting Russian nationalism, often in a messianic form. There were two groups of opinions. One group believed that Russia was a Western country and the Western experience was, in general, universally applicable. The other group represented those who believed that Russia had its own way of development; in their view, Russia could and should interact with the West but as a leader.

Nikolai Ustrialov (1880–1937) was possibly one of the most well known National-Bolsheviks who belonged to the first, west-oriented group.[20] Ustrialov began to develop his National-Bolshevik ideas during the civil war. By the end of the war, Ustrialov had concluded that despite all the calamities, the revolution had been, nevertheless, a positive development. The point is that revolution had replaced the weak elite with the strong one and had created a stronger Russian state. At the same time, at least in the 1920s, Ustrialov could not accept the Bolsheviks' policy that aimed at the total control of the state over the economy. Also at this time, Ustrialov supported the New Economic Policy and believed that it should go much further in the process of economic liberation. Private property, including the right to own land, should be finally legitimized. Similar ideas were shared by groups of émigré intellectuals known as the "Change Landmark" movement, with which Ustrialov was affiliated. All of them saw the Bolshevik Party as a force that would lead to the creation in Russia of a strong authoritarian state of the European type.

EURASIANISTS

Other groups saw the Soviet experiment differently. One of such groups was the "Eurasianists."[21] They shared a point of view, a theory that has lived through several decades and reemerged in new forms several times. Moreover, Eurasianism has continued to play an important role in the cultural and political life of post-Soviet Russia. It became especially popular in the Yeltsin era in the 1990s.[22] The interest in Eurasianism continues today.[23]

Eurasianism had emerged in the early 1920s when a small group of Russian émigrés, mostly young people, had published the manifesto, *Turn to East*. The brochure immediately attracted attention, and the influence of Eurasianism grew among ex-officers who fought against the Red Army. Later, the movement's influence spread among other segments of the exile community and reached its peak by the late 1920s.

Eurasianists, similar to other National-Bolsheviks, assumed that despite all its horrors, the Bolshevik Revolution was a positive event. The major achievement of the Bolsheviks was that they had not only restored the Russian state but also revealed the "Eurasian" nature of Russia. What was this nature? Russia—in the view of Eurasianists—was not just a state of ethnic Russians but also a country embracing all ethnic groups of the empire, including non-Slavic groups. However, Orthodox Russians were supposed to play a leading role altogether.

Russia as a part of Eurasia was also characterized by the rule of the strong authoritarian elite that drove people toward sublime, "idiosyncratic" goals. Centuries ago, the Mongols, a constructive and unifying force, had created all of these healthy attributes. They were not merely conquerors as was interpreted by the majority of Russian historians. Peter the Great who forced an "alien" European culture upon the Russian elite perverted this organic nature of the Russian-Eurasian culture. This alienated the elite from the masses and ultimately led to the Bolshevik Revolution.

In the 1930s, an opinion emerged that the Soviet Union had finally outlived its revolutionary "delusions" and become a strong power ruled by autocrats. The increasing economic and military strength of the Soviet state—at least as they perceived it—brought a sense of pride to many immigrant observers. Other groups held different views. They continued to believe that Russia in the 1930s was actually the same as it had been in 1917: a country ruled by a regime foreign to the country's national interest. The Soviet leadership was not concerned about the country's well-being. It was into its hostile plans of a worldwide revolution. These critics also did not see any economic and military improvements in the Soviet Union and regarded the regime as a colossus with feet of clay.

A SPLIT IN VIEWS

World War II and the German invasion of the Union of Soviet Socialist Republics in 1941 had widened the split among the émigrés and their perception of the new regime. For some, the regime remained an embodiment of evil. They continued to believe that any other regime would have been a better choice for their former country. Therefore, some of them were suggesting that after the military collapse of the Communist regime, the Russians could easily deal with the Germans. Others assumed that the Nazi victory would lead to the emergence of a similar, Nazi-type regime in Russia and that both countries would eventually become natural allies.

Yet other groups of immigrant observers as well as the majority of people inside the Soviet Union had different views of the Soviet regime: The war had provided the regime with its final legitimization. It became clear in the eyes of many people that the Soviet regime was the defender of the country from the mortal foreign threat. This agreement about the system "legitimization" found further justification after the victorious end of the war. The idea that the Soviet Union had become a global power appealed to a large segment of the Russian émigré community and to the majority of ethnic Russians. Many even began to commend the regime. Pavel Miliukov, a leading historian, went yet further in his praise of the regime. On his deathbed, Miliukov proclaimed that if all the horrors of the Soviet regime were needed to make Russia a great power, he was ready to accept all those horrors.

Other prominent Russian intellectuals ranging from monarchists to liberals were also ready to accept the regime's past abuses. They also believed that the brutal, despotic nature of Soviet power was a rather temporary phenomenon. They argued that the regime became authoritarian because enemies surrounded the country and the government had no choice but to respond with force. The victory in the war would give the regime a sense of security, and this would inevitably "soften" the system in the same way as the victory of the French Revolution had led to the end of terror and the rise of Napoleon. Napoleon's regime was not democratic. Yet it did not engage in terror; and the same kind of regime was expected in Russia. A slow liberalization of the system—and the elements of this liberalization were allegedly seen by immigrant intellectuals—is a point of Nicholas Timasheff's book *The Great Retreat*.[24]

Other views emerged. Some saw the Soviet Union as a threat to the global community. In their view, it was still an empire. Ethnic Russians still dominated over the minorities and the country, due in part to the messianic nature of its ideology, and remained a mortal threat to the historically democratic West. Stalinist Soviet Union, therefore, was not much different from the Tsarist Russia. Therefore, the only desirable goal for the West was the end of the Russian imperial state. In a way, these émigrés, and many of them who represented ethnic minorities, had envisioned and hoped for the disintegration of the Soviet Union.

TWO MAIN IMAGES

In the two decades following the end of the war, émigré intellectuals continued to maintain at least two major images of the Soviet Union. For some, like the writer Alexander Solzhenitsyn, the Soviet empire had been an artificial creation alien to Russia's rich culture and political tradition. The Bolshevik Party, driven by power-obsessed Jews, from his point of view, had adopted a clearly utopian paradigm. Driven by this ideological delusion, the Bolsheviks had committed unspeakable crimes because real life did not fit their abstract schemes. Solzhenitsyn echoed the ideas of some French post-modernists, such as Foucault, who thought that history was driven by such ideological paradigms.

Other groups of émigrés assumed that the Union of Soviet Socialist Republics had, indeed, been the successor of the Russian empire continuing the tradition of implementing authoritarian, imperial, and messianic ideas. Consequently, they believed that any cosmetic political changes would not make a difference in Soviet policies. Furthermore, almost everyone believed that if the Soviet regime collapsed, this would happen only in a very distant future. The end of the Soviet Union in 1991 was, thus, a great surprise to them.

CONCLUSION

Soviet immigrants did not develop a single uniform view of their country. Many changed their views with time and new émigré generations formed their own ideas. On the other hand, there were similarities between the views developing within the Soviet Union, especially among the opposition to the Soviet system, and the perceptions held by the émigrés. Western intellectuals and other observers, despite their physical distance from the Soviet Union (and most of them could not visit their homeland), conveyed the thoughts and ideas of some of their trusted friends who remained inside the Soviet Union.

It is remarkable that the perception of the Russian Revolution was changing with time as well. In 1917–1921, some saw the revolution as a short-lived anomaly, while others, primarily liberal intellectuals, saluted it as the beginning of a new era of global transformation. In the 1920s, Eurasianists began to perceive the revolution as a foundation of a new cultural and political unity of the "Eurasian"-Soviet people.

For the ideologists of the 1930s–1950s, both inside and outside Russia, the Bolshevik Revolution created a mighty state and a new global empire. A few intellectuals in the 1960s even believed that the Soviet Union's successful space program opened a new path of intergalactic revolution, thus moving mankind toward progress.

CHAPTER 3

HOMEGROWN RUSSIAN ELITES AND SOVIET REALITIES

INTRODUCTION

Since the beginning of the rapid transformation of Russia in 1917, at least two distinct types of views of the country appeared. The first was the official, government-certified description and evaluation of social and political life—the assessment that all people were expected to support. During the regime's 74 years in power, there were 28 Communist Party congresses and 19 Party conferences issuing piles of documents related to the state of the country and world's major events. Official party documents, newspaper editorials, books, and publicized speeches were the sources of official information. There was the other way to look at the Soviet Union—it was an unofficial, unauthorized outlook. An important feature of most unofficial descriptions was their critical nature. Such criticism could create serious problems for individuals attempting to disseminate it. However, despite censorship, there have been many sources of information of this kind.

Creating a positive, upbeat, and optimistic image of the Soviet Union was one of the main tasks of the Soviet leadership since the revolution of 1917. Communist ideology was a firm background for interpreting history and for reflecting on contemporary events. During the entire Soviet period, especially after the 1930s, the ruling elites repeatedly instructed social scientists that they should not be ideologically neutral. Only by accepting the officially sanctioned Marxist-Leninist theory could social scientists claim to be certifiably objective. Any attempts to avoid the Marxist approach in studying society were condemned as "bourgeois" and anti-Soviet. Marxism was the only scientific and "truthful" approach and any critical discussions of Marxism in the official sources were impossible. Scientists were constantly reminded that Marxist teachings were all-powerful because they were correct. Soviet officials, therefore, were always uneasy about empirical sociology and quantitative studies in political science (although this discipline was not sanctioned to exist in the Soviet Union). The official position was that Marxism already provided enough knowledge and intellectual tools to understand society and politics and there was no need to invent additional disciplines to study social or political institutions.

The concept of Socialist realism became the official Soviet doctrine in state-sponsored cultural policies. According to this concept or rather, an imperative, writers, poets, artists, and social scientists had an obligation to portray only "positive" elements of reality. Criticism of the Socialist system was sanctioned only in limited ways. Soviet elites received enormous opportunities to create a detailed but distorted image of reality and convey this uncritical image to ordinary people. By the 1980s, more than 20 million people, about one-sixth of the nation's labor force—including party bureaucrats, government officials of all ranks, teachers, professors, journalists, and others—were engaged in state-sponsored propaganda.

Promoting the official and polished image of the Soviet Union is a great example of the social construction of reality (Berger and Luckmann, 1967). It was a multidimensional task. In many respects, the official image did not change significantly over more than 70 years and contained numerous contradictions. The Soviet Union was officially heading toward a classless society, yet the working class' supremacy was constantly underlined in ideological documents. All ethnic groups were equal, yet the Russian people had a leading role to play. The country's international goal was global peace, yet the Soviet Union had to struggle with its sworn international enemies: free-market capitalism and western imperialism. The Soviet people were educated and constantly reminded about how free they were politically, but they had to accept the one-party system, exit visas if they wanted to visit a foreign country, residence permits, and official censorship.

Soviet political leadership also maintained two general images of their own society. This was not necessarily unique for a Communist state. The first image was open for public consumption inside and outside the country and conveyed through public speeches, the media, films, and official reports. The other was "classified," available only to the ruling elites, and distributed only through restricted channels. There were significant differences between these two images of the Soviet reality. Images designed for mass consumption did not generally contain critical information about society. The classified image was conveyed through professional reports, "off the record" letters to local Communist Party organizations, and uncensored but unpublished government statistics. This information, often containing distressing data, was available only to a selected few members of the *nomenklatura* (literally, "the named ones," shorthand for the top political and administrative leadership).[1]

THE BEGINNINGS (1917–1920S)

After their initial victory in 1917, the Bolshevik leadership quickly realized the necessity to create their own vision of the country and distort fundamental facts whenever it was necessary. The focal point of the official image was the claim that the new regime had an overwhelming popular support, which was not the case. The Communist administration portrayed itself as a main protector of the masses from the oppressors—landlords, corrupt priests, former government officials, and capitalists. The official doctrine maintained that all workers were taking an active part in the building of a new society, driven by the people's enthusiasm. Alexei Rykov (1881–1938), a close ally of Lenin, spoke in 1918 about workers and workers' intelligentsia, who would successfully manage factories and offices. Official constructions depicted the relationship between Soviet power and peasants in an idyllic way. Lenin and his close allies did not hesitate to distort the facts that a majority of peasants did not support the Bolshevik revolution, had little desire to "embrace" the working class, and did not want to voluntarily give up their harvest for the sake of the revolution. The official image also included unfounded claims that all large ethnic groups had voluntarily chosen to give up statehood and to unify themselves with Russia.

Why were these and other distortions necessary? Vladimir Lenin as a head of the new Socialist state actually borrowed this propaganda strategy from the German Social Democratic theorist Karl Kautsky (1854–1938). The core argument in this strategy was that the masses (especially the peasants) were unable to understand their own class interests unless a leading workers' party would "explain" these interests to them. Bolsheviks repeatedly declared that, after they took power in 1917, the morality of the masses improved due to the party's persistent propaganda. The Bolsheviks also repeated that people's support of the regime was manifested through the strength of the Red Army, comprising of workers and peasants.

Lenin and other top Bolsheviks described the new political system as the dictatorship of the proletariat, or a system of total rule by the working class governing on behalf of all people. They claimed the existence of a strong theoretical foundation of this new system. Nikolai Bukharin (1888–1938) stated in his famous work *The ABC of Communism* (1919) that the theoretical ideas of Karl Marx have been fulfilled in the realities of the Russian revolution. One of the most profound statements made was that the dictatorship of the proletariat was a new form of democracy and that the Soviet government was the most democratic one in the world.

The top party leaders also promoted their own positive image. They appeared in newspaper publications and other reports as enthusiastic, selfless, honest, and modest citizens totally devoted to their country and people. On the opposing side, there were the country's enemies, those who plotted against these leaders and, therefore, against the people of the country. Among these foes were "class enemies" such as rich peasants, capitalists, small business owners, priests, former government officials, demoralized proletarians, and, of course, foreign governments. The struggle against these enemies was necessary because the country was going through a very difficult period: the catastrophic fall of industrial and agricultural production, social unrest, massive unemployment, mass starvation, and the spread of diseases. Yet the official image of a new society, with a few exceptions, was optimistic especially in the sentences containing promises of change.

The Soviet leadership gradually developed an image of Russia as a country surrounded by foreign enemies and confronted by domestic traitors. For many years, this perception projected domestically became dominant and central to the image of the Soviet Union. The people were repeatedly reminded before 1953 that the war against global capitalism was unavoidable. In the 1920s, Stalin, Trotsky, and many of their party comrades had little doubt about an unavoidable military confrontation with the Western powers—most likely England or France. War hysteria in the official Soviet press reached its highest level in 1927. Warnings and threats discussed in party leaders' official speeches triggered a massive food hoarding.

The use of foreign threats in propaganda allowed the government to conduct deeply undemocratic domestic policies. On the other hand, the image of the United States was generally positive in the early years. Soviet newspapers frequently covered American achievements in technological progress and in organized labor. Yet these and other favorable descriptions of the United States and Western countries gradually disappeared in subsequent periods.

In Soviet history, the 1920s were the years of social and political transition when the government returned back to some basic market principles in its economic policies. After a period of initial prohibitions, small-business ownership and free trade was allowed again for some time and in a limited way. The country was not returning to free-market capitalism. The society was still under control of the Communist Party. Democratic freedoms were virtually absent. Political repressions continued and oppositional intellectuals were either expelled from the country or locked up in prisons.

Lenin was initially uncertain in 1921–1922 about how to label the economic policies of the central government, and he eventually called it the New Economic Policy (NEP). He first insisted on using the term *state capitalism*, which legitimized the emergence of limited private enterprises, free trade, and foreign concessions that remained under the control of the Soviet state. According to the official version, the NEP had sharpened the ongoing class struggle within Russia, which was the competition between the working class and the growing class of property owners. The Bolsheviks perceived these "owners" with resentment, envy, and open hostility (while allowing them to exist for some time). For a long period, the label "NEP-man," referring to a 1920s small-venture capitalist or a property owner, had an extremely negative meaning. These people were portrayed by the official propaganda as mean, arrogant, and rapacious.

There were significant differences in official perceptions of the rich peasant—called *kulak* in Russian, which literally meant a "fist," the label standing for someone strong and tough (Solopov, 1991). On the one hand, Bolsheviks considered *kulaks* property owners and, therefore, inherently hostile toward the Socialist state. On the other hand, prosperous rural families were legitimate evidence that the new political system was efficient. In general, Bolsheviks were not necessarily consistent in their views of social equality. In the mid-1920s, the Communist leadership did not adopt an official definition of the *kulak*. However, after the state had ordered coercive grain procurement in 1928, the Kremlin issued a special decree, *About the features of the kulak* (May 21, 1929), in which prosperous peasants were condemned as a counterrevolutionary social class. This was the beginning of the forceful agricultural collectivization, one of the most controversial and disturbing events in Soviet history.

Overall by the mid-1920s, most domestic observers and commentators agreed that the newly formed Soviet Union had already overcome the major crises of the Civil War, foreign interventions, and most important, domestic political struggles. The Communist Party and its leadership received the biggest credit from its own people for restoring the country's economy, rebuilding cities, and defending the borders. Most agreed that the Bolsheviks were the single political force in Russia able to curb anarchy and chaos. The Communists were seen as capable of mobilizing the country against foreign invasion. In addition, the changes that took place in the economy and the growing living standards of the population led many people to believe that the Communist Party and its leaders had finally created a sustainable society. There were many, however, who disagreed with these views.

EARLY CRITICS OF THE REGIME

Two groups of critics emerged almost simultaneously. The first one was the supporters of the Tsarist regime deposed in February 1917; the other one represented the extreme left, who thought that the new Soviet regime was not "communist" enough (Brovkin, 1991; Galili, 1989). Many intellectuals, despite the government's monopoly on information, were capable of developing and discussing their own views. In general terms, the critics of the Soviet Union constructed their perceptions from either antisocialist or pro-socialist positions, which became major starting points or ideologies on which they built their interpretations of the Soviet regime.

Non-Bolshevik Groups

Russian monarchists emphasized the devastations caused by the Bolshevik rule and called for restoration of the monarchy, which was their main inspiration. Pavel Miliukov (1859–1943), leader of the Constitutional Democratic party, described the new regime as illegitimate and one that was imposed on people against their will. He, as well as other monarchists, called it a dictatorship of Lenin and Trotsky (Miliukov, 1927). These critics saw the Soviet revolutionary society as a triumph of despotism, destruction, and lawlessness. These critics also underlined in their reflections the destruction of the economy and the chaos in industries in the virtual absence of factory management (Galili, 1989).

Critics from the "socialist" wing, such as the Menshevik party, also believed that the Bolshevik takeover was an anomaly and the regime was about to perish soon. One of the Menshevik leaders, Pavel Axelrod (1850-1928), wrote in one of his letters in early 1918 that the life of the Bolshevik regime would be short (Ascher, 1972). One of the main features described by the critics of the new regime was its inability to manage factory production. While the Bolshevik government blamed saboteurs for the economic difficulties, critics saw that the problem was embedded in the new inefficient social system allowing anybody to get away with anything. On the other hand, as soon as the government in Moscow began its violent crackdown against the opposition, it was accused of being nondemocratic and as betraying the ideals of Socialism and the working class (Brovkin, 1991).

Monarchists and Mensheviks also used moral arguments to criticize the new regime. They saw nothing but a moral decay of the entire society under Bolsheviks. The new leaders themselves, as their critics pointed out, quickly accepted many social benefits and privileges in a country still suffering from chronic shortages and hunger. Contrary to what official propaganda stated, the Mensheviks portrayed the new regime as unstable and opposed by hostile masses.

On the other hand, within their own ranks, the Menshevik party leaders like Fyodor Dan and Fyodor Cherevanin maintained that the elimination of democratic principles of government did not necessarily contradict the ultimately democratic essence of the dictatorship by the working class established by the Bolsheviks. Other "left-wing" members of the Menshevik party saw the system built in the Soviet Union as essentially Socialist but with serious deformations. They did not like, for example, the "new rich" appearing as a result of the New Economic Policy in the 1920s, which they considered as a backward and antisocialist trend.

The "right-wing" Mensheviks idealized Western democracy and saw the events unfolding in Russia from their own ideological angle. Pavel Axelrod equated the Bolshevik regime with Tsarist and Oriental despotism—both based on violence, nepotism, and corruption. Others emphasized that the "Bolshevik democracy" was nothing more than a special form of dictatorship by a minority. They were also confident that peasants, for the most part, disliked Bolsheviks. Yet they maintained that the essence of the Bolshevik policy was to force a dictatorship on peasants in exchange for a promise of freedom and land in some distant future. The Mensheviks were confident that the Bolshevik regime was doomed because it had almost no money in the treasury and that the collapse would occur soon (Dallin, 1922).

Another wave of partisan assessments of the new regime came from the Socialist Revolutionary Party (SR). Winning a relative parliamentary majority in November 1917, they were, in theory, the strongest political alternative to the Bolsheviks. The SR Party drew support from peasant constituencies and advocated agrarian Socialism and land reform. However, the party became more deeply divided in 1918 and could not represent a formidable oppositional force (Melancon, 1997).

THE WORKERS' OPPOSITION AND THE RIGHT OPPOSITION

Dissenting voices within the Bolshevik ranks provided another view into the Soviet society of the 1920s. One group of critics inside the party (the members of the so-called "Workers' Opposition" such as Gavri'il Miasnikov, Vladimir Antonov-Ovseenko, and Alexandra Kollontai) emphasized that almost everything that was happening in the country was the establishment of a highly bureaucratic and despotic society. They focused on corruption among party *apparatchiks,* as well as on the lack of genuine democracy in the country, including the absence of political parties (Renton, 2004; Allen, 2005). Dismissing the rosy picture provided by top government officials, the critics like David Ryazanov, Solomon Lozovskii, and Nikolai Skrypnik warned about the growth of authoritarianism in the country, which was a deviation from a Socialism they envisioned.

Leon Trotsky, a top Bolshevik leader and an active supporter of the system, changed his opinions about the direction in which the country was moving. At the end of 1923, he published an article in the party newspaper *Pravda,* suggesting that the country should have more freedom. In further letters sent to members of the Communist Party's Central Committee and the Central Control Committee, Trotsky contended that in 1923 there was less democracy in the party than there had been during the civil war (Deutscher, 1959). *The New Course,* a pamphlet published in 1923, brought all these ideas together. Trotsky advocated an alternate vision of the Soviet society, which included, among others, the election of all party officials and the acceptance of political criticism (Chernyaev, 1997). Trotsky saw the main problems in the Soviet society as stemming from the working class' passivity, wallowing in apathy and indifference to the revolutionary cause. Khristian Rakovsky (one of the most influential members of Trotsky's faction) decried stealing, bribes, violence, extortions, abuse of power, heavy drinking, and debauchery as common behavioral features of the Soviet society.

After Trotsky was removed from the Soviet Union, he continued to view the Communist Party bureaucracy as a parasitic caste within the Soviet state. Trotsky depicted the degradation of the party rank and file, the spread of corruption, and the abandonment of revolutionary ideals by majority of the ruling elite (Trotsky, 1973). Trotsky was sure that Stalin's Russia was deeply unstable and doomed to collapse as a state. He also believed that the developments in the country would eventually lead to a new revolution. In the 1930s, Trotsky (who had been expelled from the country in 1929) was also among the first observers to equate Stalinism of the Soviet Union with German Nazism.

Another opposing line of thinking within the Bolshevik party was associated with the names of Gregory Zinoviev and Lev Kamenev—prominent veterans of the Communist movement. One of their main concerns was the lack of democracy and representation within the party. They believed that it was becoming excessively bureaucratic. In

1926–1927, their criticism was most substantial and based on their strategic assessments of Soviet realities. They claimed that Stalin was using the party bureaucracy to expand his own power base, limit the activities of the opposition, and forestall critical debates (Daniels, 1960). Another disagreement with the official portrayal of the Soviet Union emerged in the Bolshevik party's "right" wing. Nikolai Bukharin, Alexei Rykov, and Mikhail Tomsky argued that the government was obsessed with economic planning. It was becoming overtly bureaucratic, too centralized, and intolerant to criticisms (see Yugov, 1929).

Overall, the top "insiders" and critics of the Soviet system were largely disappointed about the direction in which the government was taking the country. They based their views of the country on their own analysis and experience. To a great degree, their critical views of the Soviet Union were influenced by the negative perception of Joseph Stalin and his closest supporters. Almost all of them paid an ultimate price for having and expressing their critical or skeptical views of the Soviet Union, its present and future developments.

Attitudes of Soviet Elites in the 1930s–Mid-1940s

With the strengthening of Stalin's establishment, it did everything to construct the most positive image of the Soviet state. Encouraging economic news was emphasized relentlessly and information about achievements was continuously recycled. Criticisms existed as well. However, any critical information had to pass through official government "filters." To be allowed, critical facts had to be focused primarily on bureaucratic delays or inefficiency on the local level. No critical information was released about the central government, the country's top leadership (although with several exceptions), Marxist-Leninist theory, and the deficiencies of Socialism as a political system.

Official Constructions of Reality

During the Soviet Union's early years, it was common to portray the country as surrounded by multiple foreign enemies. People were constantly told through official newspapers and radio reports about the acts of sabotage committed by disgruntled, politically motivated individuals as well as by "foreign agents" who were unhappy to see the remarkable developments of the Soviet economy. By official accounts, the country was invaded by economic spies trying to steal factory secrets and most precious technologies. Many Soviet movies made in the 1930s contained plots about domestic enemies and spies organizing intrigues against Socialist industries. "Internal" enemies were frequently accused of deliberate provocations, such as hiding food or slowing down food supplies to big cities (*Pravda,* March 4, 1931).

Staged criminal trials, which were frequently open to the public, against "class enemies" were important institutionalized attempts to build up an atmosphere of anxiety and hostility against the foes of the country. Among such stage trials were political shows against the "All-Union Bureau of Mensheviks" in 1931, as well as the "Shakty case" in 1928, the purpose of which was to demonstrate the politically motivated hostility of many engineers and scientists toward the Soviet government. The trial of "the Industrial party" (in 1930) and an endless list of other staged actions against "class enemies" followed from the late 1920s until Stalin's death in 1953. While publicizing some show trials, official propagandists did not permit dissemination of information about the mass repressions taking place in the country in the 1930s. Scores of people disappeared from their workplaces and homes. They spent many years in labor camps wrongfully accused of sabotage, treason, negligence, and aiding the enemies of the Soviet Union. Very few people, for fear of prosecution, openly questioned and criticized these massive political repressions. Most people genuinely believed that such harsh repressive methods were necessary.

Government officials suppressed most facts of criminal mismanagement of the economy. When collectivization began in the countryside, the Kremlin was involved in falsifying reports about the actual status of agricultural production. Such falsifications were revealed only after Stalin's death in 1953. Yet during the high point of the collectivization campaigns from 1929 to 1934, official propaganda maintained that collectivization was generally proceeding on a voluntary basis and, despite some insignificant difficulties, was going very well. The facts of state-sponsored violence, including mass deportations, imprisonment, and confiscations were suppressed. There were practically no reports of mass starvation in the 1930s in the Ukraine, the Northern Caucasus, or in any other region of the country. Official sources were silent about mass slaughtering of cattle (peasants did not want to surrender their animals to collective farms). In addition to these omissions, government sources also gave no information about the drastic decline of agricultural production in all regions of the country under collectivization. Overall, almost all major critical facts about collectivization were thus absent from the official picture.

Political censorship had reached an extraordinary level: A reporter or a citizen could face a prison term or even a death sentence for disseminating reports about problems in the countryside. Official newspapers conveyed a rosy image of success to city dwellers and foreign guests. Most facts about problems were rejected as either exaggerated or spread deliberately by the enemies of the state. Official propaganda also exaggerated the successes of Soviet industrialization and rates of economic growth. The government declared, for example, that the First Five-Year Plan of 1928–1932 was completed as scheduled, even though this was demonstrably untrue (Medvedev, 1974: 225–229).

What was apparent, however, was that at that time most educated people within the Soviet Union including scientists, writers, doctors, professors, artists, teachers, and engineers, supported this officially authorized, rosy but distorted image of reality.

ELITE'S SUPPORT OF THE OFFICIAL IMAGE

The vast majority of the Communist Party leadership never dared to defy Stalin's orders or openly criticize his views. The supportive position taken by party *apparatchiks* and intellectuals in the mid-1930s was remarkable. Most of them, even on the eve of their pending arrest, did not cast doubt (publicly or privately in communications with their family members) about the great future of the country, the triumph of Communism, and the ultimate righteousness of the party's political course. Moreover, many prisoners of the gulag, so-called "old Bolsheviks," remained faithful Communists. Most of them kept their Marxist-Leninist outlook of history, politics, and economy unchanged.[2]

Nikolai Bukharin in his letter to future generations of Bolsheviks, which was memorized by his wife on the eve of his arrest, pledged allegiance to the Communist ideology (Larina, 1993). The fact that Soviet elites never seriously opposed Stalin's regime was humiliating to many intellectuals who finally could discuss these tragic pages of the Soviet history during the late 1980s. Some of them were searching, almost desperately, for any fact of resistance inside the party but could find very little. The evidence is clear that party leaders and numerous loyal intellectuals passively accepted the repressions. Stalin had easily expelled Leon Trotsky (to Alma-Ata in 1928, and to Turkey in 1929) without any serious opposition from his supporters. A small protest action staged by Trotsky's followers in Moscow on the eve of his exile to Kazakhstan is one of few examples of this sort.

Cultural and scientific intelligentsia also publicly supported the government and its official description of reality. Cultural elites were largely loyal to the regime in this period. Intellectuals, such as poet Boris Pasternak or physicist Lev Landau (both would become the Nobel Prize winners later), believed at that time in basic Communist ideals. Soviet literature of the 1930s (including the novels of prominent writers such as Valentin Kataiev, Valentin Kaverin, Yuri Olesha, Alexander Tvardovski, Konstantin Paustovskyy, Ilia Ehrenburg, Arkadii Gaidar, and many others) conveyed the officially approved "spirit" of enthusiasm, the relentless optimism, and the revolutionary passion of the Soviet people (Latsis, 1989). Only few dared to express their critical view of the Soviet Union.

Isolated Critics

Evidence of criticism of the system was found in several documents and eyewitness accounts. Ordinary people sent critical letters to local party committees and to newspapers.[3] There was evidence of several lower-ranking officials openly criticizing the Kremlin policies in their letters sent to each other. Moisei Frumkin (an old revolutionary and deputy minister of finance during the late 1920s) was brave enough to send an openly critical letter to the members of the Politburo in 1928. This letter was filled with arguments of loyalty to the Soviet ideology but criticized Stalin's agricultural policy. Frumkin died in the gulag in 1938 (Kossakovsky, 1990).

Scientists and writers occasionally protested too. In 1938, physicist Landau helped to prepare an anti-Stalinist leaflet, which accused Stalin of betraying Socialism (Gorelik, 1992). Famous writer Mikhail Sholokhov sent a critical letter to Stalin about the abuses of collectivization (Aksenov, 1991). In 1934, the famous scholar and the Nobel Prize winner, Ivan Pavlov, sent a critical letter to Soviet foreign minister Molotov, blasting Stalin's regime for despotism and negligence of scientific research (*Sovietskaia Kultura,* January 14, 1989).

Some other exceptional cases of documented criticism can certainly be found. However, they are few and far between. Most intellectuals generally embraced the Socialist ideology and disagreed only about specific policies and decisions (but they could discuss this only in private conversations with close friends or family members).

Stalin's Last Years

During World War II and particularly in the late 1940s, some important changes occurred in the views of Russian intellectuals and ordinary people as to the nature of their society. On the one hand, there was devastating evidence of massive military failures and loss of human life in 1941 and 1942. Many people realized that their country had entered the war grossly unprepared and militarily weak and that the government could have been better prepared to fight the aggression. On the other hand, the Soviet Union emerged victorious from the most devastating of wars. Nazism had been defeated and the Soviet flag was flying high over Berlin. People felt proud of their victory. Millions of soldiers, officers, sailors, pilots, and nurses had the chance to see Europe, where most of them were not allowed before the war. Europe, although destroyed and unstable, was a great "discovery" to many Soviet people. Only few, however, dared to discuss their positive impressions of the West.

Among the elites, not many were sufficiently daring to voice their criticism of the regime in the immediate postwar years. There is a case of two top commanders, Marshall Georgy Zhukov, a glorious military leader during the war, who did not get along with Stalin, and General Vasilii Gordov who criticized Stalin and the Soviet regime and praised Western democracy. Zhukov was removed from power and Gordov was arrested and executed in 1950 (Maximova, 1992). Among intelligentsia, there was practically nobody daring to voice any critical opinions in the immediate postwar years. Yet even the critics no longer passed negative judgment about the Soviet political system or Socialism: They were asking only for some improvements within the existing regime.

The Soviet Union's victory in the war contributed to Stalin's personality cult. Even the most serious critics of the political regime believed that Stalin was an exceptional and triumphant leader who was, from time to time, misled by some of his cabinet members and advisers. The ideological climate forming in the country after 1945, fears of persecution for disagreements with the official versions of the events, censorship, and seemingly overwhelming support of the régime by the masses—all these factors influenced the minds and actions of a small group of critics of the Soviet system (Gershenson and Grossman, 2001).

Stalin's death in 1953 did not immediately produce a significant change in the educated elites' perceptions of their own country and its political and ideological foundations. An intellectual pause was generally due to the uncertainty of the political winds blowing in the country right after Stalin was gone.

Elite's Attitudes between 1960s and 1980s

After a brief interregnum under Georgii Malenkov and a period of collective leadership of several Politburo comrades, greater social and political changes began to come about in the Soviet Union in the mid-1950s. The new Soviet leader Nikita Khrushchev's report to the twentieth Communist Party Congress in 1956 was one of the most remarkable events in Soviet history.

INITIAL CHANGES IN POLITICAL CONDITIONS UNDER KHRUSHCHEV,
AND STABLE OFFICIAL REALITIES

The Khrushchev report was significant not only and necessarily because it criticized the Soviet past. The report stood out because it challenged most Soviet citizens' views of their society, their lives, and their perception of their country's leaders. Even after Stalin's death, the majority of the Soviet people continued to believe in the official image of Soviet society, and continued to perceive Stalin as a national hero. After 1956, his statues and portraits were quickly taken out of public places and offices. The national icon was rapidly removed from the altar of reverence and fear.

Khrushchev's strong criticism of Stalin and his policies drastically changed people's perceptions of government and society. Former "enemies of the state" were now declared innocent victims of unlawful political repression. Overall, Stalin's behavior and many of his domestic policies were now presented to the Soviet people as a deviation from the normal, Marxist-Leninist course of development of a Socialist state. The ideological foundations of the Soviet state, people were told, were healthy. The problem was with Stalin's methods of governance. The leadership of the Communist Party gave itself credit for its ability to recognize and accept the mistakes of the past. As a result of new assessments, many outspoken supporters of the new policies demanded legal rehabilitation of the victims of political repressions. The government obliged.

The official doctrine launched in the early 1960s described the Soviet society as undergoing steady, rapid, and progressive development. According to the new official view, the Communist Party had learned from the mistakes of the past. The society was ready to move forward. Government leaders and their propagandists now shifted their attention to policies related to social security. It was frequently argued that the Soviet people had never experienced unemployment, inflation, economic depression, or any other unpredictable problems associated with free market. Economy, agriculture, science, education, culture, and health care were improving. Soviet propaganda used quantitative data to show the gradual growth of living standards, increasing numbers of durable goods purchased, and improving housing conditions. This new official doctrine found support in all social groups.[4] These numbers now helped the officials to argue that the Soviet Socialist system was superior to capitalism. Soviet people had to embrace a new kind of hope: Now that the obstacles of Stalinism had been removed, the Soviet society could develop rapidly to its fullest potential.

Government propaganda excluded all critical or pessimistic "elements" from the official vision of society and its future. Even purely theoretical debates in physics about the eventual end of the Earth or the universe were not encouraged. Official ideology promoted the idea of peaceful cooperation rather than confrontation with foreign powers. For example, during the Cuban missile crisis in October 1962, when the world was on the verge of a nuclear catastrophe, the Soviet people remained generally unconcerned. Only in the late 1960s, when Soviet-Chinese relations became exceptionally tense, did the fear of war reappear. A possible conflict with China became a topic of people's informal conversations with friends and family members. Yet the official Kremlin was utterly silent about a threat of war with China. As in the past, some intellectuals criticized the official policy of imposition of false social optimism. However, they did it privately. Publicly, most people supported the regime and its ideological doctrines.

The dismissal of Khrushchev from all party and government posts in 1964 was a significant political event: He was simply voted out and sent to retirement (Hosking, 1990). The failure of Khrushchev's attempts to liberalize society and his dismissal did not stop the development of a neo-Leninist ideology. Its supporters wanted to get back to the idealistic basics of Communism.

NEO-LENINISTS

The official neo-Leninist view of Soviet society, as it emerged in the late 1950s, attempted to legitimize several specific features of the Soviet social order: the Communist Party's political monopoly and rejection of a multiparty political system. Post-Stalin Leninists continued to respect the "old" party cadres and party intellectuals. However, they suggested that to guarantee immunity from another Stalin, the Communist Party should become truly democratic, by at least allowing opposing political factions within the party. The party leadership was called upon to initiate creative discussions about Marxist theory and ideology. Neo-Leninists also urged that censorship be dismantled and that the free flow of information be allowed. The Communist Party was urged to eliminate the prejudice and anti-Semitism that had flourished during Stalin's era. Among neo-Leninists were also the so-called "old Bolsheviks," which included those people who returned from Stalin's prison camps and who continued to regard themselves as true Communists, faithful to the original ideals of the revolution. Of course, they disapproved of Stalin's atrocities, but they did not wish to change the country's social and political system.

A popular journal called *Novyi Mir* (The New World) was an important source of information for the oppositional intelligentsia in the 1960s, including those of the neo-Leninist persuasion. Publications in this journal advocated a neo-Leninist image of Soviet society: The Soviet system was legitimate, but it had been weakened by serious mistakes in the past. For Alexander Tvardovski, the journal's editor in chief in the 1960s, and his assistants (including Alexander Dementiev and Vladimir Lakshin), the Socialist revolution of 1917 was a great historic event. However, they argued that Stalin and his policies had made it impossible for the Soviet people to enjoy the fruits of the revolution. Being close to these writers, Vasilii Grossman, in his book *Life and Destiny,* advocated a similar view. Alexander Solzhenitsyn also supported this view but only in the early 1960s.

Young people, mostly university students, turned to the original works of Lenin. (Lenin's *State and Revolution,* in which he forecasted the development of a socialist state, was an especially popular text.) They began to create informal discussion groups. Their main activities included regular meetings and debates. They maintained that Stalin had turned away from the original ideas of Leninism and they disagreed with the official glowing picture of the Soviet Union. Such groups began to appear in the late 1940s.[5] They multiplied in the 1950s after Stalin's death. Now, as young people believed, it was time to turn to the original, fundamental ideas of Leninism and build a new and pure society of equals. In the twenty-first century, somewhat similar processes were taking place in many Muslim countries plagued by corruption, nepotism, and injustice. Many young people turned to the fundamental principles of Islam, which became their genuine ideology and which, they believed, could guarantee the creation of a new type of society. History repeats itself multiple times.

In the Soviet example, the government did not tolerate such group activities for long. The neo-Leninist ideas suggested reforms, innovations, and a new vision of the Soviet Union, quite different from the official ideology. Although the members of these groups pledged their allegiance to Lenin, most of them were arrested, expelled from universities, and even imprisoned. The criminal charges against them were standard: anti-Soviet propaganda and conspiracy to commit antigovernment actions. Neo-Leninists vanished from the universities by the early 1970s. Their ideas reappeared again in various forms only in the 2000s.

Another point of view did not advocate the restoration of the fundamental principles of Leninism and was largely based on a combination of progressive, liberal ideas.

LIBERAL INTELLECTUALS

The ideological evolution of Soviet intellectuals into liberal thinkers was rapid after 1953. On the psychological level, many people probably wanted to compensate for more than two decades of political, cultural, and spiritual stagnation. By the beginning of the 1960s, many intellectuals had already begun to move away from neo-Leninism. This process took place together with a gradual decline of Lenin's prestige and with growing affinity between Lenin and Stalin in the minds of many intellectuals (Solzhenitsyn, 1975; Zimin, 1981). Both leaders came to be seen as responsible for the horrors in Soviet history, and Stalin was no longer considered the sole source of terror. The October Revolution of 1917 was also increasingly viewed as an unfortunate development, something that had aborted the hopes and aspirations of many true reformers who actually wanted to see Russia as a democratic country. For these critically minded intellectuals, the most promising Russian historical event was the February Revolution of 1917, which brought to power a multiparty Provisional Government under the moderate Socialist Alexander Kerensky. This event, the liberals argued, could have opened the way for different possibilities, including a free-market social democracy.

Having released themselves from the ideological magnetism of Lenin and the October Revolution, many progressive intellectuals began to question the official picture of Soviet society and the official views that Soviet society had inherent advantages over capitalism. These intellectuals began to surreptitiously discuss a very radical idea: The core of Soviet society was in its oppressive political regime. Since the mid-1960s, this point of view grew stronger among many liberal intellectuals who believed that the solution to any fundamental social or economic problem in their country would depend on changes in the Soviet political structure.

It was a dangerous point of view to express. Yet Soviet liberals did not call for an open revolt against the system. Moreover, they were convinced that the established political and economic system was practically infallible. In particular, state ownership of the major means of production, as well as the political monopoly of the Communist Party, were seen as permanent elements of the system. In the opinion of many intellectuals, the emergence of capitalism in the Soviet Union would require deeply ingrained respect for private property—a psychological condition and a legal imperative that the Soviet people had lost for good. Thus, the only choice available for future reformers was to develop a new and improved type of the "old" social, economic, and political system.

Many intellectuals became secret advocates of liberal Socialism, a system that would combine economic Socialism and political pluralism. In the 1960s, the liberal intellectuals, many of whom were still influenced by Marxism and believed in the Soviet state, could not imagine a time in the future when the Secretary General of the party (i.e., Mikhail

Gorbachev) would become a champion of privatization and would call for the dismantling of collective farms and the transformation of state enterprises into nonstate cooperatives. Back in the 1960s, debates revolved around a general question: Would it be generally possible to establish a liberal Socialist order, and would it be possible to do this under Soviet conditions in particular?

During private discussions of the 1960s, critics pointed at one of the evident fallacies of Marxism: While Marx had brilliantly described nineteenth-century capitalism, he was wrong in predicting capitalism's inevitable collapse. Capitalist societies and economies proved to be strong and flexible contrary to Marx's predictions. Young liberals of the 1960s held that Socialism, like capitalism, was characterized in its early stages by rigidity, oppression, and antagonistic contradictions. However, like capitalism, it could move into another phase. This new phase would combine the planned economy and limited private property with scientific and rational principles of government, social collectivism, and equality.

Physicist Andrei Sakharov became the main advocate of the idea of liberal Socialism in the Soviet Union. His early theoretical publication *A Reflection on Progress, Peaceful Coexistence, and Intellectual Freedom*, released in 1968, was a true manifesto of liberal Socialism. Sakharov's writings of the late 1960s and the early 1970s were filled with Marxist terminology. Marxist dogmas penetrated all the pores of the Soviet people's collective soul for a long time.[6]

One major idea propounded by the young liberals was about a new political order called, "socialism with a human face." This new order would require the individual to have a role in all spheres of life. Humanizing Soviet society was at the center of the liberals' agenda in the 1960s. Extolling individuality and personal needs, reason, and capacity to choose sensible options without directives from above, became new fixtures in many Soviet intellectuals' publications. Terms like *the individual, personality,* or *the human being* were new and exciting. Works by sociologists such as Igor Kon and Vladimir Shlapentokh, who addressed the topics of choice and individuality, aroused great interest among many members of the educated intelligentsia.

For these intellectuals of the 1960s, liberal Socialism had to guarantee free public opinion. It was thus argued that although the Soviet people were prohibited from electing leaders directly, they should have the right to express their views about various subjects, at least those unrelated to the legitimacy of the Socialist order. Newspapers and magazines should be free to give the real picture of society, to criticize any official, and to be able to generate and disseminate new social ideas. In particular, liberal intellectuals believed that conducting opinion polls would significantly enhance the quality of the Soviet mass media's contact with the public.

The liberals also wanted to modernize official ideology and rid it of a number of obsolete Communist dogmas, such as the leading role of the working class and the importance of the "class approach" to social issues. The liberal model included broadening the individual freedoms of Soviet citizens beyond freedom of speech. The intellectuals of the 1960s did not really anticipate achieving the full range of rights available to people in the West. However, they did expect that it would be possible for individuals to live and work anywhere they chose, that they could travel abroad, that people could receive greater access to Western sources of information, and that arts and literature prohibited in the past could be made available.

By the end of the 1960s, one of the prime sources of political communication among the young liberals became self-published papers called *samizdat*. In most cases, these typed papers, which were illegal, portrayed Soviet society in a critical and realistic way. The most active consumers of samizdat were young writers, poets, and artists.

Artists

During the 1960s, writers and artists represented a very diverse social stratum responsible for a critical exposure of Soviet realities. Throughout the official cultural policy's twists and turns under Khrushchev and thereafter, Soviet cultural elites learned what was allowed and what was prohibited in their depictions of reality. Acts of lone defiance from the late 1950s and into the early 1970s, some of them with major international repercussions—including Boris Pasternak and Joseph Brodsky— were highly publicized (Keep, 1996). Cultural intellectuals with critical leanings provided a more realistic picture of the West. Articles written by Viktor Nekrasov (1965) in *Novyi Mir* and by others who traveled to the West made a great impression on the average Soviet reader. The Soviet past also appeared in a different light. Alexander Solzhenitsyn and other writers provided a new picture of life in the gulag during the 1930s and 1940s, and their revelations further undermined the credibility of official ideology. Novelists including Sergei Zalygin, Vasilii Belov, and Boris Mozhaiev made early attempts to reinterpret the history of collectivization, while Pavel Nilin and Boris Kardin cast doubts about official depictions of the Russian Civil War.

A new depiction of life, different from the official version, was not only a different kind of perception and evaluation of social and political realities. The authors, who were also critical of the governing authorities, demanded the right for self-expression, which was dangerously close, from the government's standpoint, to the demands of political freedoms. In addition, artists-dissidents attracted the attention of the Western public, which obviously made these cases more political than they actually might have been. While prohibiting free expression in art and literature, as liberals suggested, the government was making a strategic mistake and undermined its own legitimacy in the eyes of many critically thinking intellectuals. Yet the masses were generally pleased with the mandatory deportation of Alexander Solzhenitsyn in 1974. The government portrayed his books as a dangerous distortion of Soviet realities. In the eyes of many, Solzhenitsyn was an attention-seeking hypocrite who deeply disliked the Soviet Union.

One of the growing trends in literature was the abandonment of the principle of Socialist realism (which required a positive, optimistic depiction of reality) and acceptance of nonideological positions. Writers Fedor Abramov, Vasili Shukshin, Viktor Astafiev, and other representatives of the "rural prose" school depicted life in the countryside without optimistic distortions and motivational slogans. Urban life was the focus of realist writers such as Nikolai Voronov, Vitali Semin, and Vasilly Aksenov, among many others. Poetry experienced a sudden boom. Young poets, such as Andrei Vosznesensky and Evgeny Evtushenko displayed their aesthetic experiments in artistic emotions, graphic illustrations, and pulsating rhyme. People packed stadiums to see these and other poets. Filmmakers were also involved in the critical exposure of official mythology. Films such as *Chairman* revealed many sordid realities of rural life, while *Our Contemporary* unmasked the shadier activities and hypocrisy of Soviet officials.

Sociologists

With the resurgence of social sciences in the Union of Soviet Socialist Republics in the late 1950s, sociologists also participated in debunking of many official images. The writings of sociologists were particularly important because, unlike the contributions of writers and filmmakers, their arguments could not be attributed to artistic imagination. Sociologists rooted their critiques in empirical evidence gathered through modern research.

Sociologists Vladimir Shubkin (1970) and Iuri Arutiunian (1968, 1970) questioned the postulate about the social homogeneity of Soviet society and the leading role that the working class played in it. Vladimir Iadov (1967), Viktor Perevedentsev (1975), and Tatiana Zaslavskaia (1970) critiqued the official idea that the Soviet workforce was motivated largely by moral and ideological commitments. Sociologists studying the mass media, like Boris Grushin (1968), Ülo Vooglaid (1967), and Vladimir Shlapentokh (1969), sought to undermine the myth of the media's effectiveness in the Soviet Union. Anatoli Kharchev (1964), Igor Kon (1967), and Sergei Golod (1975) produced evidence contradicting ideological postulates that the Soviet family was emotionally healthy and strong, and that Soviet people did not have much interest in sexuality. Finally, Vladimir Shubkin (1970) and Vadim Ol'shanski (1966) revealed the weakness of the official myths about the strong and harmonious Soviet social groups.

Overall, sociologists only began to question several essential details in the official depiction of the Soviet Union. However, they had very limited access to the media and the government could always regulate their research by allowing or disallowing particular studies.

Russian Nationalists

Soviet nationalists, or Russophiles, like their nineteenth-century predecessors, advanced the idea that Russian history had a unique nature rooted in unique culture, traditions, and morals. They also rejected the idea that Russia was just one particular case in the universal scheme of world history. They saw Russia as an exclusive country. This is a postulate, which is put forward by nationalists in almost every country. Yet Russia's strength and respect were undermined by an unfortunate chain of events in the twentieth century. To nationalists, Communism in the Soviet Union has been a deviation from a normal, natural course of development.

In fact, the idea of national exclusiveness was also fundamental in Soviet official ideology. Images of the Soviet Union as the first Socialist society and the main liberator of oppressed people were central to Soviet propaganda. Stalin recognized, above all, during the war against Germany, that it was necessary to combine the ideas of Socialist loyalty and Russian exclusiveness. After Stalin's death, however, the idea of Russian national exclusiveness was downgraded, but it has never completely vanished from official ideology. With the growing suppression of the liberal political thought in the 1970s, the beliefs in Russian exclusiveness began to grow again among some intellectuals. The most fully elaborated concept of Russian nationalism was presented by Igor Shafarevich in his *samizdat* publications of the late 1970s. Many Russophiles of the 1970s and (to a lesser extent) of the 1980s, cherished the so-called "Russian idea" formulated by émigré philosopher Nikolai Berdyaev (1874–1948). The "Russian idea" espoused Russia's moral and spiritual superiority over the world, particularly over the West. Russia's mission was to save the world from self-defeating decadence.

Yuri Davydov was probably the most prominent and eloquent defender of the "Russian idea" during the Brezhnev's period until the early 1980s. Davydov assailed the West, its modernist philosophy, and relativist morals. He preached that, in contrast to the rest of the world, the Russian people were inclined toward sacrifices for the sake of others. The theme of sacrifice was central to many authors' theories of this period. A host of publications in the late 1970s and the first half of the 1980s described the West, and especially America, as deprived of moral values, altruism, compassion, and spirituality. By the late 1980s, however, revelations that appeared during glasnost about the moral degradation of Soviet society made it difficult to defend the thesis of the moral (or any other) superiority of the Russian people.

Self-identified "Russian patriots" and "national Bolsheviks" were a distinct group among the Russophiles. Devotion to the state was incorporated into official Soviet ideology since the 1930s. Official ideology, however, linked patriotism to Socialism and in no way presented these values as being in opposition to one another. Russophiles argued differently: Even in their publications in the official press, they directly ranked patriotism as the highest moral value, independent from Socialist ideals.

Russophile patriots of the 1970s held a positive view of Stalin. To them, he was a statesman who restored Russian patriotism, and who deserved respect for creating a superpower. (This view has become popular again in the 2000s under president Putin). For this reason, "patriots" praised the 1930s and 1940s as periods in which, in contrast to the 1920s, Russian culture flourished (Nesterov, 1984). Together with their worshipping the strong state, Russophile patriots assumed that all of the problems plaguing Russia should have been solved through strengthening of Russian statehood. Consumerism and individualism endangered Russia's national interests. For the Russophile traditionalists, the main focus of Russian history has been their religion, the Orthodoxy. Traditionalists also saw the decline of religion in the Soviet Union as the main cause of their country's moral degeneration. In the 1970s, traditionalists' views found support of Solzhenitsyn and several other authors.

Although Russian nationalism was not part of the official ideology, the authorities did not consider "patriotic" nationalists and traditionalists particularly dangerous, compared to liberal intellectuals who were critical of the Soviet Union and its political system (Keep, 1996).

DISSIDENTS

How strong was the political opposition in the Soviet Union? Between 1967 and 1977, only 1,583 individuals (less than 200 per year) were sentenced, as estimated, for "anti-Soviet activity," including people persecuted for nationalist and religious activity (Bukovsky, 1995). Almost 50 percent of the punishable offenses against the state were categorized as "calumnious or politically damaging statements." The second category of offences (about 8 percent of all cases) involved people who actually wrote, produced, or distributed calumnious or politically damaging documents. The third group (about 6 percent) included people who participated in "antisocial actions."

What were the main criticisms of the open opposition? The majority of dissidents wanted to "humanize" the regime rather than to abolish it. According to official reports, more than 50 percent of those then sent to prison were formally accused of supporting bourgeois nationalism (including 17 percent labeled "Zionists"). Another 35 percent of detainees disseminated "revisionist and reformist ideologies"; another 8 percent were labeled as advocates of "religious ideology." The remaining 7 percent were a very diverse group of "others" (Bukovsky, 1995: 140).

In the early 1980s, the mood of the Russian intellectuals who thought critically of the Socialist system was gloomy (Remington, 1989). The Soviet intellectuals' lack of action and their shallow criticism of the system were based on the belief that the Soviet state would survive for decades without a change (Shlapentokh, 1990). Overall, intellectual opposition in the Soviet Union was almost fully suppressed by the early 1980s, only a few years before perestroika. The absolute majority of the regime's critics accepted roles of disgruntled but formally loyal Soviet citizens. It was Gorbachev who took a significant effort to arouse new perceptions and criticisms of the Soviet system in 1985–1987.[7]

GORBACHEV AND THE 1980S

After Andropov's death in February 1984, and a brief interregnum under Konstantin Chernenko, who died in 1985, Mikhail Gorbachev initiated the policies of glasnost and perestroika that gave the Soviet elites a real chance to speak their minds freely and declare their true moral allegiances. Political censorship was lifted, thus giving an opportunity to different opinions to flourish. What was the Soviet Union and where did the reforms lead in the minds of intellectual elites?

CULTURAL AND POLICY ELITES

Soviet journalists were in great need to earn their prestige. For many years they had to promote the official but distorted image of Soviet reality. During perestroika, they had the freedom to report almost anything they wanted and on any topic they could choose. Most of them chose critical themes.

In a growing number of publications appearing in the Soviet Union after the end of 1985, the rosy and dull reality of the Soviet Union was replaced by a nonstop reporting of problems, catastrophes, accidents, crime, and scandals. Absent before 1985, open criticism of the government became relentless (Kagarlitsky, 1988). The importance of this critical coverage—although it was to necessarily welcome many Soviet people who preferred to believe in the official ideology—was an intellectual and political breakthrough. It was an endeavour to present an alternative image of reality where both desirable and undesirable events can actually happen simultaneously (Naylor, 1988). Big and small newspapers began to publish letters from their readers, issue editorials, and journalistic reports critical of the party, government agencies, and officials of all ranks. Editors let almost anyone speak out. There were almost no forbidden political or ideological topics to discuss.

Opinions about the state of affairs in the Soviet Union were different. Both liberal intellectuals and the majority of the political leadership agreed about viewing Brezhnev's political legacy negatively. The period between the 1970s and the 1980s was assessed as a long stage of duplicity and stagnation. Most liberals advocated social populism based on the belief that several major adjustments in the party's policies should bring the country back to normalcy. At the same time, the early perestroika was the time of the resurgence of liberal Marxism that was in many ways similar to liberalism of the 1960s. Gorbachev long believed that democracy and civil rights could coexist within a one-party system, without relinquishing the Communist Party's sole hold on power. Only gradually did he accept the view that Socialism could mean the possibility of several parties competing for power (Remnick, 1993). Liberal Marxists also believed in the possibility of social and political reforms that would increase people's participation in local politics. Gorbachev supported the view that an open dialogue and exchange of opinions would unleash new creative forces in ordinary people. This was an idealistic vision of reality close to several utopian models generated in the past. These utopian theories suggested that as soon as people acquire appropriate conditions for their life and work, they could create a productive and harmonious society led by educated intellectuals. In Gorbachev's view, these intellectuals should become the core of the reformed Communist Party of the Soviet Union.

Conservatives in top leadership positions, and particularly neo-Stalinists, envisioned mainly administrative reforms to make the Soviet system work better. To them, the ongoing crisis was a sign that the old system went off course and needed some adjustments and improvements, but no more than that. They believed that the crisis of the 1980s was caused by the party's inability to adjust to the changes taking place in society. The aging party leadership was responsible for the failure. As a consequence, the Communist Party put itself on the defensive. To overcome the crisis, the party demanded responsibility and discipline from all its members. The conservatives also wanted to preserve the purity of Marxism and Leninism and to make sure that the basic principles of Socialism remained unchanged under the capricious winds of political populism, of which they openly accused Gorbachev and his supporters.

The most conservative Russophile intellectuals did not favor the idea of democracy as part of their country's future. In their view, Russia was dying under the combined effects of modernization, secularization, and Westernization—all initiated by Gorbachev and his team (Rupnik, 1989). In a broader conflict over values, the nationalists attacked the policy of glasnost, which allowed political relativism and free exchange of ideas. The Russophiles considered these ideas as damaging and irresponsible. They argued that the Russian people should return to old-style religious values, specifically the values of the Orthodox religion.[8] They opposed the expansion of political freedoms as well as anything coming out of the West including music, street fashion, entertainment, or food choices.

Many liberal intellectuals were confused about the changes of the 1980s. They always wanted reforms but did not expect the time for them to come so unexpectedly quickly. They wanted to see new, educated, and strong political leaders. Gorbachev, however, was increasingly disappointing because of his political turns and sways from romantic populism to conservative Marxism. His relentless speeches and redundant slogans that were repeated on numerous occasions were increasingly frustrating to many people. Liberal intellectuals hailed the early stages of glasnost. The support of political transparency was overwhelming in 1986. However, it became apparent that the political podium of the following years was highjacked mainly by demagogues and populists. The promises of a multiparty system remained unfulfilled. Yet scores of political organizations and communities appeared on the local level, each demanding something for their own personal gain. Meanwhile, crime flourished. Hopes for order and stability remained wishful thinking. It was easier for an average person to travel abroad but the vast majority of people did not have the money to go anywhere due to inflation. Most liberal intellectuals believed that they were witnessing the "wrong" kind of reforms. In media reports and other publications, it was common for authors to entertain a passive-aggressive attitude about the Soviet Union and Russia. The country was criticized for being incapable of undergoing any, even minor, social improvements.

Economy

The massive changes in the country's economic system have had immediate implications on the lives of the Soviet people. Uncertainty was the most common characteristic of the economic situation. Top party leaders, liberal intellectuals, and other political groups disagreed from the start about the essence and direction of the ongoing economic reforms (Kontorovich, 1987). These disagreements reflected important divisions within the different groups about private property, free market, state regulations, planning, income inequality, and job security.

Neo-Stalinists and other fundamentalists within the party's top leadership, such as Egor Ligachev, believed that the Soviet economy would respond only under a stricter administrative control through a new, strong, and centralized power structure. The market was an ideological scarecrow to the fundamentalists, so they believed that the new Soviet Socialism should continue to use planning methods. The problem with the old system was that such plans in the past were unrealistic and ideology-driven. In the late 1980s, as fundamentalists believed, central planning should be realistic. Combined with new methods of management, the new planning methods would guarantee a rapid and steady economic development.

Liberal Marxists, including Gorbachev, believed that according to their economic models, state-run enterprises should receive more responsibility for independent economic decisions. This was, a kind of economic self-management partially tied to profit. Job security should be sought but it will no longer be guaranteed. Party fundamentalists, on the other hand, perceived state-guaranteed job security as the foundation of their socioeconomic policies. The debates and political battles concerning new economic policies in the Gorbachev era were mostly about different views of social justice. Supporters of the merit-based view of justice, who were mostly in the reformist camp, believed that people should be rewarded according to their skills and the resulting social input. Their opponents, who were supporters of the fairness-based view of justice, maintained that society should provide certain guarantees to the people and the government should distribute wealth more or less equally (Shlapentokh, 1988).

Substantial evidence indicates that the Soviet general public have long remained committed to the concept of fairness-based justice and egalitarianism (Shlapentokh and Shiraev, 2002). Probably for this rationale (along with several other reasons), many liberal economists offered different reform models still containing the elements of free market and Socialism together. In their projects, it was a new economic and political system combining the essential elements of free market involving private property and competition for profit, and Socialism involving job security, stable wages, and other socioeconomic guarantees.

This belief in a possibility to converge capitalism and Socialism was perhaps best expressed in the Declaration of the Federation of Socialist Clubs, drawn up at the first meeting of informal associations in Moscow in August 1987. A portion of this manifesto devoted to economic issues, emphasized that the goals of perestroika should include the establishment of free market relations combined with safeguarding of full employment, the minimum wage, and guaranteed state pensions (Kagarlitsky, 1988). Top advisers in the Gorbachev's policy team, such as Leonid Abalkin and Abel Aganbegian, actively supported this point of view. For Gorbachev's top adviser, Alexander Yakovlev, Socialism was a giant welfare state program designed to protect people from harmful market forces (Remnick, 1993). For Gorbachev, however, the idea of Socialism also meant, for some time, state planning and state ownership.

Most Soviet nationalists unanimously condemned free market reforms on seeing in them greed and consumerism, which were, in their view, anti-Russian values. They continued to advocate self-sacrifice and asceticism as alternative values, the adherence to which would save the country. Nationalists (and organizations representing them such as *Pamiat*, for example) rapidly radicalized themselves condemning both the ongoing reforms and its leaders. They appealed to the masses claiming that free market would eventually destroy the country, the economy, and Russian culture.

Gorbachev remained in power for less than seven years. This was a very short period for his contemporaries to observe the ongoing changes and reflect on them in a systematic way. For the most part, their assessments were quick responses to the rapid changes occurring almost daily. On the other hand, however, their assessments were rooted in their deeply seated ideological beliefs ranging from Orthodox Marxism to nationalism, from liberal democracy to libertarian beliefs. It was a unique situation though: For the first time in many decades, the government allowed people to express their perceptions and beliefs freely.

CONCLUSION

For the most period of the Soviet Union's existence, its intellectual elites remained relatively loyal to the government. They accepted, on the surface, the official image of society. Certainly, their compliance with the Soviet regime was never overwhelming or voluntary. Besides, many people frequently justified "rallying around the flag," a necessary process during the time of danger or crisis. The government always tried to find or generate such troubles and crises to use them to their own advantage. Most educated people, nevertheless, believed that their country was on the right path and that it was only a matter of time, when Socialism would reveal its true socioeconomic benefits.

Soviet elites did not see their country as a pluralist society ruled by technology-savvy and educated professionals, as some intellectuals in the West tried to portray the Soviet Union. On the other hand, the Soviet elites did not actually see their country as a warmonger desiring an imminent world war to satisfy its omnipotent ideological hunger.

Beliefs about the Soviet Union began to change after the 1960s. Some accepted the Socialist foundation of the Soviet Union but hoped for cosmetic reforms. Others began to see many fundamental flaws in the regime. Some began to refer to the Soviet Union as a totalitarian society thus agreeing with totalitarianists overseas.

Despite criticism and skepticism about the nature of the reforms of the 1980s, most elite groups, nevertheless, supported glasnost and perestroika. The major exceptions were intellectuals from the radical nationalist groups. Politically liberal elites maintained a view that new policies were desirable, and that these changes could give the Soviet regime a renewed lease on life. However, intellectual elites in the 1980s remained mostly observers of the ongoing and rapid process of transformation. At the end of the 1980s, the struggle for power among the government elites, sparked by the growth of nationalist forces in the ethnic republics, overshadowed most experts' discussions of the nature of the changes.

CHAPTER 4

THE SOVIET UNION IN THE MIRROR OF AMERICAN PUBLIC OPINION FROM THE 1930S TO 1990

INTRODUCTION

During almost 40 years of scientific polling, the majority of Americans were not particularly enthusiastic or sympathetic about the Soviet Union. They did not like its social and political system. Most Americans saw the Soviet Union as an oppressive regime conducting aggressive policies. The Soviet Communist government was evidently the main cause of negative perceptions. However, in most opinion polls, the majority of Americans were also critical about Russians as people.

For instance, in one of the polls conducted in 1972, the Soviet Union was named first on the list of three countries, to which people did not want to give foreign aid. The two others were China and Egypt (ODC/Hart, October 22, 1972). This unenthusiastic opinion about the Soviet Union was so keen that, in 1985, 53 percent of Americans surveyed by *CBS* and the *New York Times* said they would rather be willing to risk the "destruction of the United States" than to be "dominated by the Russians" (*CBS/NYT,* September 19, 1985). Not all the surveyed agreed with this gloomy hypothetical scenario: 32 percent chose the lesser "evil," that is, the Russian domination. Looking at the results of this poll, any informed critic would argue that these results were not that persuasive. The survey could have asked about, for instance, a Martian invasion and the responses would have been similar: Most people do not like invasions of their homeland! However, this particular poll in 1985 reflected the critical tone of American opinion about the Soviet Union. These critical evaluations were revealed in surveys conducted as early as the 1930s. Since then, most Americans saw the Soviets as a different people. For example, in the same 1985 survey, 56 percent of respondents said that average Americans and average Russians were "quite different," in contrast to 16 percent who saw the Americans and the Soviets as "pretty much the same."

What were the particular issues and features relating to the Soviet Union, its people and policy that troubled the majority of Americans? Did the American people possess extensive knowledge about the Soviet Union, and were they able to analyze and comprehend the processes taking place in that country? Did the American people's opinions reflect direct threats from the far-away ideological and military adversary? Or, were these opinions largely xenophobic?

In this chapter, we analyze how Americans perceived and evaluated the Soviet Union. These evaluations were reflected in answers to questions posed in national opinion polls. Most of the 3,000 surveys available to us containing references to the Soviet Union were related to particular U.S. foreign policies and revealed little about the public's views of the Soviet Union as a country. Nevertheless, there is a relatively large sample of approximately 250 surveys that dealt directly with people's views of the Soviet Union. The results of these polls enable us to litmus test what "the majority of Americans" thought of Russia, its system, and inhabitants.

SIMPLE IMAGES

We begin with surveys containing questions based on "free associations." Here the respondent is given an opportunity to say any word or words that he or she feels appropriate, or to produce any association that comes first to the respondent's mind. Surveys using free association methods attempt to reveal the respondent's most salient associations and perceptions, in the sense that these are most readily accessible from memory (Converse 1964, 1970).

In 1945, a survey (*Fortune*/Roper, June 18, 1945), asked Americans to name one or two things about Russia that they thought were definitely "not so good." The most frequent response was, "I don't know" (33 percent). Next, the most often repeated answers were "communism" (13 percent) or "against religion" (10 percent). A variety of responses were also produced when people answered the question: "What one or two things about Russia do you feel are really good?" Many respondents (43 percent), once again, did not give any answer at all, which can either be interpreted as a total rejection of the Russian system having any redeeming qualities or as a lack of any associations. The Soviet military was mentioned in 10 percent of answers, which was followed by remarks related to equality and social security (8 percent), as well as related to perceived Soviet patriotism and loyalty to their country (7 percent).

Several categories of verbal associations were revealed in a 1985 survey asking the question, "Can you tell me what comes to mind when you hear the word Russia?" One set of associations included words such as "communism," "communist," or "socialist" (17 percent of answers). Another category was about the received aggressive policies: "nuclear war," "war," or "atomic bomb" (20 percent). An "enemy" category (in answers such as, "they are enemies," "trouble for us," or "rival to the U.S.") was about U.S.-Soviet rivalry, mentioned by 12 percent of respondents (*CBS/NYT*, September 19, 1985). If we consider associations such as "communism" and "socialism" as negative and reflecting significant differences between the U.S. and Soviet political systems, then nearly one half of the respondents produced some kind of negative associations related to the Soviet Union. In another survey (*Newsweek/Gallup*, November 14, 1985) "patriotism" and "loyalty" were also mentioned among particular strengths of the Soviet society (57 percent of respondents mentioned such terms). In the same survey, 55 percent of respondents mentioned a "willingness to fight" as an attribute of the Soviet people.

Over the years, there have been several polls that asked respondents to compare the United States and Russia. In 1985, Americans were asked, for example, to answer an open-ended question: "In what way are Russians and Americans most different?" (*CBS/NYT*, September 19, 1985). The answers were placed into categories. "Absence of freedom" was on the top of the list (29 percent) of major differences, followed by the obvious, "political system, government" (18 percent), and by a more general answer, "lifestyle, culture, and nationality" (11 percent). All other answer categories were in single digits, and 18 percent of the respondents did not give any answer. The further question, "In what way are Russians and Americans most alike?," was apparently more difficult than the one about differences, because more than one-third of the respondents (35 percent) did not produce an answer. A category "both just people" was mentioned most frequently (18 percent), followed by comments about both nations surviving during the war and being allies.

The Russian people were portrayed in the U.S. polls as hard-working individuals. For example, their hard work and dedication to their country were among top reasons mentioned in a 1950s poll (*Gallup*, October 15, 1957) that asked respondents to suggest a reason for why the Soviet

Union had launched a space satellite before the United States did. Russian workers were also perceived as trying harder than their American counterparts (*CBS/NYT,* September 19, 1985).[1]

According to 53 percent of respondents in the mid-1980s, Russia was doing better than the United States on job security, such as "making sure that everyone has a job," while only 33 percent gave credit to America for doing better. In addition, the crime problem was seen by 73 percent of Americans as less severe in the Soviet Union than it was in the United States (*CBS/NYT,* September 19, 1985.) Although 69 percent and 64 percent of respondents respectively mentioned Russian science and education as strengths of the Soviet Union, only 2 percent believed that Russia was doing the best job of educating its young people when compared to other countries. Most Americans (63 percent) chose Japan as the country highest in the educational area. Only few (19 percent) chose the United States (*Newsweek/Gallup,* November 14, 1985). Although these results shows that multicountry comparisons, focusing particularly on specific social issues, may not always generate compatible data, the views of the Soviet Union in America were, in general, unfavorable.

The Soviet people's hard work, patriotism, and their government's fight against crime (in addition to a few more idiosyncratic features) were thus among a few positive qualities ascribed to the Soviets in American surveys. In all other comparative aspects, most Americans evaluated the Soviet Union as being worse than the United States. Even on the issue of patriotism—a "strength" feature of the Soviet society according to most surveys—Americans rated themselves higher. Although, in one mid-1980s survey, 22 percent of respondents believed that Russians were more patriotic than Americans, still, twice as many (58 percent) disagreed. They said that Americans were more patriotic about their country than the Soviet people were (*CBS/NYT,* September 19, 1985). In any case, infrequent "positive" assessments of a few characteristics of the Soviet system or people should not overshadow the fact that many (usually most) Americans believed that the Soviet Union, as a country, was America's adversary. It was seen as an educated, hard-working, and tough opponent.

When individuals answering survey questions, use commonsensical logic to make comparisons, they normally tend to weigh the available facts in some manner before making an evaluation. In surveys, however, many responses do not necessarily act this way. They often do not have knowledge about the subject of the survey. As a result, many people give the most accessible or appropriate, within a context, answer. Consider the following question from a mid-1980s survey: "Think about what average Russians are like, and compare them to average Americans.

Who cares more about family ties, Russians or Americans?" In this survey, only 10 percent did not give an answer at all, and 19 percent said "both." Most of the responses were predominantly in America's favor, with 46 percent saying, "Americans" and 25 percent saying "Russians" (*CBS/NYT*, September 19, 1985). Yet how did all these people make these comparisons? Did they have knowledge about family ties around the globe? Or maybe such surveys simply reflect a universal tendency to evaluate one's own social group more favorably that others?

Let's look at what "average" Americans knew, or believed that they knew, about the Soviet Union.

INTEREST AND KNOWLEDGE

Historically, Americans, like people in many countries do, tend to pay more attention to domestic affairs than to the events in foreign nations, unless there is a conflict or war there. Americans' views of the Soviet Union were not an exception: Although the country was viewed as a powerful adversary and a potential threat, domestic affairs within the United States commonly drew more attention.

For example, the following question was asked in a 1976 poll: "If you had to choose, which of these problems do you think is more important to the country: Relations with Russia or crime and drug abuse?" (*CBS News/NYT*, April 15, 1976). "Relations with Russia" was chosen by just 18 percent of respondents, while 70 percent of them mentioned "crime and drug abuse." In a poll conducted in 1982 (Roper, December 11, 1982), the respondents were asked to choose two or three events from a preselected list of most important events of that year. A domestic event, a series of poisonings by Tylenol sold in supermarkets, was chosen more often than any other event (47 percent of respondents). Foreign events were rated high, although not much—the war in the Falkland Islands between Great Britain and Argentina drew serious attention (31 percent), as did the Israeli invasion of Lebanon (29 percent). The death of the Soviet leader Leonid Brezhnev in November—perhaps the most significant political event in the Soviet Union in 1982—was seventh on the list (19 percent of respondents), ahead of the ongoing NFL strike (8 percent).

On the whole, the Soviet Union drew at least moderate attention from most American people in the 1970s and later. Repeatedly, a majority of respondents reported a great deal of interest in Russian events, commonly exceeding the number of those respondents who reported little or no interest. More attention was given to bilateral relations between the United States and the Soviet Union and to issues such as negotiations about nuclear weapons and arms control agreements, such as the

SALT treaty in 1974. Many Americans, although not the majority, were generally aware of the status of Soviet-American relations and ongoing negotiations. For example, about one third of respondents (32 percent) said that their knowledge of these bilateral relationships was "good" (ABS/WP, February 12, 1986). In 1987, 25 percent of American respondents suggested that they understood "pretty well" what a nuclear arms limitation agreement with the Russians would be about; 30 percent, however, said that they did not know much about it (Roper, January 24, 1987). In contrast, Americans knew little about what was going on within the Soviet Union. Yet they often gave correct evaluations of some high-profile events. For example, Americans saw Soviet internal affair events such as the twenty-fifth Party Congress in 1976 (as well as most other Communist congresses) as a crashing bore: Many Soviet people shared the same opinion.

Although surveys indicate that the prime source of information about the Soviet Union was television, people, of course, used other sources of knowledge. In 1985, 22 percent of Americans claimed to have met a Soviet citizen at some point. About 30 percent and 18 percent, respectively, mentioned that they had seen a movie or read a book about the Soviet Union or Soviets that made a big impression on them (*CBS/NYT*, September 19, 1985). Americans could travel to the Soviet Union relatively easily, but most of them were reluctant to visit that country on vacation. Their reluctance to visit Russia was reasonable, because many Americans were aware of poor service and shortages in there (although foreign tourists in the Soviet Union received significantly better service than anyone else).

In two exemplary polls on this issue, one was conducted in the mid-1970s (*Gallup,* March 18, 1974) and the other in the 1980s (Opinion Research Corporation, August 28, 1988) only 2 percent indicated that Russia was a country they would be "most interested in visiting." The highest respondent share (17 percent) who mentioned they would at least be "very interested" in going to the Soviet Union on vacation was obtained in a poll conducted for the *Washington Post* in December of 1989. According to another survey conducted in 1988 (*USA Today/Black,* May 16), 23 percent of Americans expressed an increased interest in visiting the Soviet Union, compared with their retrospectively reported interest in doing so five years ago. Most probably, this was a result of many positive political changes that were taking place in the Soviet Union in the late 1980s.

In general, despite the existing interest and attention to the Soviet Union, Americans knew little about their overseas counterpart. The lack of knowledge should not, in all likelihood, be seen as a sign of prejudice against Russia. Pollsters repeatedly demonstrate relatively poor knowledge of the average American about many historic and political events and government-related issues, even in their own country.[2] Therefore, the fact that in 1988 only 37 percent of surveyed Americans were able to identify the Soviet Union as a member of the Warsaw Pact, and that 16 percent mistakenly believed the Union of Soviet Socialist Republics was a member of NATO, should not be particularly surprising (National Geographic Society/*Gallup,* May 8, 1988).

Table 1 displays the results of several surveys conducted by various polling organizations between the 1940s and 1991, in which respondents

Table 4.1   Americans' knowledge about the Soviet Union in the mid-1940s, the mid-1980s, and 1991: Percentage shares giving (1) correct/accurate answers, (2) incorrect/inaccurate answers, or (3) saying that they did not know the answer to the question asked (confidence intervals not reported)

- **(1) 23 percent- (2) 42 percent- (3) 35 percent** Identify the size of the Soviet Union's population (plus or minus 50 mln.) (Gallup, February 3, 1945)
- **45 percent-22 percent-33 percent** Whether every worker in Russia gets paid about the same amount of money regardless of what kind of work he does (Fortune/Roper June 25, 1945)
- **9 percent-56 percent-35 percent** That the SALT II Agreement was signed by the United States and Russia (Public Agenda Foundation May 29, 1984)
- **24 percent-11 percent-65 percent** Name of the Soviet leader (CBS/NYT, September 19, 1985)
- **40 percent-7 percent-52 percent** Name of the Soviet secret police (CBS/NYT, September 19, 1985)
- **14 percent-35 percent-52 percent** Whether U.S. troops fought in Russia against the Communists in 1918 (CBS News, New York Times, September 19, 1985)
- **56 percent-28 percent-16 percent** Whether the Soviet Union and the United States fought on the same side in WWII (CBS News, New York Times, September 19, 1985)
- **42 percent-25 percent-32 percent** Whether more Russians died or more Americans died in WWII (CBS News, New York Times, September 19, 1985)
- **45 percent-9 percent-46 percent** Name of the Soviet leader (ABC/WP, February 12, 1986)
- **48 percent-48 percent-9 percent** Whether all adults in the Soviet Union have to belong to the Communist party, or not. (ABC/WP, February 12, 1986)
- **67 percent-26 percent-7 percent** Whether or not the Soviet Union was an ally of the United States during WWII. (ABC/WP, February 12, 1986)
- **38 percent-46 percent-16 percent** Whether or not the Soviet Union was an ally of the United States after the Communists came to power. (ABC/WP, December 2, 1987)
- **76 percent-24 percent** Find the Soviet Union on a map (National Geographic Society/ Gallup May 8, 1988)
- **34 percent-66 percent** Tell who Boris Yeltsin is (Times Mirror/ PSR, May 19, 1991)

were asked to express their knowledge about particular facts related to the Soviet Union, its recent history, and policies. With a few exceptions, such as finding U.S.S.R. on the map and naming Russia as an ally during World War II, more than half of the respondents did not give correct answers.

This relative lack of knowledge has several underlying reasons. Overall, people tend to pay only some attention to international events. As discussed previously, most Americans, for example, tended to follow news about the Union of Soviet Socialist Republics and its people "casually" rather than "carefully," according to the series of surveys conducted by Roper between 1974 and 1985. Those who followed news casually, or paid only a little attention, substantially outnumbered those who followed the news closely.

The Kremlin's Iron Curtain was another important reason for the American people's lack of knowledge about the Soviet Union. In a 1985 poll (*CBS/NYT,* September 19, 1985), only 11 percent said that they had "a very good idea" about what life in the Soviet Union was; 35 percent reported that they had only "some idea"; and 50 percent said they had only "little" knowledge. In 1986, only 4 percent of respondents reported that their knowledge about the Soviet Union was "excellent." Almost 63 percent said that their knowledge of the country was either "not good" or "poor." In relation to other countries, however, the Soviet Union stood out as a country that the American people felt they knew better than many other states. To illustrate this point, in one survey, from a long list of countries, the Soviet Union was chosen by the largest share of respondents as a foreign country, which people felt they "knew most about" (52 percent), followed by the People's Republic of China (25 percent), India (24 percent), and South Korea (20 percent) (ODC/Hart, October 22, 1972).

What did these surveys reveal? Most people actually lack strong feelings on a wide variety of political and social issues. However, when people are asked to express their opinion, they tend to engage in, as psychologists say, "response construction" by choosing between the response options put in front of them by a pollster, or by generating other answers (Zaller, 1996; Tourengeau & Rasinski, 1988). People are likely to choose easily available responses, coming frequently "from the top of the head," such as facts and opinions readily available to them from memory. Lacking knowledge and interest, most American respondents kept producing such "easily accessible responses" related to the Soviet Union. These responses were predominantly negative. But if knowledge about and interest in the Soviet Union remained modest, why did most people's attitudes tend to be negative?

To answer this question, let us examine the history of polls in which Americans expressed their views about the Soviet Union.

SYMPATHIES AND DISLIKES

From the late 1930s, both the United States and the Soviet Union had to confront two powerful enemies: Nazi Germany and Imperial Japan. It is reasonable to expect that Americans should have maintained somewhat positive attitudes about the Soviet Union as a partner and the Russians as an allied nation. Table 2 displays the results of surveys relevant to this question, all taken from the mid-1930s into the mid-1940s.

Though a strong majority preferred that the Soviet Union win the war against Germany, and although anti-German antipathy in America was strong, it took some time before people in the United States started to believe that Moscow could actually win. As the survey results reveal, people's sympathies about the Soviet Union were somewhat cautious. Soon after the initial invasion by Nazi Germany into the Soviet Union in 1941, only 22 percent of polled Americans expected the Soviet Union to win against Germany, while 47 percent expected that the Nazis would defeat Moscow (*Gallup Poll,* July 14, 1941). A few months later, a small plurality (43 percent) suggested that Russia would win, with the rest of the respondents endorsing different scenarios (*Gallup,* September 17, 1941). Four years later, as the war was ending and the Red Army's military strength was undisputed, the Americans offered their support to the Soviets. Yet it was Great Britain (chosen by 73 percent), rather than the Soviet Union (30 percent), which was most often identified as being among America's most desirable principal partners after the war (*Fortune,* March 26, 1945).

Americans in 1944 and 1945 would give ambivalent answers to *Gallup* questions such as, "Do you think Russia can be trusted to cooperate with us after the war?"

Table 3 shows the dynamics of trust about the Soviet Union revealed in polls. Mistrust had been strong before and also during the war. When Gallup asked in April 1943 if Russia could be trusted to cooperate with the United States of America when the war was over, 34 percent said that it could not. The respondents were also asked to explain why they expressed such a skeptical view. About 19 percent mentioned Russia's expansionism, belligerence, and territorial ambitions. Another 19 percent mentioned the political differences between the United States of America and the Soviet Union. About 12 percent of respondents pointed

Table 4.2 Sympathy, antipathy, and other attitudes regarding the Soviet Union in a comparative perspective (from the mid-1930s to the mid-1940s). Only selected items and response shares are reported here for the Gallup polls of December 21, 1936 and July 6, 1939, as well as for the Fortune/Roper poll in November 1938: response shares thus do not summate to 100 percent

Question formulation; Survey organization and date	Response alternatives (percent)
Which of the European countries do you like best? (Gallup, December 21, 1936)	Russia 1 England 46 France 9 Germany 7
In the current boundary dispute between Japan and Russia, with which side do you sympathize? (Gallup, August 23, 1938)	Russia 44 Japan 4 Neither 31 No opinion 22
If there were a war between Germany and Russia, which side would you rather see win? (Gallup, November 16, 1938)	Russia 83 Germany 17
Toward which one of these foreign governments do you feel least friendly? (Fortune/Roper, November 1938)	Russia 5 Germany 62 Japan 13 Italy 6 Don't know 11
Toward which one of these foreign Governments do you feel most friendly? (Fortune/Roper, November 1938)	Russia 1 Germany 2 Great Britain 47 Don't know 11
If there is a war between Russia and Japan, which side would you rather see win? (Gallup, February 24, 1939)	Russia 51 Japan 9 No choice 29 No opinion 11
What country do you like best? (Gallup, July 6, 1939)	Russia 1 England 43
What country do you like least? (Gallup, July 6, 1939)	Russia 8 Germany 58 Italy 12
Which nation do you regard as the worst influence in Europe? (Roper, January 1940)	Russia 1 Germany 55 England 2 Italy 34 Other 1 Don't know 13

Table 4.2 (*Continued*)

Question formulation; Survey organization and date	Response alternatives (percent)
In the war between Germany and Russia, which side would you like to see win—Germany or Russia? (Gallup-A.I.P.O., September 17, 1941)	Russia 71 Germany 4 Neither 20 No opinion 5
If you had to choose, which kind of government would you prefer to live under—the kind in Germany, or the kind in Russia? (Gallup-A.I.P.O., October, 1941)	Russia 37 Germany 12 Unable to choose 41 No opinion 10
Which of these countries do you think has done the most toward winning the war so far—Britain, the United States, Russia or China? (Gallup, June 29, 1943)	Russia 30 Britain 11 United States 45 China 5 No opinion 8
In this argument between Russia and Poland over the Polish border) are your sympathies with the Poles or the Russians? (Gallup, January 26, 1944)	Russians 28 Poles 41 Don't know 30

to Russia's past record of political repressions as the reason for their mistrust.

What was mainly noticeable about American attitudes regarding particular Russia-related policies during and immediately after the war? The answers displayed in tables 4 and 5 reflect predominant attitudes about the Soviet Union at the time.

There was considerable popular support for certain policies, such as Russia's military operations against Germany. On the other hand, cooperation proposals were perceived somewhat skeptically. Opinions about the possibility of a postwar U.S.-Soviet military alliance were divided almost evenly (with disapproval soon increasing), loans to the Union of Soviet Socialist Republics were generally not supported, and the Soviet foreign policy was criticized. Russian emigration to the United States also enjoyed initial majority approval, although attitudes changed after the war. Most surveys revealed negative attitudes of Americans about the Soviet Union's domestic policies. In short, with some exceptions, most American respondents were repeatedly skeptical of their Soviet war ally.

Additional findings illuminate this point further. At a crucial historical moment when the entire Soviet nation's survival was at stake,

Table 4.3 The dynamics of trust in Russia during and after World War II: Shares (in percent) believing (or not) in Soviet/Russian trustworthiness in cooperating with the United States in (envisioned) postwar years (from January 1943 to October 1946)

January 14, 1943			April 8, 1943			August 25, 1943			November 11, 1943			December 17, 1943		
Yes	No	N/O	Yes	No	N/O	Yes	No	N/O	Yes	No	N/O	Yes	No	N/O
46	29	25	45	34	21	35	37	29	47	27	26	50	28	23

January 20, 1944			June 14, 1944			November 22, 1944			February 27, 1945			March 23, 1945		
Yes	No	N/O	Yes	No	N/O	Yes	No	N/O	Yes	No	N/O	Yes	No	N/O
40	37	23	47	36	17	47	35	18	60	27	13	44	40	16

May 17, 1945			August 15, 1945			August 1945			October 1945			October 24, 1945		
Yes	No	N/O	Yes	No	N/O	Yes	No	N/O	Yes	No	N/O	Yes	No	N/O
45	38	17	57	29	15	52	33	15	40	44	16	38	46	16

February 1946			May 1946			June 1946			October 1946		
Yes	No	N/O	Yes	No	N/O	Yes	No	N/O	Yes	No	N/O
41	46	12	33	52	14	30	55	15	28	59	14

Table 4.4 Wartime and immediate postwar approval or disapproval of particular policies of Russia or U.S. policies affecting Russia (in percent). *Don't know* answers are not included

Item, survey organization and date	Approval	Disapproval
Selling war materials to Russia (Gallup, August 12, 1941)	64	26
Accepting a peace if Germany were to keep only the territory won from Russia and give up France, Scandinavia, and other conquered countries (Gallup, September 1, 1941)	34	58
Try to work with Russia as an equal partner in working out the peace (Fortune Magazine, April 5, 1943)	81	9
After the war, make a permanent military alliance with Russia, that is, agree to come to each other's defense immediately if the other is attacked at any future time (Gallup, August 19, 1943)	39	37
A permanent military alliance (to agree to come to each other's defense if one is attacked) between the United States and Russia (Gallup, May 3, 1944)	35	45
Russian immigrants moving to the United States (NORC, September 1944)	56	32

Table 4.5 Wartime and immediate postwar approval or disapproval of particular policies of Russia or U.S. policies affecting Russia (in percent)

Russia actively supports individuals or groups in liberated countries (Gallup, December 20, 1944)	32	61
The way Russia handles her military campaigns (Fortune/Roper, June 18, 1945)	67	4
The way Russia handles her diplomatic relations with the United States (Fortune/Roper, June 18, 1945)	18	43
The way Russia is handling justice and legal rights of its own people (Fortune/Roper, June 25, 1945)	16	24
A loan to Russia (NORC, October 1945)	40	50
A loan to Russia (Gallup, October 10, 1945)	28	59
Russian immigrants moving to the United States (Gallup, December 12, 1945)	40	52

Americans expressed mostly pragmatic rather than sympathetic attitudes about the Soviet Union. When in September of 1941, Hitler's troops had penetrated Soviet territory to a depth of hundreds of miles, encircled Leningrad (the second largest city) and approached Moscow, when the Red Army had already sustained hundreds of thousands of casualties, only 22 percent of Americans supported the opinion that Russia should be accepted as a "full partner along with England in the fight against Hitler." A small majority, 51 percent, supported a more cautious view, suggesting the possibility of working with Russia and of giving "her some aid if we think it will help beat Hitler." Moreover, 14 percent suggested that the United States should leave Russia alone and "give her no help nor encouragement of any kind" (*Fortune*/Roper, September 1941). The same survey revealed that 35 percent of Americans believed that the Soviet government and the German government were "equally bad," and another 32 percent suggested that the Russian government was only "slightly better." Overall, almost two thirds of the respondents offered only conditional support or no support at all to the Soviet cause. By December 1941, after the Pearl Harbor attack, the share of those endorsing at least conditional support to the Soviet Union was 43 percent, with 4 percent of respondents rejecting any support (*Fortune*, December 17, 1941). The escalating war caused broader shifts of opinion in favor of the Soviets.

Disapprovals of Soviet policies and negativity toward the Soviets grew quickly in the wake of the hardening postwar superpowers' rivalry. When in 1947, Americans answered the question: "Do you think we can count on Russia to meet us half-way in working out problems together?," more than two-thirds (68 percent) said "no" and only one-fifth (21 percent) replied "yes" (NORC, October 1947). Although the Red Army had defeated the German Wehrmacht and the Soviet Union was an ally of the United States, Moscow's domestic and foreign policies were generally unacceptable to the majority of Americans. People conveniently considered the former ally as a tough opponent competing against the United States for world dominance.

Disapproval rates exceeded approval rates concerning issues such as Russia's foreign policy in the 1940s (71 percent vs. 7 percent; *Gallup,* March 20, 1946), Russian magazines and newspapers sold in the United States of America (48 percent vs. 44 percent; NORC, May 10, 1947), and America sending surplus wheat to the Russians (61 percent vs. 23 percent; *Gallup,* March 1947). Sometimes Americans were not at all enthusiastic about Russians coming to U.S. soil. A poll conducted in 1956 (NORC, April 30) showed that 37 percent of respondents could not think of any group or category of Russians to be brought to the United States on an exchange program; a fairly sizable minority, of 23 percent, did not think it was a good idea even to exchange musicians and athletes.

Americans also expressed positive attitudes about the process of arms reductions between the two countries in the 1970s. Three illustrative surveys indicate this. A poll by Harris (February 1972) yielded a 72-percent level of support for an agreement between the United States government than there was on ordinary Soviet citizens, many Americans' judgments about their Soviet counterparts were probably made according to what they thought of the government as well as of the Soviet social and political system.

OPINIONS ABOUT SOVIET GOVERNMENT

There is no extensive controversy about what Americans thought about the Soviet Union's government and its political regime. As early as in the 1940s, 67 percent of the population called Russia a dictatorship and 79 percent called it a country "without democracy" (NORC, July 1948); 83 percent of the population in another survey concurred about comparable questions (*Gallup,* February 19, 1947). *Gallup* had also conducted a 1946 survey that showed that 76 percent of the population knew—and this was an accurate evaluation—that people in Russia were not free to criticize their government publicly (*Gallup,* August 1, 1946). In 1946, 31 percent believed that a citizen of Spain—a country then under the authoritarian regime of General Francisco Franco—had more freedom than a citizen of the Communist Russia. Only 13 percent offered the opinion that a Soviet citizen had more freedom than an average Spaniard (*Gallup,* November 15, 1946).

A clear majority believed in the 1940s (65 percent, with 16 percent disagreeing) that the Soviet government made its decisions without taking much into account what its people thought (*Fortune/Roper,* June 25, 1945). Still, many Americans (42 percent) suggested that it made no difference to them what kind of government Russia had at that time (with 28 percent willing to see a change in the Soviet Union). Moreover, 45 percent said that the present government in the Soviet Union was "good," with only 26 percent objecting to such a characterization (NORC, September 1944). By 1947, however, attitudes had changed. When Americans were asked about whether they had a favorable or unfavorable impression of the present government of Russia, 76 percent indicated that their impression was "unfavorable" and just 10 percent was "favorable," with 14 percent undecided (NORC, April 1947).

Most Americans held strong negative views of political developments in the Soviet Union in later periods. When polled about human rights under the Soviet government, a "very unfavorable" view was expressed by 62 percent of respondents, and 25 percent reported a "somewhat unfavorable" view (*Gallup,* March 3, 1985). In another poll that year, a strong majority of respondents (69 percent) also considered human rights policies as a serious weakness of the Soviet Union (*Gallup/Newsweek,* November 14, 1985). The problem of human rights, however, often appeared less important to most American respondents than major security and nuclear issues (e.g., ATS/Yankelovich, July 7, 1988).

Most Americans believed that the average Soviet citizen was at odds with the government, but the ties between the people and the system were strong. Moreover, when interviewed on these subjects, a substantial number of respondents tended to believe that most Soviets would rather support their regime than go against it. In a mid-1980s assessment of possible actions and attitudes that Russians might have about their government, 62 percent of American respondents said that the "average Russian" would rather choose to have more political freedom than to have more consumer goods (*CBS/NYT,* September 19, 1985). Many Americans (51 percent) in the same poll said that the Russians disliked their system of government and would rather live in a democracy. On the other hand, a significant share of respondents (31 percent) suggested that most Russians would instead prefer strong leadership. About 40 percent of the respondents in this poll believed that if free elections were to be held in the Union of Soviet Socialist Republics in 1985, the Communist Party would have won them anyway. Although the percentage of those who suggested that the party would lose was higher (49 percent), the relatively small gap in opinions here may point at many Americans' belief in the strength of the Soviet system and the effectiveness of political socialization in this country (or at the weakness of any opposition).

Americans were aware of the fact that Moscow for many years restricted emigration from the country. In the early 1980s, 65 percent of those surveyed agreed that the U.S. government should place a great deal of emphasis on refusal of the Soviet government to allow any of its citizens to emigrate freely (*Time*/YSW, March 3, 1983). When in 1985 (*CBS/NYT,* September 19) Americans were asked to estimate (by guessing a number) how many people would leave the Soviet Union if their "government let anyone leave," the answers were distributed in the following way (table 4.9).

Overall, there was a predominant belief that as soon as the Iron Curtain was lifted, tens of millions of Russians would emigrate to seek

Table 4.9   U.S. survey estimations in 1985 on the number of envisioned emigrants from the Soviet Union upon exit liberalization

Estimate intervals	1 mln. or less	2-15 mln.	16-58 mln.	59-139 mln.	140-210 mln.	Other answers
Respondent shares (%)	10	6	14	20	22	28

Source: CBS/NYT, September 19, 1985.

refuge in the West. Forty-two percent of Americans guessed at a number of the Soviet emigrants to be between 59 and 210 million. The major reason for emigration from Russia, according to the answers, was the country's unbearable political and economic conditions.

After World War II, Americans were somewhat divided about the Soviet government's treatment of its religious groups. For instance, an early 1950s survey (NORC, June 1953) asked Americans to express their opinions on whether or not Jews and Catholics were treated worse than other people in the Soviet Union. The results revealed that a substantial share of respondents believed that these groups were treated in the same way as anyone else (32 percent believed this regarding the Jews and 40 percent did so regarding Catholics); 44 percent said that the Jews were treated worse, and 34 percent replied that Catholics were treated worse. Almost one quarter of respondents (23 percent) did not produce a definite answer. Thirty-two years later, 55 percent of Americans agreed that there was more discrimination against Jews in the Soviet Union than in the United States of America, with 27 percent believing that the situation was the same in both countries (*CBS/NYT,* September 19, 1985). Americans were divided about a suggestion that the treatment of the Jews or other minority groups was an internal matter of the Soviet Union, and none of the business of the United States of America. Almost 41 percent suggested that this was strictly a domestic matter. A slightly greater share, 48 percent, said that treatment of Soviet minorities was not necessarily a domestic Soviet affair (CCFR/Harris, December 14, 1974). The attitudes about this issue, however, reflect broader distributions of isolationist or interventionist sentiment among the Americans toward U.S. foreign policy: After Vietnam, such attitudes were almost evenly divided between those who supported a robust foreign policy and those who wanted the United States to switch its attention exclusively to domestic affairs.

Among a few things for which the Soviet government was given credit was the Soviet bureaucracy: In the mid-1980s, 46 percent agreed that state bureaucracy was the Soviet government's strength, while 28 percent disagreed on this issue (*Newsweek/Gallup,* November 14, 1985). However, over many years, most Americans believed that the Soviet military was their biggest threat.

RUSSIA AS AN OMNIPOTENT ENEMY

The Soviet Union was commonly considered a strong and expansionist country. This country underwent substantial economic changes in the 1930s, developed a strong bureaucratic machine, modernized its military, and acquired nuclear weapons. Russia had reached its ultimate strength, in the view of the Americans, after the defeat of Germany on the Eastern front in 1945. We can only speculate now about how many Americans were aware of the number of casualties that Russia sustained during the war (more than 20 million dead) and the extent of destruction within the Soviet Union caused by German occupation. We know, however, that the perceptions of the Soviet Union as a very powerful country were already in place by 1945. Along with the United States, the Soviet Union was seen as a leading world power that had its own plans and that paid little attention to the world's public opinion. For example, in 1945 only 16 percent of Americans surveyed believed that the Soviet government was concerned about what the people of the world thought about its actions. The vast majority (68 percent) believed that the Soviet government made its own decisions, without taking much into account what the rest of the world thought (*Fortune*/Roper, June 25, 1945) (table 4.10).

Especially high credit was given to the Soviet military and the country's space programs. The latter was, in fact, under the total control of

Table 4.10 Percentages of Americans supporting particular opinions of the Soviet Union (Russia). Data from various opinion polls (1945–1991)

Russia will be the leading world power after the war (not counting the United States). Gallup, February 27, 1945	70 (compare: England—21)
Russia will actually have most influence in world affairs. Gallup, February 28, 1945	27 (the United States—60)
Russia will have the most powerful peacetime Army. Fortune /Roper March 26, 1945	44 (the United States—40; don't know—13)
Russia will be ahead of America twenty years from now. Time/Roper February 20, 1948	6 (America—69; don't know/no answer—25)
Soviet Union is one of the greatest powers in the world today. Harris, June 11, 1983	68 (leader among second-rank—15; average second rank—6; other answers—11)
Soviet Union is ahead of the United States in terms of overall military strength. WAND/M&K, September 1985	35 (About even—40; United States—19; not sure—6)
Soviet Union space program is ahead of the United States space program. Time/ YCS January 28, 1988	55 (behind—24; even (vol.)—7)
Soviet Union is stronger than the United States in terms of military power. Times Mirror/Gallup February 5, 1989	23 (United States is stronger—31; about equal—43; do not know/ no opinion—3)
Soviet Union is the strongest economic power in the world today. ABC News, November 10, 1991	2 (Japan—43; United States—41; EEC—2; Other answers—16)

the Politburo and the Soviet military. However, regardless of historical timing, much smaller shares of respondents believed in Soviet world leadership or its ability to exercise diplomatic influence. And in the 1980s, when the crumbling Soviet economy began to display signs of trouble, only a very small share of respondents believed that the Soviet Union was still the world's leading economic power (table 4.11).

Table 4.11 Agreement with the opinion that Russia is a dominant and expansionist country

Russia will—after the war—try to bring about Communist governments in other European countries. Fortune Magazine, March 22, 1943	41 (will not—31, don't know—28)
Russia should have more territory than she had before the war. NORC, November 1943	27 (Oppose—56, no opinion/don't know—17)
Russia should have more territory than she had before the war. NORC, August 1944	32 (Oppose—51, no opinion/don't know—17)
Russia is imperialistic today (assessment of four countries). Gallup December 18, 1946	62 (United States—13 England—53 France—14; don't know—6)
Russia wants to spread the Communist way of life mainly because she believes it will make her more powerful. Fortune/Roper April 16, 1946	77 (different answers or don't know—23)
Russia trying to build herself up to be the ruling power of the world. Gallup May 22, 1946	58 (as protection against being attacked—31; no opinion—11)
Russia wants to spread the Communist way of life. Fortune Magazine/Roper April 6, 1946	54 (no—26; do not know—20)
Russia would like to dominate the world? Gallup, February 5, 1947	80 (Germany—15 Great Britain—14 United States—8)
Russia would like to dominate the world. Gallup July 9, 1947	78 (Others—22)
Russia trying to build herself up to be the ruling power of the world. Gallup March 10, 1948	79 (as protection against being attacked—12; no opinion—9)
Russia trying to build herself up to be the ruling power of the world. Gallup December 2, 1949	70 (as protection against being attacked—18; no opinion—12)
The Soviets are interested in nuclear advantages. CPD/P&S, October 9, 1985	74 (interested in mutual reductions—16)
The Soviets are interested in nuclear advantages. CPD/P&S, October 9, 1985	74 (interested in mutual reductions—16)
The Soviet Union is interested in world domination. ATS/MS, December 13, 1988	20 (protecting own security—77)
The Soviet Union is mainly interested in world domination. U.S.A.T./Black, May 16, 1988	33 (national security—58)

From the end of World War II until the late 1980s, opinions about the Soviet Union's aggressiveness and its desire to dominate in world affairs remained almost unchanged. Expansionism was commonly attributed to Soviet foreign policy. Only during and immediately after World War II, as well as in the late 1980s, Soviet foreign policy was seen as driven by legitimate security concerns.[5]

Early in the 1940s, a majority of surveyed Americans expressed the opinion that Soviet policies were expansionist and more than a third of the respondents in March 1943 believed that the Soviets would "export communism" after the war was over. Starting in the immediate postwar period and until the 1980s when Gorbachev started to dismantle his country's superpower status, most Americans agreed that the Soviet foreign policy was expansionist (some polls revealed 75 percent support). A significant shift in opinions about the Soviet Union as an expansionist country took place in 1988. Most people realized that world domination was no longer the Soviet Union's top priority at that time.

As a rule, as soon as a major policy shift occurs in a foreign country, the attitudes toward this country tend to change. The same trend was noticeable in Americans' views of Russia's involvement in international terrorism. In most American people's opinions, in the 1980s, the Soviet Union still received "credit" for sponsoring international terrorism. However, these beliefs had subsided by 1989, when it became apparent that Moscow could no longer maintain its superpower capabilities. In fact, the Kremlin significantly reduced by that time its support of military and authoritarian regimes and military-political movements in Africa and Central America. By the decade's end, only 2 percent of Americans surveyed suggested that the Soviet Union was responsible for most of the terrorism directed against the United States and its allies (ABC/WP, April 3, 1989) (table 4.12).

In February 1944, 71 percent of Americans expected the United States to fight another war within the next 50 years (NORC, February 1944). Almost one half of these respondents pointed to the Soviet Union as the potential country against which the United States would fight. Only 28 percent mentioned either Germany or Japan as possible enemies. The same question about a possible new war was repeated again in September 1945 (NORC). The Soviet Union was named by 66 percent of those Americans who believed that another war involving their country would take place in the next 50-year period (80 percent of those surveyed). Germany and Japan were chosen as enemies by 17 percent of these respondents. In the subsequent year, two-thirds of those surveyed agreed that a war between the United States and another country would occur (*Gallup*, July 31, 1946). At that time, 81 percent of the respondents believed that Russia would become an enemy in the future.

Table 4.12 Opinions about Russia as a potential threat, enemy, or warmonger

Do you think there is a good chance that there will be a war between the United States and Russia within the next 25 years? Gallup December 19, 1939	YES!—7 Yes—24 NO!—13 No—32 Don't know—23
Which country do you think we might have to fight (if the United States is in another war within the next 25-50 years)? Gallup, February 27, 1945	Russia—41 England—11 Germany—10 Japan—3
In which one or two of these areas, if any, do you think there is the greatest danger of trouble arising after the war that might lead to serious fighting within 20 years or so? Fortune Magazine March 26, 1945	Russia—30 South America—23 The Pacific—11 Western Europe—13 The Balkans—10 Don't know—24
Would you describe Russia as a peace-loving nation, willing to fight only if she thinks she has to defend herself—or as an aggressive nation that would start a war to get something she wants? Fortune/Roper June 25, 1945	Peace loving—39 Aggressive—38 Both (vol.)—8 Don't know—15
Would you describe Russia as a peace-loving nation, willing to fight only if she thinks she has to defend herself, or as an aggressive nation that would start a war to get something she wants? Fortune/Roper June 9, 1947	Aggressive—68 Peace-loving—13 Both (vol.)—6 Don't know—13
Who do you think will be responsible for starting the war (the United States will find itself in within the next year/next five years)? Gallup, October 27, 1950. (Asked of those who think the United States will find itself in another war within the next year/five years (58 percent)	Russia, Soviet Russia, U.S.S.R., Stalin, Communist countries—66 United States, Truman, Congress, etc.—6
Which of the following statements comes closer to your own view. . . . What worries me most about the Soviet Union is that . . . PAF, May 29, 1984	a. . . . they are a military threat to the United States—26 b. . . . their system is a threat to all our beliefs and values—freedom, democracy, religion and free enterprise—69 Not sure/Don't know—5
Do you believe the military threat from the Soviet Union is constantly growing and presents a real, immediate danger to the United States, or not? CBS/NYT, September 19, 1985	Real threat—53 Not real threat—39 Don't know/No answer—9
Generally, would you describe the Soviet Union as a peace-loving nation, willing to fight only if it thinks it has to defend itself, or as an aggressive nation that would start a war to get something it wants? CBS/NYT, September 19, 1985	Peace-loving—17 Aggressive—69 Aggressive, but won't start war (Vol.)—5 Don't know/No answer—9

(continued)

Table 4.12 (*Continued*)

Now here are some statements various people have made about the increasing acts of terrorism today. For each statement please tell me if you think it is a major reason for the increase of terrorism, a minor reason for the increase in terrorism, or not a reason at all.) . . . Professional terrorists are sponsored and financed by Russia. Roper, January 25, 1986	Major reason—34 Minor reason—25 Not a reason—19 Don't know—22
There are some statements about the Soviet Union and Communism and for each one, please tell me if you strongly agree, somewhat agree, somewhat disagree, or strongly disagree. . . . Communism threatens our religious and moral values. ATS/MOR December 13, 1988 Registered Voters	Strongly agree—33 Somewhat agree—26 Depends/Both/Neither—2 Somewhat disagree—21 Strongly disagree—16 Don't know/Refused/No answer—2

Concerns about a potential Soviet threat sometimes overshadowed some domestic problems. For instance, *Fortune* magazine (Roper, May 1945) asked Americans to mention any two of the most troublesome problems that their country would face in the next few years. Unemployment was mentioned first (33 percent), but 25 percent also said—"relations with Russia" (only 12 percent, for example, indicated "returning veterans"). Russia was believed to be the most likely country to use atomic bombs against America and was rated higher than Germany and Japan (NORC, September 1945). The Soviet Union was also perceived as a country that would not allow any inspections of its nuclear facilities (*Gallup*, November 20, 1946; 72 percent agreed). Further, a majority agreed that the United States was too "soft" in its policy toward Russia (*Gallup*, March 20, 1946; 61 percent). Such tendencies in opinions fluctuated in relation to geopolitical events: From the 1950s to the mid-1980s, Americans had many opportunities to hear from the government and the media about Soviet military threats.

OPINION ABOUT SOVIET LEADERS

Throughout many decades, American presidents and other politicians were getting constant feedback from polls about their performance and personalities. Emotions expressed about "domestic" politicians were often stronger than feelings about distant rulers from overseas. For example, when *Gallup* in September 1955 asked Americans the question: "Will you tell me the names of some men that you consider to be dema-

Table 4.13 Personal ratings and other assessments of the Soviet leaders

Khrushchev Gallup, October 23, 1960	Personal ratings: Negative—98 percent Positive—2 percent
Khrushchev Gallup May 28, 1963	Personal ratings: Negative—96 percent Positive—4 percent
Andropov Harris, June 11, 1983	Assessment of the quality of leadership: Negative—48 Positive—33 Not sure—19
Andropov Time/YSW, December 8, 1983	He is a very sick man, and may actually be dead: Agree—42 Disagree—17 No impression—31 Not sure—10
Andropov Time/YSW, December 8, 1983	He was the head of the Soviet KGB for many years, and therefore must be a very cruel and ruthless man. Agree—40 Disagree—24 No impression—26 Not sure—11
Andropov Time/YSW, December 8, 1983	He owes his position to the Soviet military, and therefore is forced to meet their wishes. Agree—41 Disagree—22 No impression—22 Not sure—15
Andropov Time/YSW, December 8, 1983	He is more westernized and knowledgeable about the world than other Soviet leaders, it is possible to reach agreements with him. Agree—35 Disagree—24 No impression—27 Not sure—14
Andropov Time/YSW, December 8, 1983	He is one of the most intelligent leaders the Soviet Union has ever had. Agree—17 Disagree—33 No impression—38 Not sure—12
Gorbachev Gallup, September 13, 1987	Is your opinion of . . . Mikhail Gorbachev . . . very favorable, mostly favorable, mostly unfavorable, or very unfavorable? Very favorable—5 Mostly favorable—34 Mostly unfavorable—21 Very unfavorable—17 Never heard of (vol.)—6 Don't know—17

gogues?," most mentioned Senator Joseph McCarthy (42 percent chose him), as well as former U.S. President Harry Truman (41 percent). Demagogues such as Hitler (13 percent) and Khrushchev (3 percent) were practically overlooked. At least two explanations can be offered. First, Americans are commonly critical of their own politicians and pay less interest to foreign leaders. Second, Hitler was long dead, and Khrushchev was not yet known to most Americans.

More standardized information about the attitudes that Americans expressed about Soviet leaders is provided in table 4.13.

While 66 percent of Americans supported the Soviet Prime Minister Khrushchev's visit to the United States in September of 1959 (20 percent opposed it), this could also have reflected the approval of the idea of the summit and not of the Soviet leader. Such opinions may also have reflected approval of President Eisenhower's foreign policy to a greater extent than sympathy for the Soviet guest (*Gallup,* August 25, 1959).

Among all top Soviet leaders (and there were six of them from the 1930s until the end of the Soviet Union), Mikhail Gorbachev enjoyed the strongest popular support in the United States. However, even Gorbachev as a person, as well as his policies—those that eventually brought down the Soviet empire—were seen with a certain degree of skepticism and mistrust. Favorable and critical impressions of him in 1987 were evenly divided—almost a fifth of respondents did not know what to say (and 6 percent said they had never heard of him). Opinions were also evenly divided in 1985 on whether his interests in peace with the West were greater than those of his predecessors. Even in 1989, only a slight plurality was willing to see his interests in democratizing Soviet society as genuine (table 4.14).

According to these surveys, Gorbachev did not exactly win the love of the American public. His popularity and approval ratings, however, were

Table 4.14 American attitudes about Soviet leaders' intentions and/or anticipated changes in Russian politics due to changes in leadership (in percent)

"Do you think there has been a real change in Russia's policy, since the death of Stalin?" Gallup, May 14, 1953	No—60 Yes, change—23 No opinion—17
Mr. Khrushchev has said that he will agree to a ban on the testing of H-bombs if that ban is part of a program for total disarmament. Do you think Mr. Khrushchev is bluffing or do you think he sincerely wants total disarmament? Gallup, November 22, 1961	Bluffing—79 Wants total disarmament—8 Don't know—14

Table 4.14 (*Continued*)

Since Russia agreed to a ban on atomic testing, some people think that Khrushchev has become more peace—minded. Do you think Russia is now really more for peace than before, or do you think there has been no real change? Harris, October 1963	No real change—63 Russians really more for peace—22 percent Not sure—15
Do you feel that with the death of Soviet leader Brezhnev and with Yuri Andropov taking over, the chances for easing tensions with Russia are better now, worse, or not changed very much? Harris, November 28, 1982	Not changed much—65 Better—15 Worse—11 Not sure—9
What effect will Andropov have on the amount of personal freedom Russian citizens will have—a positive effect, a negative effect, or not much change? Merit/A&S December 3, 1982	Not much change—61 A positive effect—8 A negative effect—12 No opinion—19
What effect do you think Yuri V. Andropov, the new leader of the Soviet Communist Party, will have on relations between the U.S.S.R. and the United States—do you think relations will get better, will get worse, or that there won't be much change? Merit/A&S, December 3, 1982	There won't be much change—56 Will get better—13 Will get worse—13 No opinion—18
What effect will Andropov have on the amount of personal freedom Russian citizens will have—a positive effect, a negative effect, or not much change? Merit/A&S, December 3, 1982	Not much change—61 A positive effect—8 A negative effect—12 No opinion—19
Yuri Andropov is no better or worse than any of the others. They are all part of the same system. TIME/Y.S.W, December 8, 1983	Agree—67 Disagree—15 No impression—11 Not sure—8
Compared to previous Soviet leaders, is Mikhail Gorbachev more interested in peace with the West, less interested, or about the same? Newsweek/Gallup November 14, 1985	About the same—38 More interested—38 Less interested—10 Don't know—13
Which do you think Gorbachev is probably more interested in maintaining peaceful relations with the West or achieving Communist domination in the world? ATS/MOR January 14, 1988	Peaceful relations—51 Domination—39 Don't know—10
Mikhail Gorbachev has publicly introduced changes to make the Soviet society more open. How much do you think the Soviet society has changed? Has it changed? United States TODAY /Black May 16, 1988	Not at all—4 Not very much—27 Somewhat—47 A great deal—18 Don't know—5
Do you think Gorbachev seriously wants to make Soviet society more open and democratic, or is he simply creating a good public image to help gain an advantage for the Soviet Union? Washington Post, November 21, 1989	Wants it open and democratic—45 Public image—42 Don't know opinion—12

significantly higher than those of Andropov, Brezhnev, and Khrushchev. Even after the death of Stalin in 1953 (and for decades afterward), most people remained skeptical of whether changing Soviet leadership made for reliable and favorable changes in policy—this trend began to change after Gorbachev's succession to power in the mid-1980s.

Overall, opinions about Gorbachev were mixed. For example, in assessing who was more interested in making progress on arms control, Gorbachev or Reagan, 66 percent of those surveyed in 1987 selected Reagan, and 20 percent chose Gorbachev (ABC/*WP,* December 2, 1987). The same question was asked about George Bush Sr. and Gorbachev in 1989. Again, the U.S. president was chosen as the leader who was more interested in arms control (by 57 percent of respondents), than the Soviet leader selected by 28 percent of respondents (ABC/*WP,* May 23, 1989). In both surveys, only 9 percent gave the same credit to both leaders.

The majority of the American public did not want to trust the new Soviet leader immediately just because of his promises of peace. National security remained a serious concern for millions of American families, and Gorbachev was still a Communist leader seeking advantages for his own country.

How divided was the American public along demographic, gender, and some other characteristics in their views of the Soviet Union?

Gender, Race, Income, Education, and Politics

Over the years, only a few national surveys provided information about various social background characteristics of the respondents. During one of several brief "thaws" in the Cold War, in 1971, Harris Polls asked the American people to give their opinion on whether they would or would not prefer to have federal funds to be spent for housing, welfare, and other assistance to the American people, at the cost of reducing the United States to a second position behind the Soviet Union in military defense (VS/Harris, October 1971). Information available here is only on gender differences. These, however, were fairly minor. Thirty percent of women and 27 percent of men were in favor of social programs over world military leadership; 47 percent of women and 56 percent of men were opposed to giving up America's military superiority. About 23 percent of women and 17 percent of men did not know what option to choose. According to another question from the same survey, men and women were equally concerned about improving relations with Russia (42 percent of women and 41 percent of men). More men (15 percent) than women (9 percent) suggested that the problem of relations with the Soviet Union was "not very serious."

Just a few months before the Soviet Union's collapse, a poll conducted in July of 1991 (*Times Mirror*/Princeton, July 14, 1991) included two questions measuring the extent to which Americans were following events in the Soviet Union; another question assessed interviewees' knowledge of a particular White House policy related to the Union of Soviet Socialist Republics. Background information was available on the response patterns by gender, racial background, party affiliation, educational levels, and income levels.

The answers show that during the course of the increasingly chaotic events in the Soviet Union of the summer of 1991, a greater share of men (48 percent) reported that they were following news stories about Russia "close," as compared to the women (34 percent). There was practically no difference in the shares of blacks (14 percent) and whites (12 percent) who "carefully" followed news from Russia in 1991. There were also no differences in responses between Democrats and Republicans. On both sides of the partisan divide, only 12 percent of respondents followed the news very closely, and slightly more than 20 percent in each camp followed the news "not at all closely."

More than twice as many women (29 percent) than men (14 percent) responded, "do not know" to the question related to U.S. financial assistance to the Soviets. The same "do not know" answer was given by 25 percent of the blacks and by 21 percent of whites, which is a fairly minor difference. The more substantial differences in this regard were related to the respondents' educational levels. Among those with a high school degree, 32 percent did not know the answer to the policy question—a share almost three times as high as those who had postgraduate degrees (11 percent) and undergraduate college degrees (18 percent).

Income also was a likely contributing factor to people's knowledge. Among Americans with an annual income of $50,000 or higher, only 16 percent said that they lacked knowledge about U.S. policy. Among those with incomes of less than $15,000 a year, 24 percent said that they had no idea what the policy was about. A greater share of Democrats (24 percent) than of Republicans (18 percent), finally, did not know about President George H. W. Bush's decision to assist the Union of Soviet Socialist Republics financially in the last year of that country's existence (*Times Mirror*/Princeton, July 14, 1991).

Differences in trust could also be related to background characteristics as seen in one survey conducted, which also included religious affiliation. In 1990, *Gallup* conducted a study measuring how much Americans trusted various groups of people. Among the groups under evaluation were the Russians, with the Americans' opinions assessed in table 4.15.

Table 4.15 U.S. respondents' trust in Russians in relation to social background characteristics. Question: "I now want to ask you how much you trust various groups of people.) Using the responses on this card, (trust completely, trust a little, neither trust nor distrust, do not trust very much, do not trust at all) could you tell me how much you trust . . . Russians?" Gallup, June 30, 1990

	Women	Men	Whites	Blacks	Liberal	Conservative	$15k & less	$40k and more
Trust completely	6	8	8	2	10	5	3	8
Trust a little	29	35	33	23	42	30	26	32
Neither trust nor distrust	38	32	35	31	34	32	27	36
Do not trust very much	12	12	12	15	7	15	15	12
Do not trust at all	7	9	7	13	3	6	18	7
Do not know	8	5	5	15	4	5	13	5

A greater share of Americans who identified themselves as politically liberal expressed complete trust in Russians (10 percent), compared to trusting conservatives (5 percent). There was also a greater share of conservatives who said they did not trust Russians at all (12 percent), compared to 3 percent of liberals who stated the same. There were no substantial differences between men and women in terms of their trust in Russians as a people in the summer of 1990. Overall, only 8 percent of men and 6 percent of women indicated that they trusted Russians completely. Most respondents from both gender groups expressed a reserved and cautious opinion: 32 percent of men and 38 percent of women gave the "neither trust nor distrust" answer. A complete lack of trust was expressed by 7 percent of women and 9 percent of men. Along religious lines, only 3 percent of American Jews expressed their complete trust in Russians. In comparison, 9 percent of the Catholics and 6 percent of the Protestants expressed their complete trust. Cautious neutrality dominated their answers: Many Jews expressed a neutral opinion (43 percent choosing "neither trust nor distrust"); 35 percent of both Catholics and Protestants said the same.

Overall, polling has revealed some differences in opinions about Russia associated with various societal background characteristics of respondents. The results support several tendencies already established in other studies. Men, compared to women, tended to be more media-oriented (Andersen 1997). The more educated and wealthier individuals paid more attention to international news than those who were less educated and well-to-do. Democratic Party affiliation and liberal political beliefs were associated with a relatively greater acceptance of the Soviet Union, compared to conservative and Republican attitudes that were associated with more skeptical and critical views of the Soviet Union and its people. Women, compared to men, were generally more pacifist than men and more willing to see better relations with the Soviet Union (Sidanius, 1996). There were some demographic differences in people's perceptions of threat and in their feelings of trust toward the Soviet Union. The differences, however, were small.

Conclusion

In the course of more than 60 years of scientific polling, a majority of Americans did not trust the Soviet Union. They were generally suspicious of Moscow's policies and distrustful of the Soviet people. There were some exceptions in attitudes, all connected to specific international developments. Most Americans expressed lukewarm attitudes about the Soviet Union during the "isolationist" period in the late 1930s before the

United States' entry into World War II. The following years of military alliance with the Soviets (1941–1945) brought some but not significant or long-lasting changes in attitudes. The battles of the cold war years enhanced the American people's negativism about the Kremlin's policies, the Soviet people, and the Union of Soviet Socialist Republics as a country.

Military competition with the United States and a number of developments within the Soviet Union, such as the lack of political freedom, human rights abuses, and the absence of a free market economy, were among the most crucial factors that determined the tone and content of the majority of Americans' attitudes. Soviet people were not counted on, or particularly trusted, in the eyes of the majority of Americans as early as in the 1940s and later. Even as late as in 1990, with the Soviet Union on the verge of collapse, only 32 percent of Americans said in a survey that they trusted Russians, but "a little." Despite this low quantity, this could have been the record-setting measure of positive feelings expressed by Americans toward Russians during the entire cold war period (*Gallup*, June 30, 1990).

Despite open access to the media, the American people were relatively uninformed about the Soviet Union. Yet many Americans gave quite reasonable and commonsensical answers to survey questions on issues related to U.S.-Soviet bilateral relations and other events involving the Soviet Union. In fact, however, Converse (1964) and his followers (Zaller 1992) have long believed that there are very few people who make informed suggestions and use comprehensive knowledge when replying to survey questions, especially on foreign-policy topics. In most cases, people generate their opinions without actually "having had" them before being surveyed. In our analysis, because the Soviet Union was a competitor and adversary of the United States during a long historical period, and because of the known facts about the repressive Communist system, American respondents should have had almost no difficulty in evaluating the Soviet Union negatively and giving critical opinions about its people and government. Besides, the media in the United States continuously conveyed mostly critical views of the Soviet Union. The lack of political freedom within the Soviet Union was not the only factor affecting American people's negative perceptions. The Soviet Union was a strategic rival of the United States for many years, especially during the cold war when both the Kremlin and the White House attempted to ensure their geopolitical aspirations around the world.

We should not ignore, of course, the existence of *Russophobia* as the core of many American people's attitudes about the Soviet Union and the Russians. From a comparative perspective, for the average Soviet citizen, the "enemies" overseas were always American warmongers and other extremists. The collective images cultivated in the Soviet Union about the United States involved mostly a few "bad" Americans: They were the militarists, the racists, the Wall Street fat cats, or the oil magnates from Texas. The average American appeared in the eyes of the average Soviet citizen as a hardworking person who was brainwashed by the U.S. propaganda machine. On the other hand, for many Americans, the enemies from overseas were *russkies,* the unlucky outcasts of Western civilization: strong and vicious yet obedient and loyal to their diabolic Communist regime (Ebenstein 1963). Russophobia was certainly part of a common cultural belief of the American people about the Soviet Union and the Russians. Xenophobia manifested from time to time in opinion polls as well as in strategic decisions of the White House and other government agencies (Shiraev and Zubok, 2001).

Nevertheless, during more than seventy years of the Soviet Union's existence, most Americans had enough information to make their own judgments, rational or emotional, about the Soviet Union, its people, and policies.

ABBREVIATIONS

ABC/WP	ABC NEWS/WASHINGTON POST
ATS/MOR	Americans Talk Security/MARKET OPINION RESEARCH
ATS/M&T	Americans Talk Security/MARTTILA AND KILEY
ATS/Yankelovich	Americans Talk Security/Daniel Yankelovich Group
Cambridge	CAMBRIDGE REPORTS, RESEARCH INTERNATIONAL
CBS/NYT	CBS News/New York Times
CCFR/Harris	Chicago Council on Foreign Relations/Louis Harris and Associates
CPD/P&S	The Committee on The Present Danger/PENN & SCHOEN ASSOCIATES
Harris	LOUIS HARRIS AND ASSOCIATES
LA Times	Los Angeles Times
Merit/A&S	Merit/AUDITS & SURVEYS
NORC	National Opinion Research Center
ODC/Hart	Overseas Development Council/PETER D. HART RESEARCH ASSOCIATES
PAF	Public Agenda Foundation

Time/Y.C.S.	Time/YANKELOVICH CLANCY SHULMAN
TIME /Y.S.W.	Time/YANKELOVICH, SKELLY & WHITE
Times Mirror/Princeton	Times Mirror/PRINCETON SURVEY RESEARCH
U.S.A.T./Black	U.S.A. TODAY/GORDON S. BLACK CORPORATION
VS/Harris	Virginia Slims/LOUIS HARRIS AND ASSOCIATES
WAND/M&K	Women's Action for Nuclear Disarmament/MARTTILA AND KILEY

CHAPTER 5

ORDINARY CITIZENS' PERCEPTIONS OF THE SOVIET SYSTEM FROM WITHIN

INTRODUCTION

The process of self-evaluation is a very complex cognitive process critically affected by immediate events and the individual's multiple appraisals of reality. This process requires not only substantial knowledge about self and society but also a particular style of conceptual reasoning. As Swiss psychologist Jan Piaget showed many years ago, not every person reaches this level of independent and critical thinking. Many assumptions about the social world around us are emotional appraisals, likes and dislikes, or just simple repetitions of what other people have told us. The Soviet people had limited access to information about other countries to be able to compare them with the Soviet Union. What they saw, read, or listened to was heavily censored. In addition, the Soviet government always kept the number of its critics down. This obviously made studying public opinion in the Soviet Union very difficult.

However, it is possible to make some generalizations about how average citizens viewed the Soviet regime over its history. Ordinary people generally supported the regime, much like the Soviet elites did. This support was never universal but it was overwhelming on the level of people's public attitudes—those that they could express and discuss openly. On another level of opinions, rarely communicated publicly, there were critical views of the country and its political system. Most people could discuss these problems, yet not always, and only within the family or among closest friends. Oppositional political views could have resulted in unwanted consequences for the person conveying them. Next, apathy and indifference constituted a third level of opinions. Many people deliberately ignored ideological and political issues, did not discuss them with friends, and preferred to focus on ordinary things of their daily lives. Finally, some social groups, for example, party bureaucrats or diehard communists always maintained the supportive attitudes of the regime and had very limited opportunities to hear opposing views.

SOME METHODOLOGICAL HURDLES

Any study of public opinion in the Soviet Union faced serious methodological hurdles. The first problem is the emotionally loaded nature of self-perception. People view their country through the prism of emotional evaluations and often make judgments about life based on their own assessments of personal success or failure. An elite worker in a prominent factory could have seen the Soviet Union differently compared to an avant-garde artist who was in trouble with authorities. People who benefited from the Soviet system evaluated it positively. People who were harmed by bureaucracy, corruption, and authoritarianism detested the system. The first group did not see the deficiencies of Soviet socialism. The other group could not say anything positive about it.

Another problem was also evident: This was the relative lack of uncensored and reliable data about what people in the Soviet Union "really thought" about the society in which they lived (Kumar, 1995). In fact, any empirical, survey-based information about the public's attitudes toward the Soviet system was scarce. How, for example, can one test a hypothesis that many Soviet people shared a common opinion that the Soviet Union was a "product" of worldwide Jewish conspiracy and that Stalin's repressions were a political payback for the "Jewish takeover" of Russia? This assumption is difficult to substantiate because of the absence of polls and surveys in the Soviet Union. There were no genuine sociological or public opinion studies conducted in the country until the 1960s. Until 1987, Soviet pollsters could not ask any questions about major political and social issues. All national and local surveys had to be approved by the official censor. Only from 1987 until the dissolution of the Soviet Union were there many opinion polls that reflected on the tendencies of the Soviet public opinion.

After 1989, when scholars gained access to some Soviet archives, new sources of information about public opinion emerged. However, the archive data were mostly relevant to single cases, and these cases were often tainted by the informers of the party and political police who frequently provided falsified reports. This fundamental methodological circumstance is often ignored by those who try to depict public opinion in Stalin's times on the basis of the archive documents.[1] Another source of information was the letters that average Russians wrote to authorities and the media. How accurate was this information? Despite the critical tone of these letters, they should not lead to broad generalizations about people's open hostility about the Soviet system. It would be mostly wrong to consider Soviet citizens' complaints about local authorities as couched critiques of the whole system as Theodore Rigby (1992) has suggested.

Could immigrants from the Soviet Union become a reliable and unbiased source of information? People who escaped or were deported from the Soviet Union were, of course, free to express their sincere views about their former homeland. For example, the findings of the 1950s famous Harvard project were based on the survey of displaced Soviet citizens after World War II. On the other hand, no sample of refugees is representative of a national sample at home. Immigrants from the Soviet Union were likely to be very critical of their country and the government. Furthermore, many respondents were definitely inclined to please their American interviewers and provide critical information of the Soviet Union at the peak of the cold war.[2]

We will start first by looking into people's attitudes about the Soviet Union from its inception and until Stalin's death.

ACCEPTANCE OF THE REGIME

Over the first years of Soviet history, public support for the regime fluctuated. Support of the establishment declined in the late 1920s and early 1930s, so did the hopes of those people who anticipated the restoration of the destroyed prerevolutionary order.

The popular attitudes toward Stalin's regime continued to improve between the mid-1930s and the early 1950s and public loyalty to the regime increased. People's support of the regime reached its peak during World War II and immediately after. On an average, one-third of the immigrants-respondents of the Harvard project reported that they were once in favor of the regime when they had lived in the Soviet Union (Inkeles and Bauer, 1968). Another study conducted in the 1970s showed that most immigrants who escaped from the Soviet Union described their life there in a somewhat "balanced" way. Of the 2,800 respondents, only 14 percent assessed the life they left behind as "very dissatisfying," and 25 percent described it as only "somewhat dissatisfied" (Millard, 1987).

Official Soviet propaganda offered optimistic and one-dimensional images of the socialist socioeconomic system. Almost until 1987, most Soviet people were told that their lives and the lives of their parents had been improving steadily. Most people believed that their lives "today" were much better than their lives "yesterday." Product and food shortages, political persecutions, and forceful collectivization were described as temporary difficulties forced upon the Soviet Union. Since the 1930s, millions of young Russians were enthusiastic about the future. Because of the lack of empirical or any other quantitative data of this period, there are only indirect sources based on diaries and eyewitness accounts that support this assumption.[3] Positive changes such as an increased social mobility, job opportunities, or improving living standards were portrayed and perceived as signs of dramatic improvements, which gave the system its new supporters, especially among the young.

Support of the regime grew among millions of party members, social activists, mid-level management officials, teachers, and a considerable part of the working class. Many of them became spirited supporters of the existing social and political order thus creating a solid social-psychological foundation in support of the socialist system. The values of socialism were not necessarily forced upon all people and they were not necessarily brainwashed against their will. In fact, millions of people were enthusiastic followers of the government and believed that their support was absolutely conscious and honest.[4]

To bring people together and boost their enthusiasm, the government began to organize (especially between 1932 and 1941) grandiose public festivals and big rallies (Malte, 2006). The great popularity of official Soviet songs was another indirect indicator of the public's acceptance of the official image of their country. These songs praised the motherland, Stalin, Moscow, the capital of the country, the happy Soviet life, the Communist Party, the Red Army, and the Soviet Union's strength vis-à-vis ever-present capitalist enemies. These songs (written by Isaak Dunaievsky, the Blanter brothers, Dmitry Pokrass, and several other composers) were put on constant rotation by state-run radio stations. The government supported these musical efforts and generously awarded the most loyal composers, poets, and singers. Many ordinary people sang these songs together at numerous informal gatherings.

The Soviet people witnessed the birth of new heroes, whose efforts received huge media coverage (radios and newspapers) and attention of top government leaders. They were pilots, Arctic explorers, miners, and record-breaking factory workers. Public welcoming parades and flashy award ceremonies for exemplary Soviet scientists, rescue workers, authors, and pilots captivated the attention of millions of people (Kurganov,

1996). The party constantly announced various mobilization campaigns to recruit volunteers to join massive construction projects or expeditions. Hundreds of thousands volunteered. Even in the 1960s and 1970s, the masses' acceptance of the official ideology and the official image of the socialist society played a substantial part in motivating many young people to answer the call of the party to participate in grandiose construction projects in Siberia, such as Baikal-Amur railroad, the "construction of the century." Thousands of young people lived for many years in very difficult conditions. Of course, high salaries and other benefits also attracted scores of people. Nevertheless, the party could always find workers who were willing to make the sacrifice not only for the evident material advantages but also because of their patriotic commitments.[5]

Many ordinary people, particularly those who lived in large cities, supported Stalin's repressions of the late 1920s and 1930s. Accepting the official Soviet propaganda's line, they saw the arrested and the persecuted as criminals, saboteurs, wreckers, and spies. Some people were even dissatisfied with the "lenient verdicts" given to some of the accused (Davies, 1997). Until the mid-1950s, few people doubted the guilt of those who were executed or sent to the Gulag. According to memoirs written by Soviet dissidents and emigrants in the 1970s and 1980s, they, as well as people around them, generally believed in fairness of the political trials and in legitimacy of mass arrests.[6] In many cases, people accepted the arrests of their close friends and family members because they perceived them as the enemies of the Soviet society.[7]

The cult of the literary character, a boy named Pavlik Morozov, who accused his peasant father of sabotage and resistance to the government, is an example of how traditional family values were reversed: A son could give up his father to authorities because of the father's unwillingness to surrender his harvest to the government. People were also told that the repressions went against corrupt state apparatchiks and traitors, and that ordinary people were not the target. Also, since the middle of the 1940s, the repressions targeted many Jews involved in management and government bureaucracy. Although there was no official anti-Semitism in the Soviet Union in the 1930s, many people, informally, were gloating about the arrests of many Jewish managers and apparatchiks.

To boost its own support among ordinary people, the government sponsored many mass organizations and established their political goals: to support the Communist Party and the Soviet government and to promote the official depiction of the Soviet Union. Young people joined several youth leagues, the largest of which was Komsomol (translated literally as the Communist Union of the Young). There were several defense-oriented organizations, and party-controlled labor unions. Many people joined these organizations enthusiastically, while others thought of repercussions in case they did not join them. Very soon, public schools and public organizations began to carry out the main function of political socialization: the transmission of political values and official perceptions to the young. The government in the Soviet Union received a virtual monopoly to conduct this transmission.

Many Soviet people supported the system wholeheartedly and were dedicated supporters of Marxist dogmas. They refused to see any deficiencies of the system and disliked the critics of the regime. Some of them were passionate about their own views and intolerant to the views of others. Alexander Solzhenitsyn's biographical story, *An Incident at Krechetovka Station,* describes a Red Army lieutenant who, in September 1941, under the devastating German air attack, continued to take notes while reading Karl Marx's *Capital.* There are facts about individuals, who, after being sent to the Gulag, continued to defend the system stubbornly.[8] However, not only sheer fanatics supported the Soviet Union. Most people supported the system because it was beneficial to them: job security, individual safety, or relative individual comfort—almost all depended on people's political loyalty to the government.

The war (1941–1945) has strengthened in people's mind the perceptions of their country and its political regime as powerful and fair. On the whole, most Soviet people felt that the victory over Germany was not only a triumph for Russia but also for the Soviet system. The sincerity of scores of Russian soldiers who crawled from trenches and propelled themselves forward, screaming, "For motherland, for Stalin!" is difficult to doubt. Most Soviet people accepted the Soviet system and adored its leader as the defender of humankind against Nazi aggressors. The Soviet Union, in their view, also inspired and unified non-Russians in the Soviet Union to fight together against the enemy. Most people were willing to struggle against a foreign aggressor who was wishing to extinguish their motherland. Nationalistic feelings grew and the war awakened Russian national self-identity (Grossman, 1970). For this reason, Stalin changed his rhetoric and official policies thus turning to Russian nationalism.

It is not a surprise that the devotion of the Soviet people to the regime reached its peak in the times of the cult of Stalin's personality, when the official propaganda disseminated his "godly" image. The cult was supported across the country in a similar fashion to Hitler's cult in Nazi Germany in the 1930s, or Mao's cult in China in the 1960s.

The image of Stalin as "the greatest leader of all countries and all times" penetrated the hearts and souls of many Russians, from apparatchiks to ordinary people.[9] This attitude reached grotesque forms in 1949 during the celebration of his seventieth anniversary. With full support of its members, each administrative unit in the country sent a telegram of congratulations to "the greatest man in the history of mankind." Many ordinary people tried to outdo each other in their attempts to commemorate Stalin's name in history. Opinions emerged to rename Moscow to Stalin City. The intensity with which the Soviet people mourned Stalin's death on March 5, 1953 was remarkable. His funeral, in many people's personal accounts, stands among the most memorable events in Soviet history.[10] Stalin was a symbol of power and glory, a human monolith, strong, and flawless.

After the shock caused by Stalin's death in 1953 and the initial period of mourning, different perceptions about the country and its most recent history began to emerge. After the critical anti-Stalin campaign launched by the twentieth Party Congress, the threat of mass terror was seemingly over. People could speak more freely without the fear of being interrogated or arrested. The ability to learn from past mistakes was largely attributed to the system's ability for self-improvement. The party was returning to the "normal" course of life and work. No repressions, no political witch-hunt, no new personality cult followed. Foreign policy was changing and a new concept of coexistence with the capitalist world had emerged. By the end of the 1950s, the quality of life improved substantially for most citizens, which was another factor affecting people's support of the regime. The country also became more open to the West. By the early 1960s, television became affordable to many Soviet families. Technology also brought opportunities to listen to foreign radio (although this was not encouraged). Government began to allow some trusted people to travel abroad and opened limited opportunities to participate in foreign exchanges, especially with socialist countries. All these developments helped people acquire a more realistic image of their life and society than it had been in the past.

Nikita Khrushchev's ascension to power and the implementation of new policies created an atmosphere of hopeful anticipation for a change. This expectation was partially reflected in people's letters to authorities. In a comprehensive survey of public letters sent by Soviet citizens to the state-run media (Magnusdottir, 2006) right before Khrushchev's visit to the United States in 1959, people showed their support for the new, more critical official image of society and for a new Soviet policy of peaceful coexistence with the West. It was a departure from the confrontational attitude of the postwar period. Moreover, people in their letters mentioned the necessity of open contacts with some Western countries, a possibility that was impossible under Stalin (Shlapentokh, 1986).

Under Leonid Brezhnev's tenure from the 1960s to 1982, as well as through Yuri Andropov's and Konstantin Chernenko's years in power until 1985, the country returned to the "old times" to some degree. The government again had suppressed and marginalized most of the intellectual opposition. Censorship was strengthened and remained effective and the Soviet people have had only limited access to western countries (through tourism) and the western media. Besides rare occurrences, in Brezhnev's times, there was basically no public mass resistance to the regime or its leaders. Public acceptance of the system and official interpretations of the Soviet Union was a widespread norm. Most Soviet people showed their formal support to the government and its leadership, no matter who occupied the highest offices in the Kremlin.

However, the post-Stalin era was also characterized by the declining prestige of official ideology and labor ethics. Mass cynicism (a mixture of skepticism and fake enthusiasm) spread steadily. The period from the late 1970s to the middle of the 1980s was a time of political apathy.

WHAT THE SOVIET PEOPLE SAW

From the beginning of their lives, especially since the 1960s, the Soviet people were repeatedly told that they were carriers of so-called "socialist" or Soviet values. The existence of such values was the principal difference between them and other people in the rest of the world. These values were hardly defined in the exact way. It was mostly a combination of collectivism, egalitarianism, helping behavior, altruism, and hard work. From early school years, the Soviet people were told that they were different because they supported collective property, social equality, and world peace. Many people believed in such a picture of Soviet society and maintained these beliefs for a long time.[11]

Look, for example, at the results of the Harvard project of Soviet émigrés. About 80 to 90 percent of all respondents believed in the superiority of state ownership of "heavy industry" and "transport" over private property in these sectors of economy as well as in the efficiency of the "cradle-to-grave welfare program." Two-thirds of the respondents also believed in the efficiency and fairness of the Soviet educational and health services. The majority of respondents hailed Soviet achievements in culture, and in the elimination of mass illiteracy.[12] At the same time, most respondents considered themselves opponents of the Soviet system. Thirty years later, in the early 1980s and in another study, Russian immigrants expressed similar perceptions of basic Soviet values. About two-thirds supported public property of heavy industries and about 75 percent endorsed socialized medicine (Millard, 1987). People who defected from the Soviet Union confirmed that most Soviet people accepted "the system" and that most people saw no better alternative.

The Soviet people accepted most images of foreign countries presented to them through the official propaganda. The Soviet people also believed that they lived in a world charged with international tensions and that the Soviet Union had nothing to do with most international problems. The main reason for tensions was the aggressive policies of other countries attempting to dominate the world and suppressing anticolonial and "national liberation" movements.

Back in the 1930s, the Soviet people supported the left in the Spanish civil war in 1936–1939. Millions of people ardently followed the course of the war from newspapers, hoping with all their hearts for the victory of the Republicans and their Communist allies.[13] People enthusiastically supported the official government position on China and North Korea during the Korean War: Koreans, according to this position, were defending their sovereignty against a foreign occupation. The Soviet people perceived the war in Vietnam in a similar fashion. The fight of North Vietnam and its southern supporters was legitimate and this struggle was an attempt to gain national sovereignty. The United States was an aggressor who should have been defeated. Many Soviet people backed the invasion of Czechoslovakia in 1968 as a necessary step to preserve the integrity of the Warsaw Pact and to protect international security. Secret documents declassified and published after 1991, acknowledge the protests in Moscow against the 1968 invasion. However, there was no massive fallout of the demonstrations demanding the withdrawal of Soviet troops from Czechoslovakia. People, in general, were supportive of the initial invasion in Afghanistan in 1979 as a necessary action of fulfillment of "international duty." The shooting of the Korean Boeing in 1983 did not cause much public concern. The absolute majority of people in the Soviet Union either ignored or condemned the behavior of political dissidents largely viewed as troublemakers, mentally ill, or Zionists paid by foreign intelligence services.[14]

Even in 1989, when official ideology was on the defensive, the people considered Lenin the greatest man in history. In a poll, Lenin garnered 70 percent of selections, while Peter the Great came in second with 40 percent. Marx received 38 percent; Engels, 20 percent; and Einstein 8 percent (in their answers, people could choose several leaders). In the same VTSIOM survey, 24 percent of the Soviet people answered the question, "What are you most proud of?," by pointing to their own "patriotism." In 1990, when the media fiercely attacked the old socialist regime, most people still expressed their support for the Soviet system.[15] In the same year the majority of the people still believed in the Soviet state as bearing the responsibility for the well-being of its citizens (Levada, 1993).

Most people believed that the socialist ideology provided them with a "right" or "correct" view of life. Historian Dmitry Volkogonov (1995), a leading critic of the Soviet ideology, wrote that a majority of people in the Soviet Union believed in the historical advantages of socialism, and deficiencies of the capitalist system. The very word "private" (*chastnyi*) in combination with "property" or "business" was officially unacceptable and stood for greed and moral corruption. The Soviet people learned from the beginning of their lives to loath private property. This alone was a grandiose ideological success. Although the attitude about private property changed dramatically during perestroika, Mikhail Gorbachev was very reluctant to talk about reinstatement of private property in Russian economy up until 1990. He and other reformers substituted this term with various euphemisms such as "cooperative property," and "life lease."

THE MEDIA

Surveys showed that considerable majorities (approximately two-thirds of the people surveyed) were satisfied with newspapers and television and believed in the accuracy of their information about the domestic and, particularly, international events (Grushin, 1980). At the same time, people were interested in other sources of information. According to the survey of the readers of three major Soviet newspapers, as much as a fifth of the respondents said that they listened to foreign radio stations (such as *Voice of America, BBC,* and *Free Europe*). In reality, the real percentage could be higher because many people probably did not want to openly admit that they listened to the Western radio, which was resisted by the Soviet authorities (Shlapentokh, 1970).

It is difficult to judge the degree to which these radio stations changed people's perception of the Soviet Union. Three behavioral outcomes emerged, according to surveys of university students conducted in the 1980s (Shiraev and Bastykin, 1988). Some listeners were suddenly confronted with a barrage of critical information about their country, its history, political system, and leadership. This new information profoundly affected their positive view of the Soviet Union and changed it to a more critical one. On the other hand, other listeners found such critical information about their country offensive and inappropriate. These people believed that the Western radio was involved in an organized smear campaign against socialism and the Soviet people. These smear campaigns, from their point of view, had to be enthusiastically rejected. And finally, the majority of listeners found only few new facts in the Western broadcasts: These Soviet listeners already knew what real life in their country was and were not particularly astounded to listen to western criticisms.

Overall, many Soviet people tended to see their country as strong and powerful, developing, growing and improving. People trusted the government to conduct foreign policy and believed in the government's version of international events. Most people valued collectivism and egalitarian values. The Soviets saw themselves as exceptional people who were proud of their accomplishments and, most importantly, optimistic about the future.

CRITICAL VIEWS

It is inaccurate to explain the behavior of the vast majority of the Soviet population as driven by fear of the omnipotent authorities. Fear, of course, played a significant role. The Kremlin attempted to isolate and marginalize the critics and to limit any free discussion of the society and its deficiencies. Although empirical data show a widespread dissatisfaction with local problems, such as the rampant bureaucracy, only few people were critical of the Soviet system. One of such sources of information about local problems was official letters of complaint.

The Soviet people sent millions of letters to the media and various institutions, issuing their complaints and their reactions to current events. Many letters sent by citizens to the media and authorities were carefully studied by the KGB and its predecessors throughout the life span of the Soviet Union. What did the critics write about? Some people expressed their discontent during election campaigns. Some criticized the Soviet election system or used facts such as food shortages, housing, and other difficulties to blame the local authorities. However, in most cases, the people focused on specific bureaucratic problems and avoided complaints that could be interpreted as anti-Soviet.

There were also unpublished personal diaries and private discussions in which individuals critiqued the regime.[16] Some people wrote long manuscripts with an unconcealed anti-Soviet content. There were private letters to friends or relatives with some critique of the regime; some of these letters were read by the KGB or other agencies. Many people were arrested for sending prohibited materials through the mail. In 1945, Alexander Solzhenitsyn, for example, was arrested for writing a letter in which he criticized Stalin; he spent eight years in prisons and labor camps and an additional three years in a mandatory "internal" exile.

One of the main groups of critics (who were quite strong in the 1920s and again in the 1980s) simply rejected the Communist ideology, its values, and official beliefs. They saw it as totalitarian and oppressive. Most probably, criticisms were more common among the people who suffered within the Communist system or whose expectations were not met. Reviewing various data in the Russian archives in St. Petersburg, Sarah Davies notes that the sharpest statements against the system in the mid-1930s were made by the poorest workers (Davies, 1997, p. 28). The number of critics was likely to increase during the periods of dwindling enthusiasm and along with the deterioration of the standard of living.

For example, religious persons saw the Soviet system as hostile to God and religion, a standpoint for which there also was factual support (e.g., Dahlke, 2002). Hatred was also awakened in those who were strongly anti-Semitic, believing that the Soviet regime was being imposed on Russia by Jews (Davies, 1997: 84–88). The world of haters included not only the various types of victims of the regime, but also the relatives of these victims as well. The number of people with critical attitudes toward the Soviet political order increased briefly after the adoption of Stalin's new constitution in 1936, which demagogically proclaimed democratic freedoms in the country. Davies cited some casual data supporting this view (1997: 102–108). Many years later, in the 1960s, a group of Soviet intellectuals headed by Alexander Esenin-Volpin founded a human rights movement with the same thrust. One of its public demands was that the Soviet leaders respect their own constitution (see Alekseeva, 1984; Shlapentokh, 1990).

On the informal level, many Soviet citizens, critical of the socialist system and its policies, frequently used the term *Sovok* (a derogative term rooted in the word, "Soviet") to consolidate all their negative perceptions of the country, the system, and its people. In general, the term *Sovok* stood for a behavioral and psychological syndrome of inadequacy, bureaucratic delays, laziness, and lack of culture. In conversations, Soviet people attached this label to anything negative identified with the Soviet Union or the socialist system. Frequently mentioned in newspaper editorials and reports, in research monographs (Gozman & Edkind 1992; Lowenhardt, 1995), mentioned by politicians (Burbulis 1992, *Argumenty I Facty*, 31, 2)—*Sovok* represented anything and everything distasteful, rigid, primitive, and provincial in Soviet society and daily life. This was a convenient term used by the critics of the regime to describe a Soviet patriot, a war veteran, a factory worker, or a Communist Party supporter. Bureaucratic delays, filth on the streets, poor service in a store, or propaganda in a television interview—all these could have been labeled *Sovok*. In general, several distinct features of this unenthusiastic image existed.

The first was *nevezhestvo* (a combination of ignorance and rudeness). Vladimir Lisovsky, a popular sociology professor from Leningrad State

University, openly called it one of the most embarrassing characteristics of the Soviet people (transcript of a lecture, November 3, 1984). This term also refers to one-sided, narrow-based knowledge instilled in the heads of millions during the Soviet times.

The second was *bardak,* a derogatory colloquial slur not used in official reports or broadcasts. This word, nonetheless, was an outstanding element in the Soviet people's daily vocabulary. Translated originally as *brothel,* the term meant everything from the lack of order and discipline to complete lawlessness. The ordinary people knew that the Soviet Union had long been known for its "poor execution of bad laws." (Smith, 1976; p.272) On the informal level, the lack of discipline and deceitfulness was often attributed by critics to the "typical" Soviet individual.[17] *Bardak* represented missed appointments, absence of transparency, empty promises, and the lack of information about anybody and anything. In the post-Soviet period, late General Lebed explained the meaning of this term quite bluntly: "Nobody obeys the law, and nobody fears the law. Nobody's afraid of not paying their debts, of not paying wages for months. They steal not only the goods in the factories but the factories as well. Why? I think it's because there's simply no law. Instead of law we have 'thieves in law'. . . . To put it bluntly, it's a complete *bardak.*" (Lebed, Ostankino radio Mayak, May 14, 1996).

Len (laziness) is another inseparable element of *sovok.* It is hard to find a classical Russian writer who would not have sketched this stereotypical feature of the Russian character: Goncharov, Gogol, Saltykov-Shedrin, or Bulgakov, to name a few, paid great attention to Russian laziness while creating their main characters. Russians sarcastically called it *mama laziness.* In the Soviet Union, laziness was frequently explained as a result of the government's inability to pay people decent salaries. "What do you expect me to do for one hundred and twenty rubles?" was a common Soviet expression referring to a person's reluctance to work hard for such a small monthly wage.

Sovok does not exist without *pokazukha* (flaunt), a feature that was sometimes criticized in Soviet leaders' official reports and speeches. "Showing off" and parade-like exhibitionism as well as relentless promotion of nonexistent achievements were the most typical attributes of socialist propaganda.

Weak Resistance

In general, open resistance to the Soviet regime was insignificant. It should be attributed not only to the efficiency of its repressive organs and reasonable social policy but also to a very great degree to propaganda that was able to inculcate a positive image of Soviet society in the minds of the majority of people.

Sources documenting a continued resistance against the Soviet government in the 1930s were mostly official documents, which, therefore, should be treated with skepticism. Still, these documents revealed the existence of "anti-Soviet agitation cases" and dissemination of unanimous leaflets containing harsh denunciation of Soviet life (Davies, 1997). Sarah Davies, for example, showed that according to archival documents, some people disseminated leaflets, containing calls for strikes in factories. These materials, in one case, were distributed throughout Leningrad after the enactment of special labor decrees of 1938 and 1940 banning people from changing jobs and punishing them for absences or tardiness.

Students in most countries, historically, represent the most active political groups. In the Soviet Union, however, since the 1930s, there were only a few students involved in some form of nonsanctioned collective action. They organized informal groups in which they discussed the ideas of Socialism and Leninism and proposed their own ideas of Soviet society. Some of these groups emerged after the war ended in 1945. However, these groups were very small and their impact on other students was insignificant.

Only few public disturbances had some political resonance including the riots in Karaganda and Novocherkassk in 1962, the riot at the sports stadium in Tashkent in 1973, and a few other incidents. Mass public disturbances were so rare that when they occurred in any part of the country they drew the complete and immediate attention of the Kremlin.[18]

In sum, most acts of resistance against the system had a predominantly individual character. Unpublished personal diaries and recollections of private discussions reveal frequent critiques of the regime. Such "private critics" came from people of all walks of life and from many social and educational groups. However, a significant number of Soviet people, despite the barrage of propaganda encouraging them to participate in public affairs at the local level, remained deeply indifferent to politics.

INDIFFERENCE

Many people suppressed their political sympathies and antipathies and preferred not to talk politics at work. Some families did not discuss politics at home. Understanding clearly that it was dangerous to speak openly about anything ideological or political, many people abstained from discussions, comments, and even friendly conversations if they related to ideological or political topics. Many people argued that they had work to do and that anything else was beyond their level of interest or comprehension. Soviet authorities during Stalin's times denounced these people as "philistines," and attempted to create an atmosphere of public intolerance for anyone who appeared disinterested in politics. However, even the disinterested were formally loyal to the regime.[19] The policy of mass political involvement changed later, during the post-Stalin era, especially since the late 1960s. There was no reason for authorities to "rock" the political consciousness of the people who appeared indifferent but remained loyal to the regime.

Death of a leader always brings a sense of uncertainty to the minds of the leaders' supporters. It was particularly true in the Soviet Union after the death of Stalin in 1953. People had a hard time imagining what type of society they would have after Stalin. He left no official proclamation about policy or instructions about his political heir. People tried to make sense of the sudden situation of loss by promising to continue Stalin's cause. Despite many people's anticipation of a societal change, there was no evidence to suggest that the country was eager to move beyond Stalin.

Post-Stalin transitions, especially during the Khrushchev years in the late 1950s and 1960s, injected a healthy measure of optimism in the Soviet people's perceptions of reality. Most of them followed the official propaganda and beliefs that after Stalin's death, the "real" principles of socialism, had been restored and that now, finally, the country was on the right path of development. The Communist ideology was, again, purified. The country was unified around the Communist Party armed with a global vision and ambitious plans. People were told that technology and education would eventually help the Soviet Union to win the battle against capitalism on the economic front. Khrushchev's slogans, such as his promises that the current generation "will live under Communism," were somewhat inspiring to many people. However, most of them did not know what Communism would be like; skepticism over this and similar promises grew rapidly. Overall, the post-Stalin era also marked the time of the decline of the prestige and acceptance of the official ideology and its major values.

Although the Soviet Union was very competitive in many fields, such as arms production and space programs, the country was far behind the West in terms of living standards of its average resident (Shiraev and Zubok, 2001). Over the course of many subsequent years, people continued to compare their lives to American and West European living standards. People in successive generations also began to recognize that, in reality, American, Swedish, or West German living standards were infinitely higher and that the gap between the Soviet Union and wealthy countries was widening. In the long run, those who looked for an explanation easily came to the conclusion that the main obstacle preventing them from achieving a comfortable lifestyle was the Soviet economic and political system (Gorbachev and Mlynar, 1994). However, because the system was well protected and people knew that any attempts at changes would eventually fail, people chose passive withdrawal as the only possible mode in their behavior (Shlapentokh, 1989). Voting also could not change anything. People felt that their votes did not matter much in the political process. In the absence of real political competition within a one-party system, voting was not considered a sign of a person's political involvement (Bahry and Silver, 1990: 837–838).

Ambivalence in the Perceptions during Perestroika

There is a common misperception that the Soviet people in 1985 were eager to embrace the Gorbachev reforms and most of the radical changes in the country. Perhaps the most profound feature of public opinion was ambivalence toward innovations (Olcott, 1987). Even if the perceptions of the Soviet reality that were coming with glasnost became more realistic and most people wanted to see changes, they were unsure which ones they wanted most. People wanted to see many policies changed, yet they did not want to see radical changes (Shlapentokh, 1989). People were not certain about the prospect of having a multiparty system in the Soviet Union (Marinov, 1989: 63). Majorities did not believe that the country could quickly overcome most of the current problems it was facing. Several surveys conducted in the 1980s indicated that Soviet citizens remained both watchful and ambivalent, displaying interest in politics, confidence in key political institutions, and clear uncertainty about the forthcoming economic and political changes (Popov, 1992).

The early years of political transition in the mid-1980s and appearance of the first, uncensored studies of Soviet public opinion in 1987 revealed an overwhelming support for changes. The rapid mobilization of the public in support of Gorbachev's political, economic, and social agenda resulted in a popular euphoria, a growing sense of empowerment, and rapidly rising expectations. Two surveys conducted in 1988 captured the optimism of the time. A *CBS/New York Times* (*CBS/NYT*) survey found that 74 percent of respondents strongly endorsed Gorbachev's reforms and 23 percent supported the reforms with some reservations. A similar survey conducted by Marttila and Kiley and Market Opinion Research (MK/MOR) found 70 percent strongly supporting the reforms and 23 percent supporting them with reservations (Willerton & Sigelman, 1991). Finifter and Mickiewicz's 1989 survey indicated widespread support for the goals of democratic reforms at this stage in the transition process. Some 95 percent of the respondents supported competitive elections (Finifter and Mickiewicz, 1992: 859).

When the Soviet system began to undergo major changes starting in 1985 with Gorbachev's accession, the overall support for the regime and its ideology remained strong. Survey data gathered in the late 1980s by VTSIOM, a major Russian polling organization showed that substantial majorities of Soviet citizens continued to support the regime on a wide range of economic and social issues. Most people acknowledged (as Gorbachev did) that the country needed transformation. However, most of the ongoing discussions were about how to improve the Soviet system and not necessarily about how to replace it with something else. National surveys revealed several reformist ideas embraced by a majority of people.

First, socialism as an economic system should be preserved. It should undergo a renovation, but not a substantial alteration. People supporting this view did not envision a massive sellout of state property into private hands and accepted state ownership of key industries. What was commonsensical at that time was a discussion about allowing people to own small businesses and allow state-owned enterprises compete with each other for profit. The main motto in the early years of perestroika was "more socialism": This meant that the main principles of Soviet socialism, in which the Soviet society was rooted, were accepted. Agreeing that bureaucracy and nonexisting economic incentives were the main obstacles destroying the Socialist economy, most people in the Soviet Union did not want to endorse free market in a classical, liberal sense. They just wanted to establish several "elements" of free market but not to witness price increases, unemployment, and unprofitable factory closures (Kontorovich, 1987).

Moreover, the Soviet publics were not convinced that free market would increase their living standards. A survey of approximately 1,000 Moscow residents published in Time magazine (April 10, 1989) showed that almost two-third of them said that from an economic standpoint, the ongoing economic reforms made no improvement in their lives or even made them worse. Asked about their expectations, 49 percent of people answered that their lives would either become more difficult or stay the same (Marinov, 1989: 63). Most people appeared to strongly favor the benefits guaranteed by the state, such as full employment or government-subsidized food prices. However, national survey data from November and December of 1989 showed that the people were almost evenly divided in their views about the state's responsibility for an individual's social and economic well-being. One half of the respondents wanted the government to accept the "big nanny" role, while the others did not support this idea (Finifter and Mickiewicz, 1992). In 1990, when the principles of egalitarianism were under constant criticism by the media, 41 percent of respondents of national polls supported "equality in income," in contrast to 38 percent who claimed it was necessary to eliminate limits on incomes and stimulate productivity (Levada, 1993: 57).

However, by 1990, it became evident that Gorbachev's attempts to reform the Soviet economy without changing its fundamentals were simply not working. The necessity of new economic reforms gained an increasing popular support. Still, according to surveys, most people supported a social-democratic version of the free market with a range of social guarantees. "Wild" forms of capitalism did not draw much of public support (Duch, 1993).

Second, the Soviet political system in the public mind needed some renovation, which would allow more freedom to criticize publicly, travel overseas, read previously "prohibited" sources, and discuss previously censored topics. Many people believed that a certain and satisfactory level of political freedom had been already achieved. In 1989, for instance, 60 percent of the surveyed Russians did not want to acknowledge the existence of "the dissident movement" in the Soviet Union probably because some people were truly unaware of the existence of the dissidents while the others did not consider them a "movement." Many people liked their country. In the same survey people were asked the question, "What are you most proud of?" Nearly a quarter of the surveyed selected "patriotism" out of 20 answer options (Levada, 1993). Opinions were divided on many issues, including how far the policy of glasnost (openness) went or should go. Although a majority was satisfied with the policy in general, 33 percent believed that it did not go far enough, and 10 percent reported that it went too far (Marinov, 1989: 62–63). The attitudes of Soviet people toward glasnost even in the late 1980s were positive enough to get them to vote for those promising to extend glasnost further.

Third, at the beginning of perestroika, the Communist Party, in the opinions of many people, should have undergone some changes as well. In particular, the party should have accepted more openness within its ranks and established new rules of self-criticism. It should have invited new thinkers, who would free it from the swamp of stagnation and bureaucracy. In later periods, opinions changed. In an August 1990 survey, the majority of people supported democratic reforms but lacked confidence in the Soviet regime, including the party (Dobson and Grant,

1992: 302). Frustration grew over the inability or unwillingness of the Communist Party to give ordinary people, as they saw it, a larger representation in the government. The party continued to maintain its monopoly on power.

By the late 1980s, antiestablishment attitudes grew along with the people's deepening disaffection with the Communist Party and the political system in general (Nepomnyashchy, 1990). In the spring of 1990, almost 30 percent of respondents of a national survey gave a nonconfidence vote to the party as an institution and the same number named top leadership responsible for the economic crisis that the Soviet Union experienced at that time. More people in ethnic republics called for a larger independence of their republics and the break-up of the Soviet Union (Zavslaskaia, 1990).

It was these increasingly critical public constituencies that enabled Yeltsin to win the June 1991 Russian presidential election, defeat the August 1991 antireformist coup, and ultimately break up the Soviet Union by the end of that year.

CONCLUSION

Throughout its long history, the Soviet regime, its leaders, and ideology had strong public support. After the Russian Civil War and since the beginning of the Soviet Union, most ordinary citizens of that country gave its institutions approval and support. Soviet citizens generally saw the existing political regime as a legitimate and powerful force that guaranteed societal order, protected them from foreign enemies, and guaranteed them social security and economic improvement.

Although support was never universal, especially at the beginning (the 1920s) and in the end (the late 1980), yet it was relatively consistent over the years. The regime conducted repressive policies to prevent and suppress criticism of the Soviet political system and its economic order. The war (1941–1945) had consolidated the people's support of the government and their belief in the socialist order. To be a critic of the Soviet system meant (in both public and legal sense) to be a traitor.

The country's increased material prosperity in the 1960s gave authorities a powerful propaganda tool to argue that the path chosen by the Communist Party and top Soviet leadership was correct. In subsequent decades, official visions of a "mature or developed socialism" coincided with a considerable public quiescence. The Soviet people entered the perestroika era of the 1980s with a relatively optimistic view of the future, hoping for some changes, and publicly supporting political and economic foundations of the Soviet Union.

Overall, the Soviet regimes succeeded in generating support from its citizens. The regime created an ideological hegemony, one global vision of the country and the world. This "official" ideology successfully conveyed to most people the belief in the righteousness of Communism and the Communist Party. People learned to accept economic difficulties and other inconveniences. They accepted the view that they lived in a hostile international environment. The Kremlin managed to persuade the majority of the people in the Soviet Union that the official picture of Soviet life was correct.

A Case in Point: Lay Discourses on Soviet Lithuania during Brezhnev Period (1964–1982)

Arunas Juska and Vladas Gaidys

In this "case in point," we would like to focus on the informal views that the ordinary Lithuanians as citizens of the Soviet Union had about the nature of society in which they lived and its political institutions. By the end of Brezhnev's period in 1982, the informal views of citizens of the nature of society and its political system in Soviet Lithuania were increasingly heterogeneous. The differentiation of viewpoints of Soviet Lithuanians was probably much greater than the spectrum of public opinion currently prevailing in postindependent Lithuania. This increasing differentiation in Soviet Lithuania during the period of "mature socialism" was influenced by social and historic conditions specific to Lithuania's incorporation in the Soviet Union. Second, the heterogeneity of Lithuanian worldviews was also affected by significant political, socioeconomic, demographic, and cultural changes that the republic underwent during the two decades of Brezhnev's rule.

From 1918 until the militarily annexation in 1940, Lithuania was an independent country with many established institutions of a modern state. Furthermore, Lithuanian culture and institutions were historically part of the Western culture and tradition. Lithuania as a country was influenced by the Roman Catholic Church, the Polish culture, and institutions prevalent in Lithuania Major (territory to the east of the Nemunas river) and by the Lutheran church, German culture, and institutions prevalent in Lithuania Minor (territory of the country to the west of Nemunas). Before the annexation, the living standards in Lithuania were higher than in the Soviet Union. Political and cultural circumstances of Lithuania's annexation certainly shaped views of the ordinary Lithuanians about the Soviet Union.

In addition to circumstances specific to Lithuania's forceful incorporation in the Soviet Union, perceptions of the Soviet regime were also significantly affected by socioeconomic, political, and demographic conditions during the Brezhnev period. Demographic changes were crucial in this respect because older generations, compared to younger ones, possessed a living memory of the independent Lithuanian statehood. The older Lithuanians also lived through the Nazi occupation as well as survived violence and deportations in the immediate postwar period. Demographic situations in Lithuania changed after the 1960s because of the rising Russian immigration in the Baltic states.[20]

STRUCTURE OF THE SUBJECTIVE KNOWLEDGE OF THE SOVIET REALITY

Our approach to perceptions is associated primarily with the Claude Lévi-Strauss (1967) study of myth and myth-like elements in a society.[21] In ethnography, myths are defined as sacred stories explaining the origins of the world or how the world and the creatures in it came to have their present form. Similarly, views of Soviet society can be analyzed as "folk stories" of origins of Soviet society or explanations of how it came to its present form. Lévi-Strauss argued that myths are made up of elemental units called *mythemes*. Through an analysis of the arrangement of themes within myths the structure of a myth is revealed.

Typically, the Soviet Lithuanian society or "us" is defined by comparison to "them" or other societies and people in West European countries such as Finland or Sweden; in East European countries such as Poland or Czechoslovakia; or with the other Soviet republics. In addition, groups within Lithuanian society can be compared with each other. Here we describe the following six mythemes.

LITHUANIA AS DEGRADED WESTERN OR EAST EUROPEAN SOCIETY

This mytheme was built on the basis of Eastern-Western comparisons, where the Western civilization represented the "golden past" of Lithuania compared with its current degraded and depended condition imposed by the "inferior" Russian East. This perception is typical to many contemporary nationalist ideologies referring to the "glorious past" of their country. For example, Serbian nationalists dream about the Great Serbia, Russian chauvinist dream about the old empire, or contemporary Israeli nationalists aspire to recover territories of the Biblical Israel.

The "golden" or "glorious" past is a mytheme, which is represented in historical myths of the origins and magnificence of the medieval Lithuanian state as well as by living memories of residents of the pre–World War II independent Lithuania. In these perceptions, Lithuania belongs to the Western Christian civilization. Lithuania is an integral part of the

West compared to the "inferior" Russian civilization belonging to the Eastern (Greek Orthodox) or Asian civilizations—the images referring to backward or barbaric cultures based on despotism and conformism. Central to the claims of "superiority" of Lithuania during the medieval ages was the reign of the Grand Duke Vytautas (1401–1430) who annexed vast Slavic territories and expanded the Grand Duchy of Lithuania from the Baltic to the Black Sea. Rarely informal gatherings of friends and family would occur without collective singing celebrating the glories of the medieval kings of Lithuania, and especially Vytautas who was "watering his horses in the Black sea."

The asserted superiority of the medieval Lithuanian civilization was reinforced by selective living memories from pre–World War II Lithuania. Older people were especially aware that their living standards were higher than in the Soviet Union. By the 1960s, because of travel and the media, Lithuanians could see Soviet Lithuania's backwardness compared to its western counterparts. At the same time, since the late 1960s, Western consumer goods and fashions were becoming increasingly important symbols of success and status. A number of Lithuanian intellectuals began to speak against the evolving consumerist society and urged people to pay more attention to their spiritual needs.

Overall, the increasing flow of information and comparisons with other countries elicited feelings of superiority and inferiority, adoration and humiliation, as many people compared their bleak day-to-day realities with a mostly mythologized Lithuanian past as well as western people's lifestyles.

Lithuania as the Soviet European West

Lithuania's own comparison with the rest of the Soviet Union provided a boost to national self-awareness and consciousness. Increasing travel of Lithuanians within the Soviet Union showed that Lithuania apparently had many advantages compared to other Soviet republics. Economically, Lithuania was better developed than most other regions. Lithuania even looked more "Western" than Russia or other Soviet republics because of street and shop signs printed in Latin alphabet; clean and tidy streets and squares (in comparison with cities in the rest of the country); and relatively lower number of red flags, propaganda posters, and Lenin's statues.

To underscore the Western character of their culture, people adopted coffee as a national Lithuanian drink. Coffee houses had proliferated. Tea, a typical Russian drink, was frowned upon by most Lithuanians. During the 1960s, the first beer pubs were open (Russians began to have them much later). Nightclubs began to function. Their presence in the cities was interpreted as a sign of a modern Western lifestyle.

Despite the official rule establishing Russian as the second official language, the functioning language of universities and other establishments of postsecondary education was Lithuanian. The Lithuanian Roman Catholic Church, although it was controlled by the Communist Party, continued to command the loyalty of many Lithuanians, thus reaffirming their ties to Western cultural and historical traditions.

Finally, compared with the other parts of the country, Lithuania did enjoy relative cultural freedom. Theaters were thriving. Innovative artistic styles were tolerated. Jazz and rock culture flourished. It was a culture with a distinct Western flavor. In the late 1960s local press in Lithuania debated the question, "Is striptease good or bad?," which could hardly be possible anywhere else in the Soviet Union east of the Lithuania borders.

LITHUANIANS AS ETHNIC MINORITY IN THE RUSSIAN-DOMINATED SOVIET UNION

Up until Gorbachev's reforms in the late 1980s, it was extremely dangerous to express publicly any nationalist views. Accusations of nationalism were probably the most serious charges that could cause a Lithuanian a career or even freedom. Despite threats of punishment, elements of nationalism were present in private conversations. Glorification of Lithuania's independent past was common. Private guests to Lithuania were often reminded about the glorious days of medieval Lithuanian state stretching "from sea to sea." Children were given names of medieval Lithuanian dukes. Every city and township in Lithuania had streets and squares named after them. Many sport teams and drinks were named after the successful medieval battles against the Germans (i.e., very popular basketball club "Žalgiris"). Official Soviet propaganda also emphasized that up until the fourteenth-century medieval Lithuania remained pagan, and fought successfully against German religious orders to convert its population to Christianity.

Lithuanians maintained old ethnic customs such as collective folk singing during informal gatherings and celebrations. Traditional folk and drinking songs strengthened communal ties and a sense of ethnic identity. Visitors to Lithuania were often reminded that Lithuanians spoke a special langauge that had nothing in common with Russian; that the Lithuanian language was very old and related to Sanskrit, the religious and classical literary language of ancient India.

By the late 1970s, the dominant positions of the Lithuanian language began to gradually erode because of the increasing Russian immigration and Moscow's attempts to promote the Russian language through mandatory policies restricting the use of Lithuanain in public places, universities, and communications (for example, scholarly papers and dissertations had to be written in Russian). However, many ethnic Russians living in Lithuania remained monoligual. As a form of protest, many Lithuanians in daily interaction did not respond to questions and requests in Russian. Mixed Lithuanian-Russian marriages were not supported thus causing relative social isolation of such couples. Migration from Lithuania was very rare bacause of the superior living conditions there.

Soviet Society as Degraded Prewar Lithuania

Many older Lithuanians who lived in the country before World War II maintained the view that Soviet Lithuania, imposed by force and annexation, was inferior to prewar free Lithuania. In the 1930s, Lithuania was predominantly an agrarian country. The older generation of Soviet Lithuanians had been born during the 1930s when the Lithuanian society was comprised of relatively homogenous rural communities.

A mixture of childhood memories and traumatic recollections of the brutal destruction of many rural communities by the Soviet Union's forceful collectivization made the 1930s a period of the "golden past." Lithuania of the prewar period was often compared with the bleakness of rural life on Soviet collective farms: low productivity, wastefulness, declining labor ethics, theft, and excessive drinking. The traditional Lithuanian worldview depicted rural lifestyle as a bearer of standards of morality and work ethics.

Soviet Lithuania as a Modernized Republic

This perception was based on somewhat ambivalent, but mostly positive evaluation of the impact of the Soviet rule on Lithuanian society, especially when compared to its prewar past. The views of the majority of the Lithuanians, thus, were pragmatic and provided a more nuanced evaluation of Soviet reality.

The modernization mytheme acknowledged the destruction and repressions brought by the Soviet regime. At the same time, it also emphasized the positive impact that the Soviet rule had on Lithuanian economy and society. Cities and new roads had been built; industries developed; the population became highly educated; standards of living increased; architecture, culture, and arts (although tightly controlled by the state) flourished; and the Lithuanian manufacturing industry and especially agriculture became the most productive in the Soviet Union.

Specifically, up until 1940, Lithuania lagged behind Latvia and Estonia in socioeconomic development. However, during the Soviet years,

Lithuania caught up with its neighbors and was even getting ahead of them. During the 1960s, large energy industry projects were implemented in Lithuania. Agriculture was undergoing rapid industrialization. Many Lithuanians believed that Lithuania's meat and milk deliveries were sufficient to feed the inhabitants of Moscow and Leningrad, the two largest Soviet cities. During the 1960s and the 1970s, Lithuania underwent serious industrialization and multiple industrial facilities were built: electronics, refrigerators, chemicals, furniture, textiles, and food processing plants were built. A new system of inter-republic highways was underway.

However, the majority of the population was ambivalent about these industrialization achivements. Supporting technological development and modernization of the rural areas, people resented large-scale drainage schemes implemented in the countryside that ruined traditional Lithuanian landscape. Forceful transfer of the rural population to centralized settlements was deplored; complaints were widespread about the lack of work incentives and work ethics. New plans to build industrial facilities in Lithuania were met with apprehension in part because of the fear that these projects would bring more Russian immigrants and further intesify the process of Lithuania's Russification.

The general public took pride in some Lithuanian brands such as TV sets "Šilelis" and refrigerators "Snaigė." However, the overall quality of goods manufactured in Lithuania was mediocre at best, especially in comparison with western standards. During the 1970s, there were quite popular stories about Westen entrepreneurs buying Lithuanian produced industrial machine-tools and then reselling them for high-quality metal scrap.

SOVIET LITHUANIA AS BASED ON POWER STRUGGLE

According to this view, the Lithuanian society was based on the coexistence and struggle for power by various clans and networks. This view emphasized the importance of informal power structures that evolved parallel to official Soviet institutions and, by the 1980s, shaped all aspects of life of the Soviet society. Networks of patronage consisted of many legal, semi-legal, and illegal interactions among its members enabling them to achieve mutual benefits. Networks of patronage and influence served as a form of protection of an individual from the state and also provided access to power, status, and resources in Soviet Lithuania.

The most powerful in the country were the networks of patronage formed by the ruling elite. High-level party and state officials usually shopped in special stores and received medical treatment in special clinics. Their children attended the best universities and studied in the most prestigious fields (medicine, law, or retail). They spent their vacations in the most prestigious resorts and received other material privileges.

Another group was comprised of various networks of "retail mafia," or managers of state-owned retail stores, services, and restaurants. These people had access to products and services, unavailable to most people, and used their status to enrich and empower themselves by monopolizing the distribution of consumer goods and services.

Finally, smaller in scope and influence, personal networks were engaged in various forms of embezzlement and theft. Pilfering became a mass phenomenon as workers were "subsidizing" their low wages by stealing products such as socks and sausages from the workplace. Elaborate informal networks were developed to distribute, trade, and exchange the pilfered property. Exchanges in kind were widespread illustrating the overall backwardness of the Soviet economy.

How did ordinary Lithuanians perceive the glaring contradiction between official statements of the omnipotence of the Soviet state and existence of semi-legal personal networks that in many respects were subverting and replacing the state? For the most part, people thought of them as "facts of life" in Soviet Lithuania. Various "back door" dealings were well known and depicted in films, books, theater plays, and newspaper cartoons. Instead of using words such as "stealing," ordinary Lithuanians talked about "coming up" with favors, goods, or services or "carrying out" the goods from their employment offices and factories. In other words, semi-illegal enrichment through various personal connections at the expense of the state was becoming "normalized" and increasingly considered as a legitimate and desirable venue, like everywhere in the Soviet Union.

Conclusion

Several inherited from the Soviet past, "mythemes" continue to influence political developments in Lithuania today. Currently, the overwhelming majority of citizens of postindependent Lithuania support the direction of Lithuania's policies: NATO and EU membership, and continuous integration of Lithuanian economy, society, and culture within the European Union. However, Lithuanian politics remains deeply divided in terms of its perceptions of the Soviet past. Political parties of center-right continue to uphold the view that the Soviet period was a violent abrogation and retardation of the country's "natural" (i.e., West European in character) course of development. In comparison, parties on the center-left tend to interpret the Soviet period, in a more pragmatic and positive way, as a period of rapid urbanization, industrialization, and social and cultural advancement of the country. This profound division of Lithuanian perceptions will most likely persist in the future and influence its domestic and foreign policies.

CHAPTER 6

Conclusion

In the famous novel by Anatole France, *Monsieur Bergeret in Paris* (1901), a group of historians argued about some episodes in ancient Egypt. The opinions of the discussants were divided. Suddenly, in the midst of the debate, the discussants switched their attention to a street brawl unfolding right before their eyes. Sitting comfortably in their armchairs, the discussants saw the entire fistfight that lasted for several minutes. When the host asked his guests to describe what had happened just seconds ago, everyone offered a different version of the story. "How you can be sure about the events that happened many thousands years ago," said the host with acerbic irony in his voice, "when you are unable to come to the consensus about the events which occurred only moments ago?"

This was a very powerful question. In our case, how can we trust these numerous studies of the Soviet Union published today, many years after its disappearance, when eyewitnesses from the past were very much in disagreement with each other in terms of what they saw and did not see in that country?

Remember how utterly different were the depictions of Soviet history offered by scholars and ordinary people in both countries? The October Revolution of 1917 was, to some of them, a popular rebellion against the much hated tsarist regime reinforced by corruption and injustice. To others, it was a lucky coup organized and completed by the Jews or undoubtedly sponsored by German brains and money.

Vladimir Lenin was one of the greatest thinkers and political leaders in history who wanted to bring peace to the feuding nations, justice to the abused, and prosperity to the poor. To other people, he was a revengeful, power-thirsty politician ready to use any means to satisfy his vindictive cravings for power.

In a similar way, Joseph Stalin was a great savior of Russia who turned this deprived country into a nuclear superpower and who crushed the

Nazi military machine. Others saw Stalin akin to Hitler. Both were paranoid and sadistic individuals blinded by an ideology and surrounded by a bunch of cowardly lackeys.

Mikhail Gorbachev appeared to some as a great reformer and visionary who had woken up the stagnant country and dared to embrace the "new thinking," a new form of liberal idealism and internationalism. To others, he was a pure demagogue, a selfish and stubborn ruler, or a collaborator with a mission to destroy the great country and sell it out to the West.

Look at the major events in Soviet history and see how they were portrayed by their contemporaries. Was the collectivization campaign an act of genocide against millions of peasants or was it the greatest success that has consolidated the country and changed the social fabric of the true socialist society?

The repressions of the 1930s appear in most accounts as a disturbing chain of events in Soviet history, as an act of political genocide. In other theories and personal evaluations, Stalin's political purges were a necessary policy aiming at political opposition and designed to consolidate the country before the war.

In official Soviet textbooks, the Soviet Union won the war against Germany thus saving Europe and the whole world from the plague of Nazism. Yet the critics saw the war as an example of military incompetence that caused millions of soldiers' deaths, diplomatic intrigues, and imperialistic inspirations, which resulted in the cold war.

Some saw the Soviet foreign policy as aggressive and ideology-driven while others believed that Moscow was only responding to military pressure coming from the United States and its allies.

Let us look now at major Soviet institutions. Was the Communist Party an oppressive organization and a major coercive machine of a totalitarian state, or was it a true leading force capable of unifying the country and playing the most important government functions?

Some believe that the KGB was just an institution within a huge government bureaucratic machine. Others equate KGB with the government thus suggesting that the Soviet Union was, in fact, a perfect example of the typical police state.

Soviet planning institutions are viewed by many as an example of an efficient mechanism that turned a backward country's economy into an efficient competitive system in just a few years. Others see the Soviet industrialization as a policy of mass coercion that turned millions of people into virtual servants of the regime and left them underpaid, abused, and ignored.

Some people admired the Soviet education and health-care systems, seeing them as first-class examples of social progressivism and genuine government's care of simple people. Others saw nothing but overcrowded schools and rundown hospitals, corrupt medical officials, shortages of medication, incompetence, and the absence of transparency.

How can we judge about who was right or wrong in these endless debates? If we suggest that everybody was equally right and wrong and that every fact has two or three sides, then we will say nothing new. Our position is somewhat different. It is also an open invitation to a discussion.

We think that the best chance to reflect the "hard reality" of the Soviet Union had been used by observers (professionals or lay people) who have carried mostly critical attitudes about Soviet society. These people were more sensitive to the problems they saw. They also knew about the main areas of distortions used by the Soviet official propaganda. Thus, from our standpoint, the dissidents inside the Soviet Union and totalitarianists in the West had a better chance to portray the facts in the most accurate way when compared to other views. However, the normalizers and domestic supporters of the Soviet regime also added important contours to the sketch of Soviet society: They saw the positive side of that country, the one that critics frequently overlooked.

We tend to see Soviet society as a "hard reality" with many objective features including the vast and omnipresent power of the Communist Party, a planned economy and government-controlled prices, a massive political police, censorship, long periods of political repressions, interventionist foreign policy, and the state monopoly in education and culture. On the other hand, there were guaranteed jobs, social security upon retirement, child benefits, paid vacations, and free education. The majority of the Soviet people favored the policies of social equality and believed in the state's responsibility to provide for basic social services including education, health care, and social security. The government of the Soviet Union censored the people's quest to see the "other side" of the reality.

Ideology plays a role in fact selection. Sociologists, political scientists, historians, or journalists, despite their good intentions of truth searching, are very vulnerable to the bias of self fulfilling prophecy, a tendency of the human mind to see and remember those facts that fit the mind's expectations and beliefs. A scholar, for example, who believes that the political repressions in the Soviet Union between the 1930s and 1950s were no different from the "red scare" of McCarthyism in the United States will certainly look for and publish the opinions and select the facts that would support the view that Stalinism in the Soviet Union and U.S. domestic policies shortly after World War II were, in fact, very similar. We believe, however, that this type of perception is largely inaccurate.

While commemorating an anniversary of Andrei Sakharov's death, Dmitry Bykov, one of several brilliant intellectuals of post–Soviet Russia, imagined what could have happened with the Soviet Union had the Soviet leadership paid serious attention to Sakharov's political writings and his vision of the facts. Sakharov saw the lack of intellectual freedom in the Soviet Union as the main obstacle to the society's progress. Bykov guessed that if the Soviet leadership treated Sakharov's beliefs seriously, if they saw them as a "fresh" perception of facts (and not as an attempt to undermine their power), and if they implemented some of his ideas, the Soviet Union would have survived as a state. Sakharov's work, *The Reflections on Progress, Peaceful Coexistence and Intellectual Freedom*, which appeared in 1968, was in many respects a "foreword" to the ideological program of Mikhail Gorbachev which he proposed less than 20 years later.

The government and most people in the Soviet Union had condemned Sakharov back in the 1970s for his alleged lies and distortions of truth about his country. His facts apparently challenged the Communist Party's version of facts. Powerful elites holding a monopoly on truth—no matter which country they live in—typically dislike those who challenge this monopoly.

For additional information about this book or to voice your opinion, please visit www.eshiraev.com

NOTES

CHAPTER 1

1. See various translations of *The Eighteenth Brumaire of Louis Bonaparte* (*Der achzehnte Brumaire des Louts Bonaparte*), written in 1852.
2. William James, *Principles of Psychology,* vol. 2, New York: Dover, 1890/1918, chap. 21, pp. 283–324.
3. Donald Campbell, *Experimental and Quasi-Experimental Design for Research,* Boston: Houghton Mifflin, 1968.
4. Only after the collapse of the Soviet Union was it possible to clarify, to some degree, what the Soviet leaders talked to one another about, both formally and informally. There were various "levels" of social reflections. For example, according to the memoirs of several ex-Soviet officials published in the 1990s, the leaders' perceptions of social life and the ordinary people's perceptions of it were not significantly different. On the other hand, Vladimir Bukovsky in his book *Jugement à Moscou* (Paris: Robert Laffont, 1995) published the minutes of the secret Politburo meetings of the 1980s. It is evident that the participants' comments and statements were very ideological and not very different from the official newspaper *Pravda*'s formal editorials. In *Stalin and Cosmopolitism, 1945–1953,* which contains numerous previously classified materials about the communications among high-level Soviet apparatchiks, the reader will find that their opinions were not much different than the materials published in the official media (*D. Nadzhofov* and *Z. Belousova, Stalin I kosmopolitism. Dokumenty Agitpropa TsKa, 1945–1953,* Moscow: Materik, 2005.).
5. Christopher Hitchens, *Why Orwell Matters,* New York: Basic Books, 2002, p. 83.
6. See Jeffrey Meyers, *Orwell,* New York: Norton, 2000, pp. 280–281; Alexander Kafka, "The Wintry Orwell," *The American Prospect,* vol. 11, no. 22, retrieved online from http://www.prospect.org/cs/articles?article-the_wintry _orwell (accessed July 21, 2008); and Stuart Hall, "Conjuring Leviathan: Orwell on the State," in Christopher Norris (ed.), *Inside the Myth: Orwell, Views from the Left,* London: Lawrence and Wishart, 1984, p. 220.
7. See, for instance, Bukovsky, *Jugement à Moscou,* pp. 70, 335, 560; Mikhail Kapustin, *Konez utopii,* Moscow: Novosti, 1990, p. 12; Mikhail Heller and Alexandre Nekrich, *Utopia in Power: The History of the Soviet Union from 1917 to the Present,* New York: Summit Books, 1986, p. 8.

8. See Vladimir Shlapentokh (ed.), *Sotsiologia Pechati,* vol. 1, Novosibirsk: Nauka, 1969; Shlapentokh (ed.), *Chitatel I Gazeta,* vol. 1, 2, Moscow: IKSI, 1969–1970; see also Shlapentokh and Olga Maslova, "K voprosu o sopostavimosti resultatov sotsiologicheskikh issledovani," *Sotsiologicheskiie Issaledovania,* vol. 3, 1975.
9. See Vladimir Shlapentokh, *Soviet Intellectuals and Political Power,* Princeton, NJ: Princeton University Press, 1990.
10. Peter L. Berger and Thomas Luckmann, *The Social Construction of Reality: A Treatise in the Sociology of Knowledge,* Garden City, NY: Anchor, 1967.
11. See V. Shlapentokh, J. Woods, and E. Shiraev, *America: Sovereign Defender or Cowboy Nation?* London: Ashgate, 2005. The project was based on surveys and media analyses conducted in six countries: Russia, Germany, Columbia, India, China, and Egypt.
12. See John Searle, *The Construction of Social Reality,* Free Press, 1997. The author argues that there are objective facts in the world that are only facts by human agreement.

CHAPTER 2

1. For our analysis, we have selected publications, which are broadly representative of American Sovietology. We have been focusing on authors whose overall production rates are highest with respect to both how often they have been cited as well as how many works they have produced (based on Social Sciences Citation Index, International Political Science Abstracts, and Sociological Abstracts). We have also selected authors based on how often and how favorably they have been reviewed in academic publications, new or repeat edition frequency, and any available information about their research design quality. We have also included the works by journalists and a few politicians selected on the basis of the rhetorical quality of their arguments (Przeworski and Teune, 1970). They were either extreme critics or die-hard sympathizers of the Soviet regime in different historical periods.
2. See, for example, Carrol, 1965: 7–8; Lash, 1962: 121; Graham, 1925: 296; and Strakhovsky, 1961.
3. Later, Pipes (1996) draws upon typical features of prerevolutionary Russian culture in explaining the political failure of Russian liberalism after 1991. Yet he does not acknowledge the roots of Bolshevism within pre–1917 Russia.
4. Malia (1994: 34) resolutely rebuffed this view and contended that the totalitarian nature of Communism should not be explained as "the prolongation of traditional Russian authoritarianism."
5. See the reprints of the works by the Civil-War-Era Russian monarchist Shulgin (1990, 1991). An enemy of the Bolsheviks, he, nevertheless, recognized their role in the restoration of a relatively "civilized state."
6. Conquest's estimate of a 1938 Gulag population of 9 million is fairly evidently absurd even if we take into account that only the 1939 size of the

Union of Soviet Socialist Republic's population (by admittedly problematic census data) was 170.6 million (TsSU SSSR, 1956: 17). Assuming that about 100 million of these people were adults and that only 50 million of these were men (the Gulag population consisted mostly of men), this would mean that almost one out of six men was in political prison. This claim, according to critics, does not jibe very well with the reality of the 1930s. However, some Soviet researchers even surpassed these estimates. Dmitry Volkogonov alluded to 4–5 million people arrested only in 1937–1938 (Senokosov, 1989: 280). Roy Medvedev (1973) and Aleksandr Solzhenitsyn (1973) referred to a much larger number of the persecuted, up to 20 million (Shatunovskaya, 1990).

7. For other revisionist estimations of mass killings and/or arrests that are to be viewed as disturbingly low, see also Hough and Fainsod (1979: 176–177) as well as Jerry Hough's (1989) directly communicated estimates cited by Alexander Cockburn in *The Nation*, where the number of purge deaths in 1937–1938 was in the range between 75,000 and 200,000 (Robeson et al., 1989: 184).
8. Thus Dallin (1973: 562) wrote: "Thus it used to be axiomatic that the Soviet system required an omnipotent dictator. Well, where is he today?"
9. See John K. Galbraith, *The New Industrial State*, Boston: Houghton-Mifflin, 1971; see also Michael Ellman, *Collectivisation, Convergence and Capitalism: Political Economy in a Divided World*, New York: Academic Press, 1984.
10. *Samizdat*, or underground and illegal dissident network of publications, used the term *totalitarian* already in the 1960s to describe the nature of the Soviet Union.
11. Michael Ellman and Vladimir Kontorovich, *The Destruction of the Soviet Economic System: An Insider's History*, New York: M. E. Sharpe, 1998.
12. The three economics textbooks that devoted more extensive analysis to the Soviet defense industry were by Gregory and Stuart (1986), Bornstein (1981), and Krylov (1965).
13. Arguments that Soviet political institutions even in Stalin's era bore similarities with pluralist democracy could continue also beyond the Soviet regime's demise (e.g., Dallin, 1992: 283).
14. In Peter Rutland's (1993: 115) work, up to five factions were identified in the 11-person body of the Politburo.
15. After 1991, some scholars continued to describe the early Soviet government, which actually banned any democratic manifestations, as "potentially one of the most democratic in history" (Suny, 1998: 23). Other Western scholars also suggested that the Soviet leadership was increasingly sensitive to the working class' constituents and their grievances (Fitzpatrick, 1992: 126).
16. According to several empirical studies, American social scientists in the 1960s were more likely to support liberal views compared to conservative ones (Lipset and Ladd, 1972; Lipset and Dobson, 1973; Lipset, 1972; Shlapentokh, 1990).
17. Walter Laqueuer was right when he joined Seymour Martin Lipset and Gyorgy Bence, authors who contended in 1992 that "although much maligned

by Sovietologists in the 1970s and 1980s [totalitarianism] has proved to be the most fruitful of the paradigms" (Laqueur, 1994: 83; cf. Lipset and Bence, 1992; Sartori, 1993).

18. See, for example, the euphoric 1993 special issue of *The National Interest* on the collapse of the Soviet regime as well as Malia (1993) and Pipes (1994).

19. National Bolshevism, for example, was well known in Germany, with Ernst Niekisch. See Hans Buchheim, "Ernst Niekischs Ideologie des Widerstands," *Vierteljahrshefte für Zeitgeschichte*, 1957, 5 (4), pp. 334–361. Louis Dupeux, "Pseudo-'Travailleur' Contre Pretendu 'Etat Bourgois l'interpretation de L'Hitlerisme par Ernst Niekisch En," 1934–1935, *Revue d'Allemagne*, 1984, 16 (3), pp. 434–449. Michael Pittwald, "Zur Entwicklung Völkischen Denkens in der Duetschen Arbeiterbewegung der National Revolutionär Ernst Niekisch," *Internatonale Wissenschaftliche Korrespondenz zur Geschichte der Deutschen, Arbeiterbewegung*, 1996, 32 (1), pp. 3–22.

20. Erwin Oberlaender, "National-Bolschewistische Tendenzen in der Russischen Intlilgenz," *Jahrbücher für Geschichte Osteuropas*, 1968, 16 (2), pp. 194–211. Mikhail Agursky, "Defeat as Victory and the Living Death: The Case of Ustrialov," *History of European Ideas*, 1984, 5 (2), pp. 165–180. Krausz Tamas, "A Nacional-Bolsevizmus alapvetése: Tőrténeti adalékok egy rendszerváltás ideológiai hátteréhez," *Multunk*, 1994, 39 (1–2), pp. 51–80. Svetlana Viktorovna Onegina, "Porevoliutsionnye politcheskie dvizheniia Rossiiskoi emigratsii v 20–30-E Gody: K istorii ideologii," *Otechestvennaia Istoriia*, 1998 (4), pp. 87–99. Viacheslav Konstantinovich Romanovski, "Nikolai Vasil'evich Ustrialov," *Otechestvennaia Istoriia*, 2002 (4), pp. 79–99. Liudmila Anatol'evna Bystriantseva, "Mirovozzrenie i obshchestvenno-politicheskaia deiatel'nost' N. V. Ustrialova (1889–1937)," *Novaia Noveishaia i Istoriia*, 2000 (5), pp. 162–190.

21. Despite the fact that Eurasianism had fascinated quite a few intellectuals in Europe, later, upon the decline of the movement, Western scholars began to pay less attention to it; the publications on Eurasianism were few. Only a handful of articles, for example, had been published for almost 20 years, since the 1960s to the middle of the 1980s, for example, the time of Gorbachev's perestroika. For examples of these early publications, see Nicholas V. Riasanovsky, "Prince N. S. Trubetskoy's 'Europe and Mankind'," *Jahbücher für Geschichte Osteuropas*, 1964, 12 (2), pp. 207–220. Georges Nivat, "Du 'Panmongolisme' Au Mouvement Eurasien," *Cahiers du Monde Russe et Soviétique* 1966, 7 (3), pp 460–478. Leonid Luks, "Die Ideologie der Eurasier Im Zeitgeschichtlichen Zusammenhang," *Jahbücher für Geschichte Osteuropas*, 1986, 34 (3), pp. 374–395.

22. It was this renewed popularity of Eurasianism among the Russian public that led to publications on Eurasianism among Western and Russian scholars. See, for example, Leonid Efremovich Gorizontov, "Evraziistvo, 1921–1931 GG.: Vzgliad iznutri," *Slavianovedenie*, 1992 (4), pp. 86–104, available online at http://src-h.slav.hokudai.ac.jp/publictn/acta/16/volodymyr/volodymyr-notes.html.

Mikhail Andreevich Robinson and Leonid Petrovich Petrovski, "N. N. Durnovo in. s. Trubetskoi: Problema Evraziistva v kontekste 'dela Slavistov,' materialam OGPU-NKVD," *Slavianovedenie*, 1992 (4), pp. 68–82, available online at http://books.google.com/books?id=uskPRW0XLwYC&pg=PA65&lpg=PA65&dq=Problema+Evraziistva+v+kontekste+%E2%80%98dela+Slavistov&source=web&ots=sJbPuZ3xOn&sig=tPEhaRAvDqpfoji9aR-nuunYFoU&hl=en&sa=X&oi=book_result&resnum=1&ct=result.

M. A. Robinson, "Pis'mo P.N. Savitskogo F. I. Uspenskomu," *Slavianovedenie*, 1992 (4), pp. 83–85, available online at http://www.google.com/search?hl=en&client=firefox-a&channel=s&rls=org.mozilla%3Aen-US%3Aofficial&q=Savitskogo+F.+I.+Uspenskomu&btnG=Search.

Vladimir Anatol'evich D'iakov, "O nauchom soderzhanii i politcheskikh interpretatsiiakh istoriosofii Evraziistva," *Slavianovedenie*, 1993 (5), pp. 101–116, available online at http://src-h.slav.hokudai.ac.jp/publictn/acta/16/volodymyr/volodymyr-notes.html.

V. V. Perkhin, "Literaturnye Spory M. Gor'kogo (1935–1936); k. kharakteristike kritcheskogo metoda," *Vestnik Sankt Peterburgskogo Universiteta, Seriia 2, Istoriia, Iazykoznanie, Literaturovedenie*, 1993 (4), pp. 50–57. Ol'ga Anatol'evna Kaznina, "N. S. Trubetskoi i krizis Evraziistva," *Slavianovedenie*, 1995 (4), pp. 89–95. Claire Hauchard, "L. P. Karsavin et le Mouvement Eurasien," *Revue des Etudes Slaves*, 1996, 68 (3), pp. 357–365. Petia Dimitrova, "Russkaia kul'turna cherez vzgliad Evraziitsev," *Bulgarian Historical Review*, 1997, 25 (2–3), pp. 205–223. Mijail Málishev and Sepúlveda Garza Manola, "Euroasiatismo: Reveses de la Fortuna de una Teoria Enterrada y Rescucitada," *Estudios de Asia y Africa*, 1997, 32 (3), pp. 559–573. Dmitry V. Shlapentokh, "Eurasianism: Past and Present," *Communist and Post-Communist Studies*, 1997, 30 (2), pp. 129–151. E. A. Gogokhiia, "Evraziiskaia mysl' ob istokakh Russkoi revoliutsii," *Vestnik Moskovskogo Universiteta, Seriia 8, Istoriia*, 1998 (5), pp. 54–66. Petia Dimitrova, "Georgi Florovski i Evraziiskata sublazun," *Istoricheski Pregled*, 1998, 54 (3–4), pp. 61–76. Emil Voráček, "Vznik Eurasijstvi: Úvod do problematiky," *Slovanské Historické Studie*, 1997, 23, pp. 35–51. E. Voráček, "Vývoj 'vrcholného' Eurasijstvi a jeho dobová reflexe," *Slovanské Historické Studie*, 1999, 25, pp. 151–188. Ryszard Paradowski, Liliana Wysocka, and Duglas Morren, translators, "The Eurasian Idea and Leo Gumlëv's Scientific Ideology," *Canadian Slavonic Papers*, 1999, 41 (1), pp. 19–32. Mazurek Slawomir, Torr, and R. Guy, translators. "Russian Eurasianism—Historiography and Ideology," *Studies in East European Thought*, 2002, 54 (1–2), pp. 105–123.

23. Viktor Aleksandrovich Shnirel'man, "Russkie, nerusskie i Evraziiskii Federalism: Evraziitsy i ikh opponenty v 1920-E Gody," *Slavianovedenie*, 2002 (4), pp. 3–20, available at www.ceeol.com/aspx/getdocument.aspx?logid=5&id=56F80012-6DBD-4270-9D87-41474E728D85.

Zola Sergeevna Bocharova, "Contemporary Historiography on the Russian Émigré Community in the 1920s and the 1930s," *Russian Studies in History*,

2002, 41 (1), pp. 66–91. Svetlana Viktorovna Onegina, "Postrevoluionary Political Movements in the Russian Expatriate Community in the 1920s and the 1930s (Toward a History of Ideology)," *Russian Studies in History,* 2002, 41 (1), pp. 38–65. E. Vorácek, "Vzestupy a pady Eurasijstvi," *Slovanský Prehld,* 2001, 87 (4), pp. 451–482. Marlène Laruelle, "Les Ideologies de la 'Troisime voie' dans les Annees 1920: Le Mouvement Eurasiste Russe," *Vingtième Siècle,* 2001, (70), pp. 31–46, available online at www.princeton.edu/~restudy/soyuz_papers/Rouland.pdf.

Viktor Shnirelman, "The Fate of Empires and Eurasian Federalism: A Discussion Between the Eurasianists and Their Opponents in the 1920s," *Inner Asia: Great Britain,* 2001, 3 (2), pp. 153–173. M. Laruelle, "Le Neo-Eurasisme Russe: L'Empire Apres l'Empire?" *Cahiers du Monde Russ,* 2001, 42 (1), pp. 71–94. V. Shnirelman, Sergei Pananin, and Caroline Humphrey, translators, "Lev Gumilev: His Pretensions as Founder of Ethnology and His Eurasian Theories," *Inner Asia: Britain,* 2001, 3 (1), pp. 1–18. Mark Von Hagen, "From Russia to Soviet Union to Eurasia: A View from New York Ten Years After the End of the Soviet Union," *Österreichische Osthefte,* 2002, 44 (1–2), pp, 43–60. Ol'ga Alekseevna Sergeeva, "Tsivilizatsionnaia kontseptsiia, 'Evraziitsev' i kritika imi Sovetskoi modeli ustroeniia obschchestva," *Vostok,* 2001 (6), pp. 56–74. Alexandra Smith, "Between Art and Politics: Tsvetaeva's Story, 'The Chinaman' and Its Link with the Eurasian Movement in the 1920s–1930s," *Soviet and Post-Soviet Review,* 2001, 28 (3), pp. 269–285. Roman Bekker, "Mezhdu revoliutsionnym konservatizmom i totalitarizmom. Dilemmy otsenki mezhvoennogo Evraziistva," *Slavianovedenie,* 2001 (5), pp. 14–27. Svetlana H. B. Rusnak, "N. V. Ustrialov i Evraziitsy," *Revue des Etudes Slaves,* 2001, 73 (2–3), pp. 317–335. M. Laruelle, "Histoire D'une Usurpation Intellectuelle: L. N. Gumilev, 'Le dernier des Eurasistes'? Analyse des Oppositions entre L. N. Gumilev et P. N. Savickij," *Revue des Etudes Slaves,* 2001, 73 (2–3), pp. 449–459. M. Laruelle, "Lev Nikolaevic Gumilev (1912–1992): Biologisme et Eurasisme dans la Pensee Russe," *Revue des Etudes Slaves,* 2000, 72 (1–2), pp. 163–189. Julia Mehlich, "Die philosophisch-theologische Begründung des Eurasismus bei L. P. Karsavin," *Studies in East European Thought,* 2000, 52 (1–2), pp. 73–117. Leonid Luks, "Der 'Dritte Weg' der 'Neo-Eurasischen' Zeitschrift Elementy: Zurück ins Dritte Reich?" *Studies in East European Thought,* 2000, 52 (1–2), pp. 49–71. Ilya Vinkovetsky, "Classical Eurasianism and Its Legacy," *Canadian-American Slavic Studies,* 2000, 34 (2) pp. 125–139.

24. Nicholas S. Timasheff, *The Great Retreat: The Growth and Decline of Communism in Russia,* New York: E. P. Dutton & Co., 1946.

CHAPTER 3

1. Initially the term *nomenklatura* referred to a system of appointments, stemming from the Russian Social Democratic Worker Party (Bolshevik)'s

Ninth Party Congress' recommendation that "party committees at all levels ... keep lists of employees suitable ... for promotion within their field. Such lists, coordinated and extended by the Secretariat, became the nucleus of the *nomenklatura* system of appointments, not just in the party, but in all walks of life" (Hosking, 1990: 89). By the late 1930s, such party-designated appointees were also attaining top leadership posts in the military as well as in major factories, educational, scientific, and legal institutions. We use the term mainly to refer to "personnel" or, more specifically, to a subset of persons therein with top or middle-level posts within either the party structure or the state's administrative structure.

2. Aleksandr Solzhenitsyn (1978) wrote at length about this phenomenon in *The Gulag Archipelago*. This "old Bolshevik phenomenon" was also brilliantly portrayed by Arthur Koestler in *Darkness at Noon* (1941), dealing fictionally (although with real-life precedents) with the arrest, interrogations, and eventual execution of its "could-have-been-real" protagonist, the old revolutionary politician Nikolai Salmonovich Rubashov. His attempts to justify himself are profoundly loyalist, reminiscent of the pledges of loyalty that many Communists put forward after being arrested for their alleged activities.

3. The Soviet historians Gennadii Bordiugov and Vladimir Kozlov (1988, 1992) have cited several letters that were very critical of Stalin, sent during the collectivization campaigns. Also Sarah Davies (1997: 38–39, 41, 53, 94–95) has cited numerous archived letters addressed to the authorities or media that evidently could be classified as challenges to the system.

4. Of all professional groups, military and political police remained loyal and uncritical during this period. Several isolated cases hardly depict any mass disobedience or political movement. For example, Victor Orerkhin, working in the Moscow directorate of the KGB, in the mid-1970s began to inform dissidents about forthcoming actions against them. He was arrested and spent eight years in prison (Khinstein, 1994). Captain Valerii Sablin, charged with mutiny, was trying to improve the socialist system from "within." General Petro Grigorenko organized several political groups, pushing at the beginning for the restoration of Leninism in the country (Keep, 1996).

5. One example of such a group was the Communist Party of the Youth (or KPM in its Russian abbreviation). This group had its origins already in the early postwar years, being founded by 53 teenagers in Voronezh in 1948—it was one of many such groups to come to light by 1988 (Zhigulin, 1988).

6. The "loyal opposition" of liberal intellectuals was relatively small and scattered across the country. Most of their activities were discussions. During the relative political "thaw" of the 1960s, the number of people who signed open letters of protest against the regime did not surpass a few hundreds. On December 5, 1968, the number of people who participated in the UN Human Rights Day demonstration was no higher than 100–200 (Alexeiva, 1984).

7. In his book, *Jugement dans Moscou,* Vladimir Bukovsky (1995) wrote that the dissident movement remained a powerful opposition to the regime until its demise. He went so far as to state that "we [the dissidents] were the major obstacle to Soviet dominance over the world," and that "the Soviet regime could not resist an opposition, even symbolic" (Bukovsky, 1995: 187). However, all of the concrete episodes and incidents of resistance that the author cites in substantiation of his thesis occur only in the 1960s and 1970s (Bukovsky, 1995), and not since the late 1970s or in the early 1980s when the dissident movement was virtually obliterated.
8. Among especially prominent advocates of the return to Russian orthodoxy at this time, we may count the novelists Viktor Astaf'ev and Vasilii Bykov. For discussion on the rabid anti-Semitism that accompanied their faith, see Olcott (1987: 118, 124–25; also Kagarlitsky, 1988: 328–329, 355).

CHAPTER 4

1. This opinion would have surprised many people in the Soviet Union, of course, if they had access to American opinion polls. The reason is that in the Soviet Union, the majority of people held the opposite view on whether it was the Russians or the Americans who worked harder. (Perhaps for American respondents, it was reasonable to assume that if the Soviet system was totalitarian, then people living under it should be working harder; further, work conditions had to be better organized because of the tight discipline imposed by the authorities on all people of the Soviet Union.)
2. For example, on repeated polling occasions in the 1960s, 1970s, and 1980s, less than half of surveyed American adults could correctly identify the duration of the U.S. Senate term, or accurately report the number of Supreme Court Justices (Jennings and Stoker, 1999; Jennings, 1996).
3. One of the authors has had personal experience about Reagan's remark when he was a member of a Soviet graduate students' exchange group that visited the United States in October 1988. The "evil empire" remark was brought to the group's attention on many occasions—mostly during seminars and discussions on university campuses. Our hosts—mostly ideologically liberal professors—blasted Reagan for his anti-Soviet rhetoric. They tried to assure the visiting Soviets that Americans did not support the president's view of the Soviet Union. As it turned out, their portrayal of the American public opinion may not have been all that accurate. (Perhaps the hosts also did not want to upset their visitors.) In addition, most people in the Soviet delegation had a very critical view of the Soviet Union's domestic policies and partially agreed with the "evil" label.
4. For example, a Yankelovich survey, on July 7 1988, contained the following statement in one of its item-framing preambles: "Even though Americans reject the communist system and there is no proven basis for trusting the Soviets."
5. In the Soviet Union, on the other side of the ocean, the concept of "capitalist encirclement" worked extremely well. The Soviets themselves were con-

vinced of the danger coming from foreign countries (in the west and in the east), and especially from the United States. The tendency of Russians to believe in various conspiracy theories, particularly in the plots driven by foreign enemies against their motherland, has long historic roots.

CHAPTER 5

1. Sarah Davies's book on public opinion in Stalin's Russia is based on the study of the Leningrad archive. She carefully evaluated the validity of her sources and compared them with each other, trying to come up with a clear idea about the representativeness of her data based on letters and other written documents (Davies, 1997: pp. 9–17).
2. Three quarters of the respondents of the Harvard project claimed (in some cases, probably in order to please their American interviewers) that they or some member of their family had been arrested (Inkeles and Bauer, 1968: pp. 35–36).
3. Various memoirs written by opponents of Stalin's regime show that the regime was popular. Many dissidents who published their books in the West before the end of the Soviet Union (R. Orlova, 1983; L. Kopelev, 1975, 1978; P. Grigorenko, 1982, to name a few) supported the view about the mass support of the Soviet system.
4. Vaclav Havel, former president of the Czech Republic, wrote that the Stalinist system "deliberately created a specific structure of values and models of behavior," which were "a perverted structure, one that went against all the natural tendencies of life." However, he conceded that "society nevertheless internalized it, or rather was forced to internalized it." (Vaclav Havel, "The Post-Communist Nightmare," *New York Review of Books,* vol. 40, no. 10, p. 8.)
5. Bukovsky's assertions that "Soviet society lived on a volcano" (p. 133) and that millions of Russians were ready to join the struggle against the Kremlin if they had been encouraged by the West and the Russian intelligentsia (p. 134) are intriguing but "utopian" assumptions about the situation in the Soviet Union (Bukovsky, 1995).
6. The movies made in the 1930s, such as Fridrikh Ermler's *A Great Citizen* (1938–1939), as well as historical movies, such as Sergei Eisenstein's *Alexander Nevsky* and *Ivan the Terrible* (1945) and Petrov's *Peter the Great* (1937–1939), substantiated the necessity of the fight against "domestic" enemies. Most people accepted these movies and drew historic parallels between then and now (see Dmitry Shlapentokh and Vladimir Shlapentokh, *Soviet Cinematography 1918–1991,* New York: Aldine, 1993: pp. 108–110).
7. See the memoirs of Soviet dissidents Piotr Grigorenko (1982), Raisa Orlova (1983), and Galina Vishenveskaia (1984).
8. The people's real perceptions of Soviet reality were manifested quite well in the first hours, days, and even long after their arrests. Most people seized by the political police in the 1930s believed that they were arrested by

mistake. Later, having coped with the arrest, many people continued to support the official picture of Soviet society. In the *First Circle,* Solzhenitsyn described the fiery debates about the nature of Soviet society among prisoners in the so-called "Sharashchki," a privilegious prison for professionals involved in the construction of new weapons. Rubin, whose protagonist was writer Lev Kopelev, passionately defended the existing order against the committed enemies of the Soviet system (Solzhenitsyn, 1968; Medvedev, 1974: p. 832).

9. Vladimir Stavsky, an official writer in the 1930s, in his diary was overwhelmed with his feelings toward a woman, apparently his mistress. He used the most passionate words, remembering with rapture their trysts. In his eulogy of his carnal love, he enmeshed the name of Stalin as a god who protects their love: "I want to love, together with the epoch, together with Stalin, together with you, my beloved, my darling" (Garosse, 1995: p. 241).

10. See Evgenii Evtushenko's movie *Stalin's Funeral* (1990).

11. The attitudes of the Russian masses toward the media can be treated as an indirect sign of popular attitudes toward the system. People identified the media with power. In general, the attitudes toward the media were positive among most Russians. No less than two-thirds of the Soviet people were satisfied with newspapers and TV before 1985 (see Grushin, 1980).

12. Alex Inkeles and Raymond Bauer, *The Soviet Citizen: Daily Life in a Totalitarian Society,* New York: Atheneum, 1968, pp. 234, 236, 238, 239.

13. Alexandr Solzhenitsyn recalled that this war was "a dear war of my generation." He continued, "And this amazing influence of this political ideology, of this heartless earthly religion of socialism, with what force it sweeps away young souls, with what spurious lucidity it shows them a simple solution to any problem!" (Solzhenitsyn, "Razmyshlenia po povodu dvukh grazhdanskikh voin," *Komsomolskaia Pravda,* June 4, 1991).

14. In 1989, Levada found that 70 percent of people under the age 20, and 60 percent of older people had never heard about the dissidents. Even in 1988, only 1.5 percent of the respondents offered Andrei Sakharov as the man of the year in a VTSIOM survey (Levada, 1993: p. 194–195, 258).

15. Forty-one percent of the respondents of a VTSIOM survey directly supported "equality in income," against 38 percent who emphasized the necessity of a differentiation in income as the stimulus for productivity (Levada, 1993: p. 57).

16. Some people, who were torn between the necessity of expressing their feelings and the fear of doing so, resorted to coding their diaries much like the classic historian Solomon Lurie, who encoded his diary in 1947 using Latin and "Cyprian syllabary" (R. Davies, 1997: pp. 188–189).

17. Alexander Yakovlev, a prominent reformer, wrote in a weekly newspaper: "This is our old sin: Do not work but steal" (Yakovlev, *Argumenty I Facty,* #12, March 1997, p. 11). Yuri Bondarev, Russian famous writer and critic of the reforms, explained the meaning of Russian freedom and democracy referring to "permissiveness," "anarchy," and "pluralism of stupidity" flour-

ishing in the society and the forces that could substitute any ideology. He continued: "Russian pluralism is all about breaking ties, savagery, indifference." (*Argumenty I Facty,* #27, 1993, p. 6)

18. The day after the start of the strike in Novocherkassk on June 1, 1962, almost half of the members of the Politburo (Kozlov, Mikoian, Kirilenko, and Polianskii), the deputy chairman of the Council of Ministers (Shelepin), as well as the head of the KGB, Semichastnyi, arrived in the city to take the necessary measures (Trubin, 1991).

19. V. Kisilev took a straw poll among people who were adults during the 1940s and 1950s asking them how people living in those times would have answered the question: "Do you support the leader and his policy?" All of his respondents said that 100 percent of the people would have said "yes" (*Nezavisimaia Gazeta,* June 4, 1993).

20. By 1979, proportion of ethnic Russians and other Slavs in Lithuania reached 11.5 percent. (Goskomstat SSSR, 1989: p. 194). Russian concentration was especially high in the biggest cities such as Vilnius and Klaipeda. The growing presence of and increasing competition with ethnic Russians for jobs and housing; the need of the native population to adapt to newcomers (primarily by becoming bilingual, while Russians remained monolingual); and gradual erosion of Lithuanian language from public life, mass media, and education in a fundamental way influenced the critical attitudes of ordinary Lithuanians about the Soviet Union.

21. See Claude Lévi-Strauss, *Structural Anthropology,* New York: Anchor Books, 1967.

Bibliography

Adams, Arthur, and Jan Adams. 1971. *Men versus Systems: Agriculture in the USSR, Poland and Czechoslovakia.* New York: Free Press.
Agursky, Mikhail. 1980. *Ideologiia national-bolshevizma.* Paris: YMCA Press.
Aksenov, Yurii. 1991. "Stalinism: Polslevoennyie utopii i realii." Pp. 39–61 in Vitalii Zhuravlev (ed.), *Trudnyie voprosy istorii.* Moscow: Gospolitizdat.
Alexeiev, Sergei. 1995. "Miatezh na 'Storozhevom'." *Moskovskie Novosti,* December 31.
Alexeieva, Ludmila. 1984. *Istoriia inakomysliia v SSSR: Noveishii period.* Benson, VT: Khronika Press.
Allen, Barbara. 2005. "Alexander Shliapnikov and the Origins of the Workers' Opposition, March 1919–April 1920." *Jahrbucher für Geschichte Osteuropas* 53 (1): 1–24.
Andersen, Kristi. 1997. "Gender and Public Opinion." Pp. 19–36 in Barbara Norrander and Clyde Wilcox (eds.), *Understanding Public Opinion.* Washington, DC: Congressional Quarterly Press.
Arendt, Hannah. 1951. *The Origins of Totalitarianism.* London: Secker and Warburg.
Armstrong, J. A. 1961. *The Politics of Totalitarianism: The Communist Party of the Soviet Union from 1934 to the Present.* New York: Random House.
Aron, Raymond. 1962. *Dix-huit leçons sur la société industrielle.* Paris: Gallimard.
Arutiunian, Iuri. 1968. *Opyt sotsiologicheskogo izuchenia sela.* Moscow: Izdate'lstvo MGU.
Arutiunian, Iuri. 1971. *Sotsial'naia struktura sel'skogo naselenia SSSR.* Moscow: Mysl'.
Ascher, Abraham. 1972. *Pavel Axelrod and the Development of Menshevism.* Cambridge, MA: Harvard University Press.
Bahry, Donna, and Brian D. Silver. 1990. "Soviet Citizen Participation on the Eve of Democratization." *American Political Science Review* 84 (3): 821–847.
Bell, Daniel. 1973. *The Coming of Post-Industrial Society: A Venture in Social Forecasting.* New York: Basic Books.
Berger, Peter L., and Thomas Luckmann. 1967. *The Social Construction of Reality: A Treatise in the Sociology of Knowledge.* London: Allen Lane, Penguin Press.
Bergson, Abraham. 1964. *The Economics of Soviet Planning.* New Haven, CT: Yale University Press.

Berliner, Joseph. 1972. *The Innovation Decision in Soviet Industry.* Cambridge, MA: MIT Press.
Bialer, Seweryn. 1980. *Stalin's Successors: Leadership, Stability, and Change in the Soviet Union.* New York: Columbia University Press.
Bialer, Seweryn. 1981. "The Harsh Decade: Soviet Policies in the 1980s." *Foreign Affairs* 59 (5): 999–1020.
Bialer, Seweryn. 1983. *The USSR after Brezhnev.* New York: Foreign Policy Association.
Bialer, Seweryn. 1987. *The Soviet Paradox: External Expansion, Internal Decline.* New York: Vintage.
Birman, Igor. 1981. *Secret Incomes of the Soviet State Budget.* The Hague: Martinus Nijhoff.
Bordiugov, Gennadii, and Vladimir Kozlov. 1988. "'Revolutsia sverskhu' i tragedia 'chrezvychishchiny'." *Literaturnaia gazeta,* October 12.
Bordiugov, Gennadii, and Vladimir Kozlov. 1992. *Istoriia i koniunktura: Subektivnye zametki ob istorii sovetskogo obshchestva.* Moscow: Politizdat.
Bornstein, Morris (ed.). 1981. *The Soviet Economy: Continuity and Change.* Boulder, CO: Westview.
Brovkin, Vladimir (ed.). 1991. *Dear Comrades: Menshevik Reports on the Bolshevik Revolution and the Civil War.* Stanford, CA: Hoover Institution Press.
Brzezinski, Zbigniew. 1956. *The Permanent Purge: Politics in Soviet Totalitarianism.* Cambridge, MA: Harvard University Press.
Brzezinski, Zbigniew. 1966. "The Soviet Political System: Transformation or Degeneration?" *Problems of Communism* 15 (1): 1–15.
Brzezinski, Zbigniew (ed.). 1969. *Dilemmas of Change in Soviet Politics.* New York: Columbia University Press.
Brzezinski, Zbigniew, and Samuel Huntington. 1964. *Political Power: USA/USSR.* New York: Viking Press.
Bukovsky, Vladimir. 1995. *Jugement à Moscou.* Paris: Robert Laffont.
Burbank, Jane. 1991. "Controversies over Stalinism: Searching for a Soviet Society." *Politics and Society* 19 (3): 325–340.
Burbulis, Gennadii. 1992. " Interview." *Argumenty i fakty* 31 (2): 1.
Burnham, James. 1941. *The Managerial Revolution.* New York: J. Day.
Carros, Veronique, Natalia Korenevskaya, and Thomas Lahusen. 1995. *Intimacy and Terror: Soviet Diaries of the 1930s.* New York: New Press.
Chamberlin, William. 1930. *Soviet Russia: A Living Record and a History.* London: Duckworth.
Chamberlin, William. 1944. *The Ukraine: A Submerged Nation.* New York: MacMillan.
Chernyaev, Vladimir Iu. 1997. "Trotsky." Pp. 188–196 in Edward Acton, Vladimir Iu. Chernyaev, and William G. Rosenberg (eds.), *Critical Companion to the Russian Revolution, 1914–1921.* London: Arnold.
Cohen, Stephen. 1973. *Bukharin and the Bolshevik Revolution: A Political Biography, 1888–1938.* New York: Alfred A. Knofp.
Cohen, Stephen. 1979. "The Friends and Foes of Change: Reformism and Conservatism in the Soviet Union." *Slavic Review* 38 (2): 187–202.

Cohen, Stephen. 1985. *Rethinking the Soviet Experience: Politics and History since 1917.* New York: Oxford University Press.
Colton, Timothy. 1986. *The Dilemma of Reform in the Soviet Union.* New York: Council on Foreign Relations.
Conquest, Robert (ed.). 1967. *The Politics of Ideas in the USSR.* London: Bodley Head.
Conquest, Robert. 1968. *The Great Terror: Stalin's Purges of the Thirties.* London: MacMillan.
Conquest, Robert. 1975. "A New Russia? A New World?" *Foreign Affairs* 53 (3): 482–497.
Conquest, Robert. 1990. *The Great Terror: A Reassessment.* London: Hutchinson.
Conquest, Robert. 1993. "Red to Go." *Times Literary Supplement,* July 9.
Converse, Philip E. 1964. "The Nature of the Belief System in Mass Publics." Pp. 206–261 in David E. Apter (ed.), *Ideology and Discontent.* London: Free Press of Glencoe.
Dahlke, Sandra. 2002. "Kampagnen fur gottlosigkeit: Zum zusammenhang zwischen legitimation, mobilisierung und partizipation in der Sowjetunion der zwanziger jahre." *Jahrbücher für Geschichte Osteuropas* 50 (2): 172–185.
Dallin, Alexander. 1973. "Biases and Blunders in American Studies on the USSR." *Slavic Review* 23 (3): 560–576.
Dallin, Alexander. 1992. "Causes of the Collapse of the USSR." *Post-Soviet Affairs* 8 (4): 279–302.
Dallin, David. 1922. *Posle voin i revoliutsii.* Berlin: Grani.
Daniels, Robert V. 1960. *The Conscience of the Revolution: Communist Opposition in Soviet Russia.* New York: Simon and Schuster.
Daniels, Robert V. 1967. *The Red October.* New York: Charles Scribner.
Daniels, Robert V. 1987. "Russian Political Culture and the Post-Revolutionary Impasse." *Russian Review* 46 (2): 165–175.
Davenport, Christian, and Allan Stam. 2003. "Rashomon Goes to Rwanda." Paper presented at the meetings of the American Political Science Association, Philadelphia.
Davenport, Christian, and Marika F. X. Litras. 2000. "Rashomon and Repression: A Multi-Source Analysis of Contentious Events." Paper presented at the annual meetings of the American Sociological Association, Washington, DC.
Davies, Joseph. 1942. *Mission to Moscow.* London: Victor Gollancz.
Davies, Robert W. 1997. *Soviet History in the Yeltsin Era.* London: MacMillan.
Davies, Sarah. 1997. *Public Opinion in Stalin's Russia: Terror, Propaganda, and Dissent, 1934–1941.* Cambridge, UK: Cambridge University Press.
Davis, Nancy J., and Robert V. Robinson. 2006. "The Egalitarian Face of Islamic Orthodoxy: Support for Islamic Law and Economic Justice in Seven Muslim-Majority Nations." *American Sociological Review* 71 (2): 167–190.
Davydov, Yurii V. 1970. *Glukhaia pora listopada.* Moscow: Molodaia Guardia.
Deriabin, Peter, and T. H. Bugley. 1990. *KGB: Masters of the Soviet Union.* New York: Hippocrene Books.

Deutscher, Isaac. 1950. *Soviet Trade Unions: Their Place in Soviet Labor Policy.* London: Royal Institute of International Affairs.
Deutscher, Isaac. 1959. *The Prophet Unarmed: Trotsky, 1921–1929.* London: Oxford University Press.
Dobson, Richard B., and Steven A. Grant. 1992. "Public Opinion and the Transformation of the Soviet Union." *International Journal of Public Opinion Research* 4 (4): 302–320.
Duch, Raymond M. 1993. "Tolerating Economic Reform: Popular Support for Transition to a Free Market in the Former Soviet Union." *American Political Science Review* 87 (3): 590–608.
Duranty, Walter. 1935. *I Write as I Please.* New York: Simon and Schuster.
Duranty, Walter. 1944. *USSR: The Story of Soviet Russia.* London: Hamish Hamilton.
Ebenstein, William. 1963. *Today's Isms: Communism, Fascism, Capitalism, Socialism.* Englewood Cliffs, NJ: Prentice-Hall.
Eley, Geoff. 1986. "History with the Politics Left Out—Again?" *Russian Review* 45 (4): 385–394.
Ellman, Michael. 1984. *Collectivisation, Convergence and Capitalism: Political Economy in a Divided World.* New York: Academic Press.
Fainsod, Merle. 1953. *How Russia Is Ruled.* Cambridge, MA: Harvard University Press.
Fainsod, Merle. 1958. *Smolensk under Soviet Rule.* Cambridge, MA: Harvard University Press.
Fainsod, Merle. 1963. *How Russia Is Ruled* (Rev. ed.). Cambridge, MA: Harvard University Press.
Finifter, Ada W., and Ellen Mickiewicz. 1992. "Redefining the Political System of the USSR: Mass Support for Political Change." *American Political Science Review* 86 (4): 857–874.
Fischer, Louis. 1941. *Men and Politics: An Autobiography.* New York: Duell, Sloan and Pearce.
Fitzpatrick, Sheila. 1984. "Cultural Revolution as Class War." Pp. 7–40 in Sheila Fitzpatrick (ed.), *Cultural Revolution in Russia, 1928–1931.* Bloomington: Indiana University Press.
Fitzpatrick, Sheila. 1986. "New Perspectives on Stalinism." *Russian Review* 45 (4): 357–373.
Fitzpatrick, Sheila. 1994 [1982]. *The Russian Revolution.* New York: Oxford University Press.
Fitzpatrick, Sheila. 1992. *The Cultural Front: Power and Culture in Revolutionary Russia.* Ithaca, NY: Cornell University Press.
Freund, Heinrich Alexander. 1945. *Russia from A to Z: Revolution, State and Party, Foreign Relations, Economic System, Social Principles, General Knowledge.* Sydney: Angus and Robertson.
Friedrich, Carl J., and Zbigniew Brzezinski. 1956. *Totalitarian Dictatorship and Autocracy.* Cambridge, MA: Harvard University Press.
Fürst, Julianne. 2002. "Prisoners of the Soviet Self? Political Youth Opposition in Late Stalinism." *Europe-Asia Studies* 54 (3): 353–375.

Galbraith, John Kenneth. 1967. *The New Industrial State*. London: Hamish Hamilton.
Galili, Ziva. 1989. *The Menshevik Leaders in the Russian Revolution: Social Realities and Political Strategies*. Princeton, NJ: Princeton University Press.
Gershenson, Dmitriy, and Herschel I. Grossman. 2001. "Cooption and Repression in the Soviet Union." *Economics and Politics* 13 (1): 31–47.
Getty, J. Arch. 1985. *Origins of the Great Purges: The Soviet Communist Party Reconsidered*. Cambridge, UK: Cambridge University Press.
Getty, J. Arch, and Roberta Manning. 1993. "Introduction." Pp. 1–20 in J. Arch Getty and Roberta Manning (eds.), *Stalinist Terror: New Perspectives*. Cambridge, UK: Cambridge University Press.
Gleason, Abbot. 1995. "Totalitarianism and the Cold War: A Personal View." *Newsnet: The Newsletter of the AAASS* 35 (4): 1–3.
Goldthorpe, John. 1997. "Current Issues in Comparative Macrosociology: A Debate on Methodological Issues." *Comparative Social Research* 16: 1–26.
Golod, Sergei. 1977. "Sotsial'no-psykhologicheskie i nravstennyie tsennosti sem'i." Pp. 57–84, in D. Valentei (ed.), *Molodaia sem'ia*. Moscow: Statistika.
Goodman, James. 1994. *Stories of Scottsboro*. New York: Pantheon Books.
Gorelik, Gennadii. 1992. "Za chto sidel Lev Landau." *Izvestia*, January 8.
Gozman, Leonid, and Alexander Etkind. 1992. *The Psychology of Post-Totalitarianism in Russia* (Roger Clarke, trans.). London: Center for Research into Communist Economies.
Graham, Stephen. 1925. *Russia in Division*. London: MacMillan.
Granick, David. 1960. *The Red Executive: A Study of the Organization Man in Russian Industry*. London: MacMillan.
Gregory, Paul, and Robert C. Stuart. 1974. *Soviet Economic Structure and Performance*. New York: Harper and Row.
Griffiths, Franklyn. 1972. *Images, Politics and Learning in Soviet Behavior toward the United States*. Ph.D. dissertation, Columbia University.
Grigorenko, Piotr. 1982. *Memoirs*. New York: W. W. Norton.
Grossman, Vasilii. 1970. *Vse techet*. Frankfurt: Posev.
Grushin, Boris. 1968. *Mir mnenii i mneniia o mire*. Moscow: Politizdat.
Grushin, Boris, and Lev Onikov (eds.). 1980. *Massovaia informatsiia v sovetskom promyshlennom gorode*. Moscow: Politizdat.
Gustafson, Thane. 1981. *Reform in Soviet Politics: Lessons of Recent Policies on Land and Water*. New York: Cambridge University Press.
Harper, Samuel N. 1929. *Civic Training in Soviet Russia*. Chicago: University of Chicago Press.
Harper, Samuel N. 1931. *Making Bolsheviks*. London: Cambridge University Press.
Harper, Samuel N. 1938. *The Government of the Soviet Union*. New York: D. Van Nostrand.
Hayek, von Friedrich. 1944. *The Road to Serfdom*. London: G. Routledge.
Hazard, John N. 1953. *Law and Social Change in the USSR*. London: Stevens.
Heider, Karl G. 1988. "The Rashomon Effect: When Ethnographers Disagree." *American Anthropologist* 90 (1): 73–81.

Hewett (ed.). 1988. *Reforming the Soviet Economy: Equality versus Efficiency.* Washington, DC: Brookings Institute.

Hideo, Hama. 1999. "Ethnomethodology and the Rashomon Problem." *Human Studies* 22 (2–4): 183–192.

Hindus, Maurice. 1929. *Humanity Uprooted: An Account of the Results of the Revolution in Russia.* London: Jonathan Cape.

Hindus, Maurice. 1931. *Red Bread.* London: Jonathan Cape.

Hindus, Maurice. 1933. *The Great Offensive.* London: Victor Gollancz.

Hollander, Paul. 1981. *Political Pilgrims: Travels of Western Intellectuals to the Soviet Union, China, and Cuba 1928–1978.* New York: Oxford University Press.

Horowitz, Irving L. 1985. "The Rashomon Effect: Ideological Proclivities and Political Dilemmas of the International Monetary Fund." *Journal of Inter-American Studies and World Affairs* 27 (4): 37–55.

Hosking, Geoffrey. 1990. *A History of the Soviet Union.* London: Fontana Press.

Hough, Jerry. 1971. "The Party Apparatchiki." Pp. 47–92 in H. Gordon Skilling and Franklyn Griffiths (eds.), *Interest Groups in Soviet Politics.* Princeton, NJ: Princeton University Press.

Hough, Jerry. 1972. "The Soviet System: Petrification or Pluralism?" *Problems of Communism* 21 (2): 25–45.

Hough, Jerry. 1977. *The Soviet Union and Social Science Theory.* Cambridge, MA: Harvard University Press.

Hough, Jerry. 1980. *Soviet Leadership in Transition.* Washington, DC: Brookings Institution.

Hough, Jerry. 1987. "Gorbachev Consolidating Power." *Problems of Communism* 36 (4): 21–43.

Hough, Jerry, and Merle Fainsod. 1979. *How the Soviet Union Is Governed.* Cambridge, MA: Harvard University Press.

Howe, Irving. 1982. *A Margin of Hope: An Intellectual Autobiography.* San Diego: Harcourt Brace Jovanovich.

Hubbard, Leonard E. 1938. *Soviet Trade and Distribution.* London: MacMillan and Col.

Hunter, David. 1991. *Culture Wars: The Struggle to Define America.* New York: Basic Books.

Huntington, Samuel P., and Zbigniew Brzezinski. 1964. *Political Power: USA-USSR.* New York: Viking Press.

Husserl, Edmund. 1969 [1931]. *Ideas: General Introduction to Pure Phenomenology* (W. R. Boyce Gibson, trans., 5th ed.). London: George Allen and Unwin.

Inkeles, Alex. 1968. *Social Change in Soviet Russia.* Cambridge, MA: Harvard University Press.

Inkeles, Alex, and Raymond Bauer. 1968. *The Soviet Citizen: Daily Life in a Totalitarian Society.* New York: Atheneum.

Jennings, M. Kent. 1996. "Political Knowledge over Time and across Generations." *Public Opinion Quarterly* 60 (2): 228–252.

Jennings, M. Kent, and Laura Stoker. 1999. "The Persistence of the Past: The Class of 1965 Turns 50." Paper presented at the annual meeting of the Midwest Political Science Association.

Kacowicz, Arie M. 2005. "Rashomon in the Middle East: Clashing Narratives, Images, and Frames in the Israeli-Palestinian Conflict." *Cooperation and Conflict* 40 (3): 343–360.

Kagarlitsky, Boris. 1988. *The Thinking Reed: Intellectuals and the Soviet State, 1917 to the Present.* New York: Verso.

Keep, John. 1996. *Last of the Empires: A History of the Soviet Union, 1945–1991.* Oxford: Oxford University Press.

Kenez, Peter. 1986. "Stalinism as Humdrum Politics." *Russian Review* 45 (4): 395–400.

Kennan, George F. 1961. *Russia and the West under Lenin and Stalin.* London: Hutchinson.

Kharchev, Anatolii. 1964. *Brak i sem'ia v SSSR.* Moscow: Mysl'.

Khinstein, Alexander. 1994. "Dobry kapitan gosbezopasnosti." *Moskovskii Komsomolets,* October 15.

Kiecolt, Jill, and Laura E. Nathan. 1985. *Secondary Analysis of Survey Data.* New York: Sage.

Kim, Maksim. 1983. *Problemy teorii i istorii real'nogo sotsialisma.* Moscow: Nauka.

Kolakowski, Leszek. 1978. *Main Currents of Marxism.* Vol. 3 of 3. New York: Oxford University Press.

Kon, Igor. 1967. *Sotsiologia lichnosti.* Moscow: Politizdat.

Kontorovich, Vladimir. 1981. "Forecasts of the Soviet Economy: Upward Bias in 1976–1980 and the Prospects to 1985." Paper presented at the Department of Economics Planning Workshop, University of Pennsylvania, October.

Kontorovich, Vladimir. 1987. "Labor Problems and the Prospects for Accelerated Economic Growth." Pp. 23–49 in Maurice Friedberg and Heyward Isham (eds.), *Soviet Society under Gorbachev: Current Trends and the Prospects for Reform.* Armonk, NY: M. E. Sharpe.

Kontorovich, Vladimir. 1996. "Economic Sovietology and Its Subject's Collapse." Unpublished book chapter manuscript, Haverford College, Pennsylvania.

Kopelev, Lev. 1975. *Khranit' vechno.* Ann Arbor, MI: Ardis.

Kopelev, Lev. 1978. *Sotvorim sebe kumira.* Ann Arbor, MI: Ardis.

Kossakovsky, Igor. 1990. "Opponent Stalina." *Literaturnaia Gazeta,* December 26:14.

Krylov, Constantin. 1965. *The Soviet Economy: How It Works.* Lexington: Heath.

Kuran, Timur. 1995. *Private Truths, Public Lies: The Social Consequences of Preference Falsification.* Cambridge, MA: Harvard University Press.

Kurganov, Oskar. 1996. "Zhdite." *Izvestiia,* August 24:1.

Lapidus, Gail. 1975. "Political Mobilization, Participation, and Leadership: Women in Soviet Politics." *Comparative Politics* 8 (1): 90–118.

Lapidus, Gail. 1984. "Ethnonationalism and Political Stability: The Soviet Case." *World Politics* 36 (4): 555–580.

Laqueur, Walter. 1994. *The Dream That Failed.* Cambridge, UK: Cambridge University Press.
Larina, Anna. 1993. *This I Cannot Forget: The Memoirs of Nikolai Bukharin's Widow.* London: Hutchinson.
Lash, Joseph. 1962. *Dag Hammarskjold: A Biography.* London: Cassel.
Latsis, Otto. 1989. "Stalin protiv Lenina." Pp. 55–87. in X. Kabo (ed.), *Kul't Stalina.* Moscow: Progress.
Leontief, Wassily. 1960. *The Structure of American Economy, 1919–1929: An Empirical Application of Equilibrium Analysis* (3rd ed.). Cambridge, MA: Harvard University Press.
Levada, Yuri. 1993. *Sovetskii prostoi chelovek.* Moscow: Interntsentr.
Lévi-Strauss, Claude. 1967. *Structural Anthropology.* Garden City, NY: Anchor Books.
Levy, Philip. 1987. "Modelling Cognition: Some Current Issues." Pp. 3–20 in Peter E. Morris (ed.), *Modelling Cognition.* Chicester: Wiley.
Lewin, Moshe. 1974. *Political Undercurrents in Soviet Economic Debates.* Princeton, NJ: Princeton University Press.
Lipset, Seymour Martin. 1972. "Academia and Politics in America." Pp. 211–289 in T. J. Nossiter (ed.), *Imagination and Precision in the Social Sciences.* London: Faber.
Lipset, Seymour Martin, and Everett Carl Ladd. 1972. "The Politics of American Sociologists." *American Journal of Sociology* 78 (4): 67–104.
Lipset, Seymour Martin, and Gyorgy Bence. 1992. "Anticipations of the Failure of Communism." Paper presented at the annual meeting of the American Sociological Association, Pittsburgh, August.
Lipset, Seymour Martin, and Richard B. Dobson. 1973. "Social Stratification and Sociology in the Soviet Union." *Survey* 88 (Summer): 114–185.
Lowenhardt, John. 1995. *The Reincarnation of Russia: Struggling with the Legacy of Communism, 1990–1994.* Durham, NC: Duke University Press.
Lubrano, Linda L., and Susan G. Solomon (eds.). 1980. *The Social Context of Soviet Science.* Boulder, CO: Westview Press.
Lynch, Michael P. 2006. *True to Life: Why Truth Matters.* Cambridge, MA: MIT Press.
Lyons, Eugene. 1935. *Modern Moscow.* London: Hurst and Blackett.
Lyons, Eugene. 1940. *Stalin, Czar of All the Russias.* Philadelphia: J. B. Lippincott.
Lyons, Eugene. 1966. *David Sarnoff: A Biography.* New York: Harper and Row.
Magnusdottir, Rosa. 2006. "'Be Careful in America, Premier Khrushchev!': Soviet Perceptions of Peaceful Coexistence with the United States in 1959." *Cahiers du Monde Russe* 47 (1–2): 109–130.
Malia, Martin. 1993. "A Fatal Logic." *National Interest* 31: 80–90.
Malia, Martin. 1994. *The Soviet Tragedy: A History of Socialism in Russia, 1917–1991.* New York: Free Press.
Malte, Rolf. 2006. "Das sowjetische Massenfest im Stalinismus (1932–1941)." *Geschichte und Gesellschaft* 32 (1): 69–92.
Marinov, Vselovod. 1989. "What the Comrades Say." *Time,* April 10, 62–63.

Maximova, Ella. 1992. "Podslushali i rasstreliali." *Izvestia,* July 16.
Mazur, Allan. 1998. *A Hazardous Inquiry: The Rashomon Effect at Love Canal.* Cambridge, MA: Harvard University Press.
McCormick, Anne O'Hare. 1929. *Communist Russia: The Hammer and the Scythe.* London: Williams and Norgate.
Medvedev, Roy. 1973. *Let History Judge.* New York: Vintage.
Medvedev, Roy. 1974. *K sudu istorii: Genezis i posledstviia stalinizma.* New York: Alfred A. Knopf.
Melancon, Michael. 1997. "The Socialist-Revolutionary Party (SRs), 1917–1920." Pp. 281–290 in Edward Acton, Vladimir Iu. Chernaiev, and William G. Rosenberg (eds.), *Critical Companion to the Russian Revolution, 1914–1921.* London: Arnold.
Meyer, Alfred G. 1970. *Marxism: The Unity of Theory and Practice; A Critical Essay.* Cambridge, MA: Harvard University Press.
Miliukov, Pavel. 1927. *Rossiya na perelome.* Paris: Collier Books.
Millar, James R. (ed.). 1987. *Politics, Work, and Daily Life in the USSR: A Survey of Former Soviet Citizens.* New York: Cambridge University Press.
Mills, C. Wright. 1958. *The Causes of World War Three.* New York: Simon and Schuster.
Naylor, Thomas. 1988. *The Gorbachev Strategy: Opening the Closed Society.* Lexington, MA: Lexington Books.
Nepomnyashchy, Catharine Theimer. 1990. "Famine in the Time of Feast: Soviet Literary Publishing under Glasnost." *Harriman Institute Forum* 3 (3): 3–7.
Olcott, Anthony. 1987. "Glasnost and Soviet Culture." Pp. 125–139 in Maurice Friedberg and Heyward Isham (eds.), *Soviet Society under Gorbachev: Current Trends and the Prospects for Reform.* Armonk, NY: M. E. Sharpe.
Orlova, Raisa. 1983. *Memoirs.* New York: Random House.
Perevedentsev, Viktor. 1975. *Metody izucheniia migratsii naseleniia.* Moscow: Nauka.
Pipes, Richard. 1984. *Survival Is Not Enough.* New York: Simon and Schuster.
Pipes, Richard. 1990. *The Russian Revolution.* London: Collins Harvill.
Pipes, Richard. 1994. *Communism, the Vanquished Spectre.* Cambridge, MA: Scandinavian University Press.
Pipes, Richard. 1996. "Russia's Past, Russia's Future." *Commentary* 101 (6): 30–38.
Podhoretz, Norman. 1979. *Breaking Ranks: A Political Memoir.* New York: Harper and Row.
Popov, Nikolai P. 1992. "Political Views of the Russian People." *International Journal of Public Opinion Research* 4 (4): 321–334.
Porket, Josef L. 1977. "The Soviet Model of Industrial Democracy." *Annals of the American Academy of Political and Social Science* 431 (1): 123–132.
Pratto, Felicia, Lisa M. Stallworth, and Jim Sidanius. 1997. "The Gender Gap: Differences in Political Attitudes and Social Dominance Orientation." *British Journal of Social Psychology* 36 (1): 49–68.
Przeworski, Adam, and Robert Teune. 1970. *The Logic of Comparative Social Inquiry.* New York: Wiley-Interscience.

Putnam, Robert. 2007. "*E Pluribus Unum:* Diversity and Community in the Twenty-First Century—The 2006 Johan Skytte Prize Lecture." *Scandinavian Political Studies* 30 (2): 137–174.

Remington, Thomas F. 1989. "Gorbachev and the Strategy of Glasnost." Pp. 56–82 in Thomas Remington (ed.), *Politics and the Soviet System.* New York: St. Martin's Press.

Remnick, David. 1993. *Lenin's Tomb: The Last Days of the Soviet Empire.* London: Penguin Books.

Renton, David. 2004. *Dissident Marxism: Past Voices for Present Times.* New York: Zed Books.

Richie, Donald S. 1971. *Japanese Cinema: Film Style and National Character.* Garden City, NY: Doubleday.

Richie, Donald S. (ed.). 1972. *Focus on Rashomon.* Englewood Cliffs, NJ: Prentice-Hall.

Rigby, Thomas. 1992. "The Reconceptualising of the Soviet System." Pp. 33–56 in Stephen White, Alex Pravda, and Zvi Gietelman (eds.), *Developments in Soviet and Post-Soviet Politics.* Durham, NC: Duke University Press.

Robeson, Paul, Robert Conquest, and Alexander Cockburn. 1989. "Exchange." *The Nation* 249 (5): 154 and 181–184.

Rorty, Richard. 1991. *Objectivity, Relativism, and Truth: Philosophical Papers.* Cambridge, UK: Cambridge University Press.

Rosenberg, William G. 1988. "Identities, Power, and Social Interactions in Revolutionary Russia." *Slavic Review* 47 (1): 21–28.

Ross, Edward A. 1918. *Russia in Upheaval.* New York: Century.

Rostow, Walt. 1953. *The Dynamics of Soviet Society.* London: Secker and Warburg.

Rostow, Walt. 1967. *The Dynamics of Soviet Society.* New York: W. W. Norton.

Roth, Wendy D., and Jal D. Mehta. 2002. "The Rashomon Effect: Combining Positivist and Interpretivist Approaches in the Analysis of Contested Events." *Sociological Methods and Research* 31 (2): 131–173.

Rupnik, Jacques. 1989. "The Empire Breaks up." *The New Republic,* February 20, 22–24.

Rutland, Peter. 1993. "Sovietology: Notes for a Post-Mortem." *National Interest* (Spring): 109–122.

Sarnoff, David. 1968. *Looking ahead: The Papers of David Sarnoff.* New York: McGraw Hill.

Sartori, Giovanni. 1993. "Totalitarianism, Model Mania and Learning from Error." *Journal of Theoretical Politics* 5 (1): 5–22.

Schapiro, Leonard B. 1960. *The Communist Party of the Soviet Union.* London: Eyre and Spottiswoode.

Schuman, John T. 1957. *Machine Shop Work.* London: Technical Press.

Schutz, Alfred. 1962. "On Multiple Realities." Pp. 207–259 in Alfred Schutz, *Collected Papers: The Problem of Social Reality.* The Hague: Martinus Nijhoff.

Sears, David O. 1996. "Symbolic Politics: A Socio-Psychological Theory." Pp. 113–149 in Shanto Iyengar and William J. McGuire (eds.), *Explorations in Political Psychology.* Durham, NC: Duke University Press.

Senokosov, Yuri P. 1989. *Surovaia drama naroda: Uchenye i publitsisty o prirode stalinizma*. Moscow: Izd-vo politicheskoi literatury.
Shatunovskaya, Olga. 1990. "Falsifikatsiia." *Argumenty i Fakty* 22 (May): 3.
Shiraev, Eric, and Alexander Bastrykin. 1988. *Fashion, Idols, and the Self.* Leningrad: Lenizdat.
Shiraev, Eric, and Vlad Zubok. 2001. *Anti-Americanism in Russia: From Stalin to Putin*. New York: Palgrave.
Shlapentokh, Dmitry, and Vladimir Shlapentokh. 1993. *Soviet Cinematography 1918–1991*. New York: Aldine.
Shlapentokh, Vladimir. 1970. *Sotsiologiia dlia vsekh*. Moscow: Sovetskaia Rossiia.
Shlapentokh, Vladimir. 1986. *Soviet Public Opinion and Ideology*. New York: Praeger.
Shlapentokh, Vladimir. 1988. *Soviet Ideologies in the Period of Glasnost: Responses to Brezhnev's Stagnation*. New York: Praeger.
Shlapentokh, Vladimir. 1989. *Public and Private Life of the Soviet People: Changing Values in Post-Stalin Russia*. Oxford: Oxford University Press.
Shlapentokh, Vladimir. 1990. *Soviet Intellectuals and Political Power*. Princeton, NJ: Princeton University Press.
Shlapentokh, Vladimir. 2001. *A Normal Totalitarian Society: How the Soviet Union Functioned and How It Collapsed*. London: M. E. Sharpe.
Shlapentokh, Vladimir, and Eric Shiraev (eds.). 2002. *Fears in Post-Communist Societies: A Comparative Perspective*. New York: Palgrave.
Shubkin, Vladimir. 1970. *Sotsiologicheskie Opyty*. Moscow: Mysl'.
Shulgin, Vasilii. 1990. *Gody; Dni; 1920*. Moscow: Novosti.
Shulgin, Vasilii. 1991. *Tri Stolitsy*. Moscow: Sovremennik.
Skilling, H. Gordon. 1966. "Interest Groups and Communist Politics." *World Politics* 18 (3): 435–451.
Skilling, H. Gordon, and Franklyn Griffiths (eds.). 1971. *Interest Groups in Soviet Politics*. Princeton, NJ: Princeton University Press.
Skocpol, Theda. 1979. *States and Social Revolutions: A Comparative Analysis of France, Russia and China*. Cambridge, UK: Cambridge University Press.
Smith, Hedrick. 1976. *The Russians*. New York: Quadrangle/New York Times Book.
Solomon, Susan G. (ed.). 1983. *Pluralism in the Soviet Union: Essays in Honour of H. Gordon Skilling*. London: MacMillan.
Solopov, Alexander. 1991. "Kogo schitali kulakom v 1924–1926 godakh." Pp. 83–100 in Vitalii Zhuravlev (ed.), *Trudnyie voprosy istorii*. Moscow: Politizdat.
Solzhenitsyn, Alexandr. 1973. *Arkhipelag Gulag 1918–1956: Opyt khudozhestvennogo issledovaniia*. Paris: YMCA Press.
Solzhenitsyn, Alexandr. 1975. *Bodalsaia telenok s dubom*. Paris: YMCA Press.
Solzhenitsyn, Alexandr. 1978. *The Gulag Archipelago, 1918–1956: An Experiment in Literary Investigation* (Vol. 3). London: Fontana Press.
Sorokin, Pitirim. 1964. *Social and Cultural Mobility*. New York: Free Press.
Steffens, Lincoln. 1938. *The Letters of Lincoln Steffens* (Vol. 2). New York: Harcourt, Brace.

Strakhovsky, Leonid I. 1961. *American Opinion about Russia, 1917–1920.* Toronto: University of Toronto Press.

Suny, Ronald. 1998. *The Soviet Experiment: Russia, the USSR and the Successor States.* Oxford: Oxford University Press.

Sztompka, Piotr. 1993. *The Sociology of Social Change.* Oxford, UK: Blackwell.

Talmon, Jacob L. 1952. *The Origins of Totalitarian Democracy.* London: Secker and Warburg.

Taracouzio, Timothy A. 1940. *War and Peace in Soviet Diplomacy.* New York: MacMillan.

Thurston, Robert. 1986. "Fear and Belief in the USSR's 'Great Terror': Response to Arrest, 1935–1939." *Slavic Review* 45 (2): 213–234.

Tourangeau, Roger, and Kenneth A. Rasinski. 1988. "Cognitive Processes Underlying Context Effects in Attitude Measurement." *Psychological Bulletin* 103 (3): 299–314.

Trotsky, Leon. 1937. *The Revolution Betrayed.* Garden City, NY: Doubleday, Doran.

Trotsky, Leon. 1973. *The Class Nature of the Soviet State: The Workers' State and the Question of Thermidor and Bonapartism.* London: New Park.

Trubin, Nikolai. 1991. "Kak eto bylo." *Pravda,* June 3: 3.

TsSU SSSR. 1956. *Narodnoe Khoziaistvo SSSR: Statistichsekii sbornik.* Moscow: Gosstatizdat.

Tucker, Robert C. 1961. "Toward a Comparative Politics of Movement Regimes." *American Political Science Review* 55 (2): 281–293.

Tucker, Robert C. 1981. "Swollen State, Spent Society: Stalin's Legacy to Brezhnev's Russia." *Foreign Affairs* 60 (2): 414–435.

Tucker, Robert C. 1990. *Stalin in Power: The Revolution from Above, 1928–1941.* New York: W. W. Norton.

Ulam, Adam B. 1963. *The New Face of Soviet Totalitarianism.* Cambridge, MA: Harvard University Press.

Vishenveskaia, Galina. 1984. *Galina.* New York: Random House.

Vishnevskii, Anatolii. 1989. *V chelovecheskom izmerenii.* Moscow: Progress.

Volkogonov, Dmitry. 1995. *Sem vozhdei.* Moscow: Novosti.

von Mises, Ludwig. 1951. *Socialism: An Economic and Sociological Analysis.* London: Jonathan Cape.

Vooglaid, Iulo. 1967. *Metodologicheskie problem issledovania massovoi kommunikatsii.* Tartu: Tartu University.

Webb, Sidney, and Beatrice Webb. 1937. *Soviet Communism: A New Civilization.* London: Longmans.

Welch, William. 1970. *American Images of Soviet Foreign Policy: An Inquiry into Recent Appraisals from the Academic Community.* New Haven, CT: Yale University Press.

Werth, Alexander. 1942. *Moscow '41.* London: Hamish Hamilton.

Willerton, John P., and Lee Sigelman. 1991. "Public Opinion Research in the USSR: Opportunities and Pitfalls." *Journal of Communist Studies* 7 (2): 217–234.

Willkie, Wendell. 1943. *One World*. New York: Simon and Schuster.
Wolfe, Bertram. 1981 [1957]. "The Durability of Soviet Despotism: Forty Years of Revolution." Pp. 281–297 in Bertram Wolfe, *Revolution and Reality*. Chapel Hill: University of North Carolina Press.
Workers' Library Publishers. 1931. *The Menshevik Trial*. New York: Workers' Library Publishers.
Yadov, Vladimir (ed.). 1967. *Chelovek i ego rabota*. Moscow: Mysl'.
Yanov, Alexander. 1978. *The Russian New Right: Right-Wing Ideologies in the Contemporary USSR*. Berkeley: University of California, Institute of International Studies.
Yugov, Aaron. 1931. *Pyatiletka* [The Five-Year Plan]. Berlin.
Zaller, John R. 1992. *The Nature and Origins of Mass Opinion*. New York: Cambridge University Press.
Zaller, John R. 1996. "The Myth of Massive Media Impact Revived: New Support for a Discredited Idea." Pp. 17–78 in Diana C. Mutz, Paul M. Sniderman, and Richard A. Brody (eds.), *Political Persuasion and Attitude Change*. Ann Arbor: University of Michigan Press.
Zaslavskaia, Tatiana. 1990. Comments at lecture in Zaslavskaia's capacity as adviser to Soviet premier Mikhail Gorbachev and director of the All-Union CPOS. 201 International Center, Michigan State University, May 21.
Zaslavskaia, Tatiana (ed.). 1970. *Migratsiia sel'skogo naseleniia*. Moscow: Mysl'.
Zhigulin, Anatolii. 1988. "Chernie kamni, avotoviograficheskai povest." *Znamia* 7–8.
Zimin, A. (pseudonym). 1981. *Sotsializm i neostalinizm*. New York: Chalidze.

Subject Index

Afghanistan 40, 92, 93
  invasion in 91, 121
agriculture 33, 62, 136, 137
American
  American elites 20
  American "left," 15, 28
  American people x, xiii, xiv, 20, 78, 81, 84, 94, 100, 106, 110, 111
  American Public Opinion 77, 152
  American social science 4, 5, 7, 8, 9, 14
  American Socialists 15
  American Sovietology 16, 20, 39, 146
anti-Semitism. *See* Jews
Arabs xii
Armenia xii
  Armenian genocide xii
arms control 106
  production 127
  reductions 90, 99
artists 50, 59, 67, 68, 91
attitudes 5
  attitudes of the Russian masses toward the media 154
  critical attitudes about Soviet society 5, 72, 143
authoritarianism 1, 44, 45, 46, 47, 95, 100, 114
  authoritarian methods 22, 56, 100, 114, 146
  authoritative traditions 24

backwardness of Russia and USSR 23, 30, 138
Bolshevik x, xi, 15, 18, 22, 23, 24, 40, 43, 44, 45, 47, 48, 51, 53, 54, 55, 56, 57
  National-Bolsheviks 43, 44, 45, 70
  National-Bolshevism 43, 44, 148
  old Bolsheviks 59, 63, 151
Bolshevism 16, 146
bureaucracy 19, 22, 29, 43, 56, 57, 97, 114, 117, 123, 129, 130
  bureaucratic methods 19, 56, 57, 97, 123, 124, 142

capitalism 14, 16, 17, 28, 29, 33, 50, 52, 53, 62, 65, 66, 75, 127, 130, 147
  capitalist principles 5, 19, 20, 29, 51, 52, 53, 66, 116, 119, 122, 152
censorship xv, 11, 28, 29, 30, 42, 49, 50, 58, 61, 63, 71, 120, 143
central planning. *See* economy in the Soviet Union
China 7, 28, 35, 41, 63, 77, 84, 87, 118, 121, 146, 150
  Cultural Revolution 26
Civil War (in Russia) 14, 18, 42, 43, 44, 53, 56, 67, 121, 131, 146

cognition   xiii, xv, xvi, 2, 3, 4
  cognitive mechanisms   4, 8, 113
  cognitive revolution   3, 4
  cognitive sociology   7
cold war   xii, xiv, xv, 13, 20, 28, 34, 37, 39, 40, 41, 42, 84, 91, 94, 106, 110, 115, 142
collectivism   16, 66, 120, 123
collectivization   xv, 11, 19, 25, 26, 53, 58, 60, 67, 116, 136, 142, 151
  kulaks   26, 27, 53
Communism   xiv, 7, 15, 28, 30, 34, 39, 42, 52, 59, 63, 69, 77, 78, 79, 92, 100, 102, 127, 132, 146
  Communists   xiv, 15, 16, 22, 24, 26, 30, 31, 54, 56, 59, 63, 67, 79, 82, 83, 99, 101, 117, 114, 121, 127, 151
  global Communist revolution   19, 22, 93
  global Communist system   11, 23
  ideology   14, 23, 49, 59, 124, 127
  as a system   13, 14, 16, 46, 50, 95, 105, 110, 111, 124, 152
Communist Party, the   xiii, 16, 32, 41, 42, 49, 51, 53, 54, 56, 59, 61, 62, 63, 65, 72, 73, 83, 96, 105, 116, 117, 127, 130, 131, 132, 135, 142, 143, 144, 151
  apparatchiks   35, 56, 59, 117, 118, 145
  leaders   51, 52, 53, 99, 106
consumerism   70, 75
corruption   31, 55, 56, 64, 114, 122, 141
  corrupt system   xiii, 16, 51, 117, 143
coup   22, 24, 131, 141
crime   31, 47, 72, 73, 80, 81
  criminal   ix, 9, 37, 58, 64, 117
Cuban Missile Crisis   40, 63
culture   ix, xiii, 31, 45, 47, 62, 69, 70, 75, 79, 120, 124, 132, 134, 135, 136, 138, 143, 146

cultural   xi, 8, 9, 45, 50, 59, 65, 67, 71, 91, 111, 132, 135, 139
  multicultural   8, 34
Czechoslovakia   29, 40, 133
  invasion of 1968   121

deconstructivism   8, 9, 30
democracy   16, 21, 23, 34, 35, 36, 55, 56, 61, 65, 72, 73, 75, 95, 96, 101, 105, 147
  absence of   15, 16, 56, 95
  democratic   x, 34, 36, 37, 40, 41, 46, 51, 52, 53, 54, 55, 63, 65, 105, 109, 124, 129, 130, 147, 150
  proletariat democracy   36, 52, 55, 154
dissidents. *See* resistance or opposition to regime
diversity   ix, xii, 67, 71
  cultural diversity   ix, xi
  diversity of opinions   x, xi, xii, xiii, xv, 36

economy in the Soviet Union   xiv, xv, 11, 17, 20, 21, 22, 28, 29, 31, 32, 33, 34, 38, 44, 45, 53, 54, 57, 58, 59, 65, 66, 74, 75, 99, 110, 120, 122, 129, 130, 131, 138, 142
  central planning   11, 17, 21, 33, 57, 66, 74, 143
  economic policies   17, 44, 52, 53, 74
  economic principles   11, 14, 17, 18, 21, 22, 23, 24, 25, 33, 38, 39, 43, 45, 62, 65, 74, 75, 97, 98, 127, 128, 129, 130, 131
  economic problems   xiv, xv, 33, 42, 54, 62, 65, 131, 132
  economic reforms   38, 39, 74, 129, 130
  economists   3, 21, 33, 38, 75

Subject Index

education xiv, 11, 21, 28, 29, 36, 42, 62, 80, 106, 127, 135, 142, 143, 155
 educational 14, 29, 35, 36, 80, 91, 107, 120, 126, 151
egalitarianism 14, 74, 120, 123, 130
elites xiii, 4, 6, 11, 49, 50, 57, 59, 61, 67, 71, 75, 76, 94, 113, 144
emigration 87, 96, 97
 émigré 32, 43, 44, 45, 46, 47, 69, 97, 117, 120, 148, 149 (see also immigration)
empirical 1, 4, 5, 7, 10, 31, 35, 50, 68, 114, 116, 123, 147
 empirical validity 5, 6, 7, 8, 12, 153
empiricism 1, 2, 4
epistemology 3, 4, 8
ethnic
 cleansings 26, 28
 groups 10, 45, 47, 50, 51, 94, 135
 policies 31, 34
 republics 76, 131
 Russians 45, 46, 136, 155
 tensions 37
Eurasianism 44, 45, 47, 148

famine 17
Five Year Plan 17, 59
foreign policy of the Soviet Union v, 2, 23, 27, 34, 35, 37, 41, 87, 90, 92, 100, 102, 110, 119, 123, 142, 143
 expansionism xiv, 20, 24, 41, 73, 85, 97, 99, 100
 foreign enemies 52, 57, 131, 153
 threats 52
free market x, 11, 62, 74, 75, 129, 130
 free-market capitalism 16, 17, 28, 33, 50, 53
 reforms 75
 societies x, 65, 110

French structuralism 8
Functionalism 3, 4, 26

Gallup polls 5, 79, 80, 82, 83, 85, 86, 87, 89, 90, 91, 92, 95, 97, 98, 99, 100, 101, 102, 103, 105, 107, 110
gender 9, 106, 107, 109
 discrimination ix, 28
Germany xiv, 2, 4, 18, 24, 40, 69, 85, 86, 87, 89, 98, 99, 100, 101, 102, 118, 142, 146, 148
 Nazi Germany 18, 26, 27, 41, 85, 92, 118
 Nazism xiv, 18, 20, 21, 24, 27, 40, 46, 56, 61, 85, 118, 133, 142
glasnost 70, 71, 73, 76, 128, 130
Gorbachev's reforms 128, 135
Gulag 11, 25, 31, 32, 59, 60, 67, 117, 118
 Population of 147

Harris polls 90, 91, 97, 98, 103, 105, 106, 111, 112
Harvard project 115, 120, 153
Holocaust xii
human rights ix, 95, 110, 124, 157
Hungary invasion of 1956 40

Ideology xii, xiii, 5, 6, 7, 12, 23, 41, 43, 46, 54, 63, 64, 71, 72, 74, 117, 120, 121, 127, 129, 131, 132, 133, 142, 143
 ideological factors xii, xiii, xiv, 6, 10, 12, 13, 14, 22, 25, 28, 35, 37, 39, 41, 47, 50, 55, 61, 62, 63, 64, 65, 69, 72, 75, 76, 78, 114, 122, 126, 127, 144, 145
 Soviet ideology 14, 21, 22, 23, 24, 32, 41, 44, 47, 49, 59, 60, 69, 70, 122, 124
immigration 43, 133, 135
 immigrants 32, 43, 46, 47, 89, 115, 120, 137

imperial   21, 22, 23, 24, 44, 46, 47, 85, 99, 142
imperialism   30, 50
individualism   11, 15, 70
industrialization   18, 19, 28, 59, 137, 139, 142
intelligentsia   25, 26, 51, 59, 61, 63, 66, 153
  liberal intellectuals   xiv, 14, 20, 30, 47, 64, 65, 70, 71, 72, 73, 74, 151
    prosecution of   25, 26
  Russian intellectuals   6, 11, 15, 42, 44, 48, 53, 59, 60, 63, 65, 66, 67, 68, 69, 71, 73, 124, 144
  Western intellectuals   11, 14, 17, 18, 21, 24, 47, 72, 76, 148
international Socialist movement   40, 41
Israel   xi, xii, 10, 81, 133

Japan   80, 85, 86, 98, 100, 101, 102
Jews   xii, 47, 97, 109, 117, 124, 141
  anti-Semitic   124
  anti-Semitism   18, 63, 117, 152
  Jewish   18, 114, 117
  Zionists   71, 121

Khrushchev era   25, 27, 61, 62, 67, 103, 104, 105, 106, 127
  dismissal of   35, 63
  reforms   xv, 119
  Twentieth Party Congress   62, 119
Komsomol (The Youth Communist League)   16, 37, 117

labor camps   58, 123
labor unions   37, 117
Leninism   7, 64, 73, 126, 151
liberal intellectuals. *See* intelligentsia
liberalism   34, 40, 72, 146
Lithuania   132, 133, 134, 135, 136, 137, 138, 139, 155
  backwardness   134
  incorporation in the Soviet Union   132, 136
  living standards in   132
  migration from   136
  Russification   137

Marxism   xiii, 8, 9, 19, 22, 24, 49, 50, 63, 65, 66, 72, 73, 74, 75, 118
  Marxist internationalism   22
  Marxist-Leninist   49, 57, 59, 62, 73
mass terror and repressions   ix, xi, 11, 17, 19, 25, 26, 30, 31, 32, 53, 58, 59, 62, 71, 87, 114, 116, 117, 119, 136, 142, 143, 147, 153
  political trials   19, 117
  show trials   15, 17, 58
Media   11, 14, 21, 29, 30, 36, 37, 40, 50, 67, 69, 73, 102, 110, 115, 116, 119, 120, 121, 122, 123, 130, 134, 145, 146, 151, 154, 155
Mensheviks   15, 54, 55, 58
Methodology   6, 8, 36, 114, 115
military policies
  competition with the United States   52, 110
  militarization of the Soviet Union   11, 21, 24, 33, 34, 38, 45, 46, 60, 79, 85, 97, 98, 99, 100, 103, 106, 151
  operations   87
  strength   28, 38, 39, 43, 45, 91, 106
  threat from the Soviet Union   38, 97, 101, 102, 109
modernization   28, 73, 136, 137
Molotov-Ribbentrop Pact   xiv, 18, 20
monarchists   24, 46, 54, 55
multi-perspective approach   9, 10

Subject Index

multi-realities approach 9
Muslims x, 64

Nationalism 22, 24, 41, 44, 69, 70, 75, 118, 135
  nationalist opposition 37
  nationalists 69, 70, 73, 75, 146
Nazi. *See* Germany
Neo-Leninists 63, 64
Neo-Marxists 4
Neo-Stalinists 72, 74
New Economic Policy (NEP) 44, 53, 55
nomenklatura 51, 150, 151
"normalizers," 13, 14, 20, 26, 27, 28, 31, 32, 34, 35, 36, 37, 38, 41, 42, 143
nuclear arms xii, 22, 37, 40, 81, 82, 91, 92, 93, 96, 97, 99, 102, 112
  catastrophe 63, 79
  limitation agreement 82
  race xii, 96

October Revolution xi, 14, 15, 16, 19, 23, 24, 41, 43, 45, 47, 48, 49, 51, 52, 63, 64, 65, 93, 141
  dictatorship of the proletariat 51, 52

Palestine xii
patriotism 24, 70, 79, 80, 117, 121, 124, 130
peasants xv, 17, 26, 51, 52, 53, 55, 58, 142
perestroika xv, 71, 72, 75, 76, 122, 128, 129, 130, 131, 148
phenomenology 4
  phenomenological revolution 4
pluralism 34, 35, 154
  pluralist society 16, 34, 76, 155
  political pluralism 27, 30, 34, 42, 65

Poland x, 87, 92, 93, 133
Politburo 35, 60, 61, 99, 145, 147, 155
political correctness 5
political police (Cheka, KGB, NKVD) 11, 21, 31, 32, 83, 103, 114, 123, 142, 143, 149, 151, 153, 155
political system of the Soviet Union xv, 11, 16, 27, 34, 51, 53, 57, 61, 62, 63, 65, 70, 75, 77, 79, 89, 95, 113, 122, 128, 130, 131, 132
  popular political participation 34, 36
  Soviet government xi, 12, 15, 20, 31, 32, 37, 52, 58, 59, 90, 92, 94, 95, 96, 97, 98, 113, 117, 126, 147
positive attitudes about the Soviet Union 18, 85, 90
positivism 4, 30
post-Stalin period 43, 63, 120, 127
postmodernist xiv, 8
private property xv, 11, 15, 21, 33, 44, 65, 66, 74, 75, 92, 93, 120, 122
privatization 66
propaganda in the Soviet Union 7, 14, 24, 36, 42, 50, 51, 52, 53, 55, 58, 62, 69, 115, 117, 118, 121, 124, 125, 126, 127, 131, 134, 135, 143
public opinion 5, 66, 98, 132
  in the Soviet Union 94, 113, 114, 115, 128, 153
  U.S. public opinion 91, 152

race 9, 106
rationalism 1, 2
Red Army 45, 51, 85, 89, 90, 116, 118
rehabilitation 62
relativism xiv, 9, 10, 12, 70, 73

religion xv, 3, 4, 21, 70, 73, 78, 101, 124, 154
  Russian Orthodoxy 45, 70, 73, 152
  Soviets' disbelief in God 92
  treatment of religious groups 97
resistance or opposition to regime 14, 15, 26, 27, 34, 37, 47, 54, 55, 57, 70, 71, 96, 120, 125, 142, 151, 152
  anticommunist campaigns 25
  anti-Stalin campaign 119
  dissidents 11, 32, 34, 68, 70, 71, 117, 121, 130, 143, 151, 152, 153, 154
  letters of protest 151
  mass disobedience 151
  riots 126
  workers' opposition 55, 56
revisionists 13, 21, 25, 27, 32, 34
Russian traditions 22
Russophiles 69, 70, 73
Russophobia 110, 111

samizdat 67, 69, 147
science ix, 1–5, 7, 8, 9, 11, 21, 30, 43, 50, 62, 68, 80, 146
self-perception 114
social construction 7, 8, 50
social equality 9, 53, 66, 79, 120, 130, 143, 154
social inequality xv, 74
social psychology 4
Socialism 16, 17, 18, 19, 23, 27, 28, 29, 30, 41, 44, 55, 56, 57, 60, 61, 65, 66, 70, 72, 73, 74, 75, 76, 79, 114, 116, 122, 126, 127, 129, 131, 132, 154
  Socialist ideas 22, 24, 41, 70
  Socialist system xiv, 33, 50, 62, 71, 116, 124, 151
Socialist realism 50, 68
Socialist Revolutionary Party (SR) 15, 55

Soviet-American relations 20, 37, 39, 81, 82, 89, 91, 102, 105, 106, 109, 110
  U.S. foreign policy toward Russia 31, 40, 89, 91
Soviet leaders 22, 35, 45, 102, 103, 104, 105, 124, 125, 131, 144, 145
Soviet Union
  academic and cultural exchanges with 91
  administrative reforms 72
  backwardness 15, 23, 30, 138
  collapse of xiv, 23, 39, 42, 47, 107, 110, 114, 131, 145
  Constitution of 1936, 17, 124
  deficiencies of 114
  domestic policies 52, 62, 87, 143, 152
  image of 40, 49, 50, 52, 57, 92
  information about 82
  "normal" society 13, 25
  Soviet values 120
sovok 124, 125
space program x, xi, 38, 48, 98, 127
Spanish civil war 121
stability ix, xii, 13, 24, 33, 73
Stalinism 26, 56, 62, 143
  personality cult 61, 118
  regime xi, 59, 60, 115, 153
  Stalinist 46, 60, 72, 153
  Stalin's repressions xi, 32, 114, 117
Strategic Defensive Initiative xii
surveys 5, 6, 7, 78, 80, 81, 83, 84, 85, 87, 90, 91, 92, 93, 94, 104, 106, 111, 114, 122, 128, 129, 130, 146
symbolic interactionism 7

television 82, 119, 122, 124
terrorism 30, 100, 102
  international terrorism 100
totalitarianism ix, 14, 21, 27, 30, 148
  ideology 6, 30

regime   ix, 25, 27
totalitarian nature of the Soviet
   state   6, 11, 12, 16, 20, 21,
   27, 34, 40, 43, 124, 142, 146, 152
totalitarianists   13, 14, 21, 22, 23,
   24, 25, 26, 27, 31, 34, 37, 38, 41,
   42, 76, 143
trade unions   16
transformation   9, 28, 47, 49, 66,
   76, 129
Trotskyites   16
trust   31, 85, 88, 106, 107, 108,
   109, 141
Tsarist Russia   46, 54
Turkey   xii, 59
Twentieth Party Congress. *See*
   Khrushchev era
Great Depression   17, 40

urbanization   28, 139

values   x, xvi, 3, 5, 7, 8, 70, 73, 75,
   92, 101, 102, 116, 117, 118, 120,
   123, 124, 127, 153
desirable values   5, 7
family values   117
values of socialism   116
Vietnam   40, 41, 97
   war in   121
violence   ix, 15, 22, 55, 56, 58, 133

working class   19, 50, 51, 53, 55, 56,
   67, 68, 116, 147
World Values Survey   7, 8
World War II   17, 19, 22, 24, 31, 45,
   60, 84, 88, 94, 97, 100, 110, 115,
   118, 133, 134, 136, 143

Xenophobia   111

Yankelovich survey   152

Name Index

Abalkin, Leonid 75
Abramov, Fedor 68
Adams, Arthur 33
Adams, Jan 33
Aganbegian, Abel 75
Aksenov, Vasilly 68
Andropov, Yuri 31, 71, 103, 105, 106
Antonov-Ovseenko, Vladimir 56
Aristotle 1
Aron, Raymond 28
Arutiunian, Yuri 68
Astafiev, Viktor 68, 152
Axelrod, Pavel 54, 55

Bell, Daniel 28
Belov, Vasilii 67
Berdyaev, Nikolai 69
Berger, Peter 7
Bergson, Abraham 34
Bialer, Seweryn 33
Bondarev, Yuri 154
Bordiugov, Gennadii 151
Brezhnev, Leonid xv, 27, 70, 72, 81, 105, 106, 119, 120, 132, 133
Brodsky, Joseph 67
Brzezinski, Zbigniew 22, 38
Bukharin, Nikolai 27, 52, 57, 59
Bukovsky, Vladimir 145, 152, 153
Burnham, James 16
Bush, George H. W. 106, 107
Bykov, Dmitry 144, 152

Campbell, Donald 5
Chamberlin, William 16

Cherevanin, Fyodor 55
Chernenko, Konstantin 71, 120
Clinton, William 40
Cohen, Stephen 26, 27
Conquest, Robert 22, 25, 27, 39, 42, 147
Crane, Charles 18

Dallin, Alexander 32, 41, 147
Dan, Fyodor 55
Davenport, Christian 10
Davies, Joseph 20
Davies, Sarah 124, 126, 151, 153
Davydov, Yuri 70
Descartes, Rene 1
Deutscher, Isaac 24
Dreiser, Theodore 15
Durante, Walter 17

Eisenhower, Dwight David 104
Eley, Geoff 34
Esenin-Volpin, Alexander 124
Evtushenko, Evgeny 68

Fainsod, Merle 24, 27
Feuerbach, Ludwig 3
Feyerabend, Paul 8
Finifter, Ada W. 129
Fischer, Louis 20
Fitzpatrick, Sheila 26
Foucault, Michael 8, 46
Franco, Francisco 95

Name Index

Freund, Heinrich Alexander 17
Frumkin, Moisei 60

Galbraith, John Kenneth 33
Getty, J. Arch 27
Gleason, Abbot 40
Golod, Sergei 69
Gorbachev, Mikhail xv, 42, 66, 71, 72, 73, 74, 75, 100, 103, 104, 105, 106, 122, 128, 129, 130, 135, 142, 144
Gordov, Vasilii 61
Gouldner, Alvin 4
Granick, David 33
Gregory, Paul 33
Grigorenko, Petro 151, 153
Grossman, Vasilii 64
Grushin, Boris 69

Harper, Samuel 16
Havel, Vaclav 153
Hazard, John N. 24
Hellman, Lillian 15
Hewett, Ed 34
Hindus, Maurice 19
Hitchens, Christopher 6
Hitler, Adolf 18, 26, 41, 89, 90, 92, 104, 118, 142
Hobbes, Thomas 2
Hollander, Paul 27
Hough, Jerry 35, 147
Huntington, Samuel 38
Husserl, Edmund 4

Iadov, Vladimir 68

James, William 4

Kamenev, Lev 56
Kant, Immanuel 2
Kardin, Boris 67
Kautsky, Karl 51
Kennan, George 23
Kerensky, Alexander 65
Kharchev, Anatoli 69

Khrushchev, Nikita xv, 25, 27, 35, 38, 61, 62, 63, 67, 103, 104, 105, 106, 119, 127
Kisilev, V. 155
Koestler, Arthur 151
Kohn, Melvin 5
Kollontai, Alexandra 56
Kon, Igor 66, 69
Kopelev, Lev 154
Kosolapov, Richard 31
Kozlov, Vladimir 151
Kuhn, Thomas 8

Landau, Lev 59, 60
Lansing, Robert 18
Lapidus, Gail 31, 36
Laqueuer, Walter 147
Lebed, Alexander 125
Leibnitz, Gottfried 2
Lenin, Vladimir 18, 22, 23, 27, 51, 53, 54, 64, 65, 121, 134, 141
Leontief, Wassily 33
Levada, Yuri 154
Lévi-Strauss, Claude 8, 133
Lewin, Moshe 38
Ligachev, Egor 74
Lipset, Seymour Martin 147
Lisovsky, Vladimir 125
Lozovskii, Solomon 56
Luckmann, Thomas 7
Lyons, Eugene 16, 42

Malenkov, Georgii 61
Malia, Martin 23, 39, 146
Manning, Roberta 27
Mao, Zedong 118
Marx, Karl 3, 7, 52, 66, 118, 121
McCarthy, Joseph 104
Medvedev, Roy 147
Meyer, Alfred 29
Meyers, Jeffrey 6
Miasnikov, Gavri'il 56
Mickiewicz, Ellen 129
Miliukov, Pavel 46, 54
Mills, C. Wright 29

Name Index

Molotov, Viacheslav 60
Morozov, Pavlik 117
Mozhaiev, Boris 67
Musolini, Benito 17

Napoleon, Bonaparte 46
Nekrasov, Viktor 67
Niekisch, Ernst 148
Nilin, Pavel 67
Nixon, Richard 40

Ol'shanski, Vadim 69
Orerkhin, Victor 151
Orlova, Raisa 153
Orwell, George 6

Pasternak, Boris 59, 67
Pavlov, Ivan 60
Perevedentsev, Viktor 68
Peter the Great 45
Piaget, Jan 8, 113
Pipes, Richard 22, 24, 39, 42, 146
Plato 1
Putin, Vladimir 70

Rakovsky, Khristian 56
Reagan, Ronald xii, xiv, 40, 91, 92, 106, 152
Reed, John 15
Rigby, Theodore 115
Ross, Edward 15
Rostow, Walter 22, 23, 28
Rubashov, Nikolai 151
Rutland, Peter 147
Ryazanov, David 56
Rykov, Alexei 51, 57

Sablin, Valerii 151
Sakharov, Andrei 66, 144
Sarnoff, David 42
Schapiro, Leonard 24
Schutz, Alfred 4
Searle, John 11
Semichastny, Vladimir 155

Semin, Vitali 68
Shafarevich, Igor 69
Shiraev, Eric 111, 127, 166
Shlapentokh, Vladimir xv, 6, 66, 69
Sholokhov, Mikhail 60
Shubkin, Vladimir 68, 69
Shukshin, Vasilii 68
Shulgin, Vasilii 146
Sinclair, Upton 15
Skrypnik, Nikolai 56
Solzhenitsyn, Alexander 32, 47, 64, 67, 68, 70, 118, 123, 147, 151, 154
Sorokin, Pitirim 29
Spinoza, Benedict 2
Stalin, Iosif x, xi, 18, 19, 20, 22, 23, 24, 25, 26, 27, 31, 32, 34, 52, 57, 58, 59, 60, 61, 62, 63, 64, 65, 69, 70, 101, 104, 106, 116, 118, 119, 123, 127, 141, 142, 151, 154
Stavsky, Vladimir 154
Steffens, Lincoln 15
Stuart, Robert 33

Timasheff, Nicholas 46
Tomsky, Mikhail 57
Trotsky, Leon 19, 52, 54, 56, 59
Truman, Harry 104
Tucker, Robert 23
Tvardovski, Alexander 64

Ustrialov, Nikolai 44

Vishenveskaia, Galina 153
Volkogonov, Dmitry 122, 147
von Hayek, Friedrich 21
von Mises, Ludwig 21
Voogl, Ülo 69
Voronov, Nikolai 68
Vosznesensky, Andrei 68

Walling, William 18
Weber, Max 3

Werth, Alexander 20
Willkie, Wendell 20
Wilson, Woodrow 15

Yakovlev, Alexander 75, 154

Zalygin, Sergei 67
Zaslavskaia, Tatiana 68
Zhukov, Georgy 61
Zinoviev, Gregory 56
Zubok, Vlad 111, 127

CPSIA information can be obtained at www.ICGtesting.com
Printed in the USA
LVOW09*2245080515

437741LV00009B/22/P